How the 1975 Boston Red Sox Embodied Baseball's
Ideals—and Restored Our Spirits

The Boys of October

DOUG HORNIG

McGraw-Hill

New York   Chicago   San Francisco   Lisbon   London   Madrid   Mexico City
Milan   New Delhi   San Juan   Seoul   Singapore   Sydney   Toronto

Library of Congress Cataloging-in-Publication Data

Hornig, Doug.
     The Boys of October: how the 1975 Boston Red Sox embodied baseball's ideals and restored our spirits / Doug Hornig.
        p.   cm.
     Includes bibliographical references and index.
     ISBN 0-07-140247-0 (hardcover) — ISBN 0-07-143193-4 (paperback)
     1. Boston Red Sox (Baseball team)—History.   2. World Series (Baseball) (1975)

   GV875.B62.H674   2003
   796.357'64'0974461—dc21   2003043838

For Doug Sr. and Uncle Oscar,
who inflicted upon my innocent childhood soul
the curse of lifelong Red Sox fanhood.

Thanks a lot, guys.

1 2 3 4 5 6 7 8 9 0   AGM/AGM   3 2 1 0 9 8 7 6 5 4

ISBN 0-07-140247-0 (hardcover)
ISBN 0-07-143193-4 (paperback)

McGraw-Hill books are available at special quantity discounts to use as premiums and sales promotions, or for use in corporate training programs. For more information, please write to the Director of Special Sales, Professional Publishing, McGraw-Hill, Two Penn Plaza, New York, NY 10121-2298. Or contact your local bookstore.

This book is printed on acid-free paper.

Contents

Acknowledgments

When I first conceived of this project, it was my goal to meet all of the members of the 1975 Red Sox. Unsurprisingly, and despite my fondest wishes that it be otherwise, this turned out not to be feasible. The force of circumstance intervened, as it will. I lacked the money to travel to the more distant parts of the country; the whereabouts of some players continued to elude me; others turned me down; still others, I just didn't get to. In the end, though, I did make contact with a majority of the players and coaches of that special team. I am very happy with, and grateful for, the story they gave me to tell.

So, first and foremost, thanks to the boys of October.

To Bill Lee, Bernie Carbo, and Don Zimmer, who invited a perfect stranger into their homes and treated him most kindly. To all the others who made time for face-to-face interviews: Juan Beniquez, Jim Burton, Denny Doyle, Dick Drago, Dwight Evans, Rogelio Moret, Johnny Pesky, Luis Tiant, and Carl Yastrzemski. To those I spoke with only by phone: Doug Griffin, Darrell Johnson, Fred Lynn, Rico Petrocelli, Jim Willoughby, and Rick Wise.

My apologies to those I couldn't find, or didn't get to for one reason or another: Tim Blackwell, Rick Burleson, Reggie Cleveland, Cecil Cooper, Bob Heise, Rick Miller, Bob Montgomery, Dick Pole, and Diego Segui.

To the guys who blew me off, Jim Rice and Carlton Fisk, I can only say that I wish I would have met you.

Outside of the boys themselves, I am most indebted to Dick Bresciani, Red Sox vice president for media relations. Dick put a lot of time and effort into helping me locate players, allowed me to roam around Fenway Park, arranged press credentials when I asked for them, gave me copies of his personal score sheets from the '75 Series, and shared his own reminiscences. He's a prince. Thanks also to Dave Jauss of the Red Sox, who did his best to hook me up with Jim Rice, and legendary GM Dick O'Connell.

Media people who lent a helping hand were Steve Conroy, Joe Fitzgerald, Hank Hernowitz, Tim Horgan, and Tony Massarotti of the *Boston Herald*; Dan Shaughnessy and Larry Whiteside of the *Boston Globe*; and Charlie Scoggins of the *Lowell Sun*. Jeremy Jones of the Baseball Hall of Fame kindly provided a missing game tape. And the folks at SABR were overwhelmingly responsive to my questions.

I wouldn't have gotten anywhere in Puerto Rico without the dedicated assistance of Felix Cardona, Oswaldo Gil, and Enrique Sued.

Thanks for helpful telephone interviews to writer and former Phillie Larry Colton and Hall of Famer Ferguson Jenkins; to Richard Pine (Larry Colton's agent); to Rick Cerone of the Yankees for arranging the Zimmer interview; to Bob Dowdell for locating Dick Drago; and to agent Dick Gordon for finally putting me with Yaz (assist: Dwight Evans).

Finally, thanks to agent Philip Spitzer and editors Rob Taylor and Matthew Carnicelli for believing in the project and making it happen; to Helen and Christina for tending the home fires while I went gallivanting around; and Derek and Brian for thinking that having a writer for a dad isn't entirely uncool.

Introduction:
The Unexpected Gift

Twenty-eight years later.

It's a fading memory now, but in the summer of 1975, the nation was exhausted, adrift, in the doldrums. A palpable "malaise," as Jimmy Carter would later describe it, had settled over the land like a cloud of noxious, yellow industrial smog.

The military action in Vietnam, a seemingly irresolvable conflict that had consumed the energy of the American people, was finally over. It had been the most divisive war since Abraham Lincoln vowed to keep the union together, whatever the cost. Yet, when the last American troops were withdrawn in April, there was no jubilation. There was barely even a sense of relief.

Rather, as we watched the end of this, the first television war, most of us were badly shaken by the final nightmare vision of the stricken land that had become our own personal hell: U.S. helicopters, rising into the air with terrified human beings clinging desperately to their struts.

Millions of Vietnamese had, by their reckoning, regained their home-land, at the cost of countless others losing theirs. The same home.

On the domestic front, things weren't noticeably better. Whatever good feelings had been engendered by the youthful music and flower worship of the sixties had long since dissipated, its adherents worn and weary or dead of drug overdoses.

The public was still reeling from the Watergate scandal. Richard Nixon had been forced from office the year before. In January, his three closest henchmen, John Mitchell, H. R. Haldeman, and John Ehrlichman, were found guilty of criminal activity during the cover-up. And in June the Rockefeller panel affirmed what many already suspected, that the previous administration had used the CIA to spy on individuals and groups who had opposed the president's policies.

Washington—at least as represented by the grand white house that lay at its center—had been exposed as a den of criminals, and from that focal point the people's disdain had spread to virtually everything governmental. The city was increasingly viewed as a strange and vile place, apart from the rest of the country.

The changes at 1600 Pennsylvania Avenue didn't help, either. Many Americans were profoundly uneasy that, for the first time in history, they were represented in the nation's capital by a president and vice president, neither of whom had received a single vote for the offices they held.

The nation's home had no welcoming hearth.

With politics in the pits, it would've been nice to be able to celebrate some of our social achievements in compensation. But it was hard. True, there had been substantial progress in the areas of civil rights and equality for women. Yet, after a decade and a half of accomplishment, most of us had grown weary of hearing the ceaseless litany of our social ills, and of groups clamoring to be recognized, and of change itself.

Struggles that had seemed close to resolution began to appear as unending as the small crises of every day. School busing, ordered by Judge Arthur Garrity in a last-ditch attempt to ensure classroom desegregation, was about to meet with a violent backlash among affected white Bostonians.

Economically, too, we were in pretty crummy shape.

The Arab oil embargo, with its accompanying backups at the gas pumps, had only recently eased. Some were predicting that the world's reservoirs of oil had been about pumped dry. Others blamed the sheikhs or claimed it was a conspiracy by powerful multinational companies to run up the price of crude and enrich their bottom lines.

Recession was the catchword for all financial and social ills. Its latest incarnation had dragged on for two years and, even though in hindsight we can see that it had been lifting in 1975, nobody knew that then. There were those who feared that we might be sliding back into something that more closely resembled the thirties than the go-go sixties.

Bolstering that view was the situation on Wall Street. As a proxy for the relative robustness of the private sector, it was a disaster, with stocks mired in a prolonged bear market. We know now that they were beginning to inch their way out, but here again it was anything but obvious at the time.

In my own life, I could well have served as poster boy for the state of the union.

I was, for example, essentially unemployed. I'd run through just about all my available options in the local job market and found myself driving a cab on the night shift in order to keep body and soul together. I hated it, having to deal day in and day out with rudeness and traffic and ill-tempered alcoholics and the enervating effects of sitting on my butt for ten hours straight.

I was also getting divorced after eight years of marriage. It had been an impetuous youthful thing, and probably I should have been pleasantly surprised that it had as much staying power as it did. But I wasn't. I was bummed out.

It was my initial encounter with a very bleak realization. I'd been raised, like most of my peers (the white ones, anyway), with the Nelsons as a model of the ideal family. Ozzie and Harriet, David and Ricky. Tiny black-and-white figures who stuck together through the good and the bad (well, not *really* bad). These kids dressed neatly and when they got into trouble, it was for minor youthful indiscretions. These parents not only tolerated rock 'n' roll culture but embraced it. Cool.

My marital breakup was the first indication to me that, despite our Nelsonian conditioning, my peers were not like that. In a big, big way. Sadly, for at least half the members of my generation, relationships were just not going to last.

We felt lost and, in some very critical ways, we were lost. Where we were headed, we didn't know, nor what we would find when we got there, nor even how to recognize the destination. Now, I have an inkling. Though we couldn't possibly have articulated it back then, what we had embarked upon was a quest for someplace to call home. It would prove to be a lengthy journey.

The hostilities in Southeast Asia had played their part in this, as so many felt like displaced persons in their own country. What was the point in even trying to create a stable family, only to see it torn apart by strife? The far-away, undeclared war had raged on and on for more than a decade, and more than one person truly believed that it would not end in our lifetime.

Vietnam hangover afflicted me as much as it afflicted anyone in '75. I had lost childhood friends, seen others come back maimed in body or spirit or both, and worked hard to bring the troops home for good. I was still angry, and bitter. But mostly, I was tired. If it wasn't the best of times for the country, you could sure prove it by me as well.

Fortunately, though, I was living in Massachusetts, where I'd spent my childhood and to where I'd returned when I couldn't think of anywhere else to go. The commonwealth wasn't a more pleasant place to be than other areas; in fact, it was more economically depressed than most and was about to burst into flame over Garrity's busing decision. But it felt like home.

And it had a diversion, one that both engaged my present and transported me back to a misery-free time that could never come again. For me, the summer of '75 was the summer of the Red Sox. And, as the dog days bled into fall, that magic season played itself out in a grand finale, the World Series, that hardly could have had a better story line if it had employed the most hyperbolic Hollywood hack.

Objections will now be raised, very legitimate ones. OK. Let me admit at the outset that it may be presumptuous, if not completely fatuous, to speak of a sporting event in the same breath with war, economic distress, racial inequities, and political turmoil. That's a given, and it's not something I'm about to debate here, even if I could decide which side I'd be on. Nor am I inclined (or equipped) to launch some scholarly discussion on the various roles of organized sports in society. Nevertheless, it has struck me, over the years, how often people define periods of their lives according to the seasons or eras of their favorite baseball teams, and how specific on-field incidents seem tethered to someone's own personal drama.

I'm reminded of Robin Williams explaining to Matt Damon in the film *Good Will Hunting* how his search for true love came into conflict with attending the '75 Series, how he had to choose between the two, and how he opted for love. Or of the friend who knew how high were the barriers between him and his soon-to-be-ex-wife when she didn't understand why he was letting the kids stay up past midnight to watch the end of 1975's scintillating Game 6.

Further, because I know for certain that the Red Sox came through for me at a time when I desperately needed them in *my* life, then I believe a persuasive case can be made that they (along with the Cincinnati Reds) also delivered the goods for society at large, in that for twelve wonderful days a meaningful segment of the population could put aside its more serious concerns and become entranced by what was happening on two small fields of green.

In the process, the players involved helped restore a love of the game to many for whom it had begun to slip away. For baseball, rather like myself and the country, was in one of its periodic stagnant phases. Other, more pressing matters had been competing for our attention. The national pastime had, in large measure, been displaced from its natural home, which is the hearts of those who have followed the progress of each passing season since they were in first grade.

But then '75 came along. As Boston sportswriter Dan Shaughnessy put it: "The 1975 World Series changed the way Americans felt about baseball. Watching these games was like blowing the dust off a favorite book and reading it for the first time in twenty years."

Yes, it was.

But most of all, we were given this gift: for that lovely, long October moment, we became as children once again.

And that is a gift of incalculable value.

The gift arrived in the form of a showdown between two teams that could not have been more different. We had no idea what was about to unfold—and certainly weren't expecting a Series that is widely considered the best ever—but some of us probably had a sneaking suspicion that there might be a classic in store.

On the one hand, there was the finely tuned Big Red Machine, a Cincinnati juggernaut that had cruised to 111 victories and an easy pennant and was already being ranked among the greatest teams of all time. And on the other, there were our guys, the rather more ragtag Red Sox. This was a group whose fans, those few remaining who carried a living memory, had last experienced a championship in 1918.

The managers of the two teams were polar opposites. Cincinnati boasted Sparky Anderson, a highly experienced, effusive, media-friendly genius and future Hall of Famer. The Red Sox were guided by Darrell Johnson, a reserved, poker-faced, highly stressed man who had been working at the major league level for only two years and who would lose his job nine months later and sink quietly back into the obscurity from which he had barely emerged.

Then there were the players.

The Reds had *players*, to be sure. But the Sox . . . it would be more descriptive to say that they had *characters*.

And what a cast of characters it was. Whereas Cincinnati fielded a bunch of guys named Johnny and Joe and Pete and George, Boston countered with Pudge and Yaz, Carbs and Willow, Señor and the Spaceman.

The Reds were an arrogant lot, a group of clean-cut, disciplined, highly professional athletes at the peaks of their careers. The Sox were, well, something else. Their money pitcher was an overweight, cigar-chomping fellow who sported a Fu Manchu mustache and spoke in an incongruous high-pitched voice with a nearly impenetrable Spanish accent; their non-pareil pinch hitter was a party animal who traveled everywhere with an enormous stuffed gorilla; and the organization's finest left-hander in twenty-five years was a politically outspoken pot smoker.

Not that the Red Sox didn't have a pretty good club. They'd won their division and then blown past an excellent Oakland A's team in the league championship series, three games to none. (Cincinnati had brushed off Pittsburgh by the same margin.)

But on paper the Reds were clearly superior.

They had three future Hall of Famers playing (Johnny Bench, Tony Perez, and Joe Morgan), plus one in the dugout (Sparky Anderson). They also had Pete Rose, who'd be a shoo-in for the Hall if he hadn't started salivating every time he saw a betting line. Their other position players were also imposing: sluggers George Foster (23 homers in the regular season) and Ken Griffey Sr. (who had hit .305), along with speedy defensive sparkplugs Davy Concepcion and César Geronimo.

Their starting pitching was solid, with Don Gullett in particular having had a stellar season. (In fact, Sparky had tabbed him a sure thing for Cooperstown, a certainty that failed to materialize when Gullett's career abruptly ended due to arm trouble.) And the bullpen, anchored by Rawley Eastwick, the National League leader in saves, was excellent.

True, the Sox had a couple of future Hall of Famers of their own, Carl Yastrzemski and Carlton Fisk, and a pitcher who clearly belongs there (Luis Tiant). But up and down the lineup they had less punch, especially after the loss to injury of their power-hitting rookie leftfielder, Jim Rice. They weren't as good defensively, their pitching staff was thinner, and they lacked a true closer.

As if all this weren't enough, there was also the dreaded Curse of the Bambino hanging over their heads like an anvil on a frayed rope.

This spell, legend has it, was laid upon the team for selling the game's greatest player, Babe Ruth, to the hated Yankees in 1918 for the paltry sum of $100,000. The sale purportedly came about because then-owner Harry Frazee's true love was Broadway, and he needed some cash in order to keep a production of *No, No Nanette* from going under. The show closed anyway and New York, understandably enough, failed to offer to return the Babe.

Since this terrible deal was consummated, according to the Curse, the Red Sox have been doomed, never again to win a World Series until someone figures out a way to lift the hex. Rational people may scoff at such things, yet the fact remains that a Series title *has* remained out of their grasp since Ruth pitched them to victory just before he was sold. And the bizarre ways in which they have come so close, only to lose, stretches one's belief in coincidence to the breaking point.

Certainly the team often appears beaten prior to the fact. Writer Thomas Boswell once proposed an "almost inexorable baseball law: A Red Sox ship with a single leak will always find a way to sink. . . . No team is worshipped with such a perverse sense of fatality."

Thus came the underdogs, demonstrably deficient in both managerial and on-the-field talent and, as if that were not enough, subject to the possibility that nearly six decades earlier one of their number had committed an offense of biblical proportions. It was quite a burden. Under the circumstances, the 1975 matchup should have been over before it began. No contest. Fuggedaboudit. A stroll in the park for the dreaded Beast from the Midwest.

Instead, viewers were treated to a seesaw battle without parallel. Four of the seven games were won in the final inning; six were come-from-behind victories; and five, including the nail-biting finale, were decided by a single run. The spectacle won the attention and admiration of millions.

Yet baseball is more than sport, more than spectacle, more than merely a contest in which one group of twenty-five wins and another loses. Baseball is greater than it seems. Its stately, orderly progressions touch parts of ourselves that lie deep within, places we do not expect to be reached by our pastimes.

Baseball is built upon a profound and emotionally satisfying metaphor. As Bart Giamatti, the late commissioner of baseball and unofficial poet laureate of Red Sox Nation, always reminded us, it's "about going home, and how hard it is to get there and how driven is our need. It tells us how good home is. Its wisdom says you can go home again but that you cannot stay. The journey must always start once more, the bat an oar over the shoulder, until there is an end to all journeying. *Nostos*; the going home, the game of nostalgia, so apt an image for our hunger that it hurts."

Giamatti had a flair for the dramatic—OK, the melodramatic—but that doesn't belie his vision.

For baseball *is* about going home. Why else would its focal point be called "home" instead of the more logical "fourth base"? And why would its defining event—the only one that mandates both the leaving and the return during the same at-bat—be called a "home run" or "homer," rather than a "quadruple"?

You can search all the historical texts you want, but you won't find the answer to these questions. No one knows. So why not assume that, back when the originators came to the naming of parts, there was someone like Bart present, and that he understood?

It is a true journey, this game and series of games, composed (like most journeys) of fits and starts, ecstatic highs and devastating lows, bursts of adrenaline and stretches of tedium. In the taking of it, it creates a tale, a tale that can be told and retold, and with each retelling we enter yet more deeply the realm of myth. For that is where the game most securely resides. There, and in our own inner home.

With that in mind, I set out on a very personal quest at the dawn of the new millennium, in 2000, the twenty-fifth anniversary of the 1975 World Series and the ninety-ninth year of the Red Sox' existence as a professional baseball team.

What, I wondered, had happened to those Boston teammates who had so charmed us back then? Had they somehow made it back home—despite the inflexible path charted by the nature of the game, ballplayers are, if nothing else, surely wanderers—after they left friendly Fenway?

Who had they been, these children now grown old? Where did they come from? What struggles had they endured in order to arrive at the Show, and how did they feel when they made it? What did they now think of their younger selves, and of those with whom they shared the experience?

What did they remember of their moments in the national spotlight? Did the experience change them significantly or, perhaps, not at all?

Then there were those special games themselves. Would the participants be willing to re-create them for me? Would they detail their performances, their emotional shifts over the course of the Series? Would they analyze what went right and wrong, engage in some second-guessing, reveal what they would have done differently if they could go back?

Finally, there was this: these particular boys of October were my peers. For the most part, they were members of the same rock 'n' roll, Vietnam, power-to-the-people generation as I. I wanted them to place their lives in the context of the times for me. I wanted to examine my life through their eyes. And I wanted to discover what tricks time had played upon them during the final two and a half decades of the twentieth century.

These were the kinds of questions that tickled my curiosity until I had no choice but to pursue them and the only people who could provide the answers—the members of the 1975 Red Sox. Happily, and a bit surprisingly, my first research revealed that every member of that team was still living. One by one, I set out to meet them.

Baseball began in a bright green field with an ancient name when this country was new and raw and without shape, and it has shaped America by linking every summer from 1846 to this one, through wars and depressions and seasons of rain. . . .

The game is quintessentially American in the way it puts the premium on both the individual and the team; in the way it encourages enterprise and imagination and yet asserts the supreme power of the law. Baseball is quintessentially American in the way it tells us that much as you travel and far as you go, out to the green frontier, the purpose is to get home, back to where the others are, the pioneer ever striving to come back to the common place. A nation of migrants always, for all their wandering, remembers what every immigrant never forgets: that you may leave home but if you forget where home is, you are truly lost and without hope.

—A. BARTLETT GIAMATTI
"MEN OF BASEBALL, LEND AN EAR"

The Chortling Buddha

Any baseball is beautiful. No other small package comes as close to the ideal in design and utility. It is a perfect object for a man's hand. Pick it up and it instantly suggests its purpose; it is meant to be thrown a considerable distance—thrown hard and with precision. Its feel and heft are the beginning of the sport's critical dimensions; if it were a fraction of an inch larger or smaller, a few centigrams heavier or lighter, the game of baseball would be utterly different. Hold a baseball in your hand . . . feel it, turn it over; hold it across the seam or the other way, with the seam just to the side of your middle finger. Speculation stirs. You want to get outdoors and throw this spare and sensual object to somebody or, at the very least, watch somebody else throw it. The game has begun.

—ROGER ANGELL, "ON THE BALL"

Back in September of '75, if devoid of good fortune in most areas of my life, I was at least lucky with regard to the World Series. I won the opportunity to see a part of this classic in person.

I was living some eighty miles from Boston, on the bicep of the arm that is Cape Cod. It had been a rough summer, one that the Sox helped me endure. As October loomed and it appeared that we might be celebrating our third pennant since the loss of the Babe, I very much wanted to be there. And, surprisingly by present-day standards, I could. Back then, team management made it possible, at least in theory, for Joe Average Fan to attend a World Series game. That's how it was in Boston, anyway.

All you had to do was submit an application for tickets, along with a check for the requisite amount, and wait. Your name would be put into a lottery, along with everyone else's; I envisioned a huge fishbowl and, in that misty, nearly forgotten past before the computer revolution, there may actually have been one. Then there would be a drawing. Most folks just got their checks returned, I imagine. But if fate was with you, a pair of tickets came back in the mail.

I can remember as if it were yesterday, opening the post office box on that fall afternoon and seeing the envelope from the big city. I couldn't believe that I was going to the World Series. Twenty-eight years later, it still feels miraculous. But there they were. Two tickets. Game 1. Fenway Park. Center-field bleachers. Third row from the top, as I would later find out.

I don't have a clear idea how things are handled these days, but I know it's not like that. There are no more lotteries. Not in New England, prob- ably not anywhere. You need to be a season ticket holder, or have a lot of money, or be politically well connected. No matter how passionate a par- tisan you are, if you don't measure up in one of those departments, then come October you're going to be watching your team on TV along with all those just like you.

Not me, though. Not that particular fall. I had my pair of tickets, and the only remaining question was who I was going to invite to go with me. I thought about my brother and my girlfriend, both of them fans, both of them deserving. But in the end, it was no contest. The only possible choice was my Uncle Oscar.

Oscar was a crusty old New England native whose ancestors first set foot on the region's stony soil almost three and a half centuries earlier and who had seldom ventured off-Cape after making a home there in the late 1940s. An outstanding semipro shortstop, he'd been forced out of baseball by the economic realities of the Depression. Once upon a time, he'd kindly tried to teach me how to pitch. He failed.

He succeeded at a lot of other things, though. He took care of our fam- ily when my father was suffering through some hard times, and he helped me get a job more than once.

Oscar was my man. I owed him. Besides, baseball and the Sox had bound us together for many, many years. We talked about the team, year in and year out. He was old enough to remember, if dimly, the last time the Sox had won a world championship—1918, which was also the year of the great Spanish flu epidemic that took the life of his father. He was seven.

Now, for only the third time since Oscar lost his dad, Boston would have another chance. He needed to be there.

I knew when I offered him the ticket that he was going to resist, which he did. At first he tried, typically, to convince me that one of the other candidates was actually more deserving. Then he floated that old mantra about the ills that were certain to befall any real Cape Codder who dared cross the Canal to "the Mainland." But I wouldn't budge. He was going to make it to Fenway in '75 if I had to truss him up and drag him there.

And in the end, he gave in.

So it was that we set off, the old shortstop and I, for Fenway Park on a raw, blustery October day.

It was fitting that the first game should be played there, in one of the last of the traditional parks, rather than in Cincinnati. Fenway had history and character. Riverfront Stadium had neither. It was one of those new-fangled hybrids, designed to accommodate both baseball and football and capable of doing neither job well. Sox pitcher Bill Lee sniffed that it was "a concrete jungle made by a pharmaceutical company."

Riverfront, let's face it, was plug-ugly, an entirely fitting home for the superefficient, businesslike Reds, a team that had been termed a "machine." (It is a measure of the nature of fandom in Ohio that the appellation was considered a compliment.)

Then there was Fenway, which with Wrigley Field in Chicago is one of the two patriarchs of major league playing fields. It had been dedicated way back on April 16, 1912, which coincidentally was two days after the sinking of the *Titanic*. Or maybe it was more than coincidence. . . .

Whatever the case, to enjoy a game at Fenway Park is to partake of the essence of baseball, which is itself more attuned to the rhythm of the seasons, and to changes in the weather, than any other sport. It is meant to be played outdoors, on real grass, exposed to the vagaries of sun and shadow, wind and rain. In Boston, that's what you get.

Now, let it be said up front that there are any number of bad seats in Fenway, behind posts and under roof overhangs and whatnot. We admit this. The interior is dank and gloomy as well. And noxious odors are, in places, assaultive. However, the old ball field makes up for these deficiencies in other ways.

For one thing, the amount of foul territory is the smallest in the major leagues. This serves to reduce the number of foul outs batters can make, giving them more pitches to swing at, and thereby creating one of the best of the hitter's parks. Combined with the compact nature of the place, it also means that you're close to the action, no matter where you are. You can see the players' faces, even from the back rows of the bleachers, where I would sit. The cheap seats are a great place from which to watch a game.

Fenway has more quirks than anyplace else in baseball. Notably, of course, there's the Green Monster, the left-field wall that's 37 feet high but barely 300 feet from home plate. (Management's insistence on the official distance of 315 feet is generally disbelieved.) Whatever the truth, the Wall giveth and the Wall taketh away. It turns windblown pop flies into homers, while monster line drives are often reduced to singles that, as nowhere else, begin their lives with a thwacking sound.

There are also pockets of dead space in left and center, where the bounces can drive a fielder crazy; jutting edges to the stands; and a couple of doorways that play havoc with an orderly flight path.

And there are the fans. They can be brutal. But no others are more knowledgeable, or more willing to show their appreciation of a fine play, even if it's made by an opponent.

There is nothing quite like baseball in Boston, at Fenway Park, whether it's during a gentle April drizzle; the hot, muggy days of July; or the windy chill of October. Whether the team is winning or losing. Whether you walk down Commonwealth Avenue or take the "T" (and you better not look for parking; there isn't any). Anytime is a good time to go out to the Fens.

But best of all is the exquisite joy of attending a World Series game there. That is truly special, if for no other reason than that it happens so seldom: four times in 1967, three in 1946, not once in the twenty-eight years prior to that.

Oscar and I felt privileged to be a part of it.

As the Series commences, consider for a moment the characteristics of this gracious, this great and glorious game.

Unlike other team sports, its drama is enacted not upon a cold grid of rigid shape and proportion, but within a great circle whose center is called "home" and whose arc is intersected by lines that define "fair" and "foul" fields of play—the terms suggesting the unpredictable changeability of the weather. These are lines that, in theory, can be stretched to infinity. A batted ball could be hit a mile and still be honestly judged either a home run or a long strike.

Baseball was originally played not in jackbooted Romanesque *stadia* (Yankee Stadium be damned!) but in pastoral places named Ebbets *Field* and Sportsman's *Park* and the Polo *Grounds*.

It is a game unlike others in that it determines its own pace, never dependent on the ticking down of minutes or seconds subdivided into tenths and hundredths. (In fact the action, proceeding as it does counter-clockwise, thumbs its nose at common time.) There will be three outs to a half-inning, and there will be at least eight and a half innings to a game. If this keeps the spectators in their seats past midnight, as it will in Game 6 of this Series, then so be it.

It is a game that, like the country from which it sprang, exalts both the individual over the group and the group over the individual. It involves a continual confrontation between two men, one at home plate and one on a low hill a very short distance away—a primal confrontation that has the latter heaving a rocklike spheroid in the direction of the former, who is armed with a blunt, heavy club with which to defend himself. Yet it is still a contest in which the lone participant's fate is utterly dependent on the support provided by his teammates—save with the home run, the defiant sole exception that proves the rule.

It is a game of mystical numerological significances, primarily based on holy trinities: 3 outs per inning, 3 strikes per batter, 3 outfielders, 9 players (3^2), 9 innings per game, 27 (3^3) outs per side to the conclusion.

In addition, its fixed dimensions are all divisible by three. The pitcher's rubber is twenty-four inches by six inches. The mound is fifteen inches high, in the center of a circle with a diameter of eighteen feet. The pitcher stands sixty feet six inches from home plate. The base paths are ninety feet long.

To these, perhaps for counterpoint, is added a sprinkling of harmonious fours: four balls for a walk, four bases, four infielders, four sides to the infield and to each of the three bases that lie within it.

There is also a profusion of shapes to be seen. Circles: the pitcher's mound, the on-deck areas, the sectioned circle that constitutes the entire field. Squares: the bases. Rectangles: the pitcher's rubber, the batters' boxes, the dugouts and bullpens, the strike zone.

And the one mysterious, irregular figure: the pentagon of home plate. Why a pentagon? I don't know. Its geometric irregularity is certainly jarring at first. Yet on reflection it seems appropriate that the plate be somehow different from the other bases. It is the starting point of all action, as well as the place to which a player must return in order to score. It is "home" not just to one side but to both, a quaint notion entirely incompatible with territorially based conquest games such as football, basketball, hockey, and soccer.

At the heart of the field of play lies a great square turned on its corner point: the diamond. The most precious of gemstones. Universal symbol of clarity, strength, beauty, purity, and the capacity to endure.

All other major sports are played on rectangles and feature contestants who travel back and forth in a mostly linear fashion. The diamond produces a circular path, from home to home. Within it, there are small, ninety-foot straight-line movements, with an abrupt change of direction at the end of each, climaxed by the confrontation (at home) between the base runner and the only armored defender, the catcher.

The Buddha's most revered teaching is called the Diamond Sutra. In it, he says: "A bodhisattva should practice virtue without regard to appearances, unsupported by sights, sounds, smells, tastes, tactile sensations, or mental attachments. A bodhisattva should practice virtue without attachment to externals." This (with no offense meant to believers in the faith) is rather similar to an athlete's description of being in "the zone."

The truth of the matter is that the game of baseball found a design so nearly perfect that it seems impossible to have been arrived at by chance.

Take as an example, that on a simple ground ball, cleanly handled, the batter will almost be able to beat it out, but not quite; this is true (most of the time, anyway) even of Ichiro Suzuki, who gets a running start when he swings and goes from home to first in 3.8 seconds, fastest in the majors. Or that on a routine fly to left or right, a runner will generally score from third, but perhaps not. Or that with the mound positioned as it is, the pitcher is at a proper distance to bring his best stuff, without it either resembling a beach ball or being completely unhittable (well, unless you're a left-hander facing Randy Johnson).

The mound-to-plate distance, as constituted, means that the batter has a tiny window of opportunity instinctively to react to a pitch. Four-tenths of a second, to be precise—which is how long it takes a ninety-mile-per-hour fastball to travel from the point of release to the strike zone.

That is sufficient time for the human nervous system to respond to a stimulus, but just barely. The hitter certainly can't think about it; if he does, the pitch is past him. The best he can hope for is to see the ball and manage a good swing at it.

The swing will consume two-tenths of a second, but that is the least important consideration. Assume that a right-handed batter swings cleanly, with power, taking dead aim on the center-field bleachers, and this is his margin of error: if the swing is $1/100$ of a second too early, the ball will go foul down the left-field line; if it is $1/100$ of a second too late, the ball will go foul down the right-field line.

Quarterbacks know how hard it is to make the football's flight intersect with the receiver; basketball players know how hard it is to stick a twenty-foot jumper with a defender in your face; and golfers surely know how hard it is to propel even a stationary ball in a straight line.

But the man standing alone in the batter's box has it the worst. Not only must he make contact with a thrown ball that's due to arrive in less than half a second, but he must adjust for speeds varying between about 75 and 100 miles and hour, and for spins that cause the ball to deviate from a straight line, in myriad combinations of up and down, left and right, with thousands of screaming people pressuring him to either succeed or fail. Or, as Ted Williams succinctly put it, "The most difficult feat in sports is to hit a pitched ball."

Thus it comes as no surprise that even the very best fail to reach base safely seven times out of ten, ensuring a kind of parity between the two who face each other and also ensuring that relatively few games will turn into out-and-out slugfests.

But baseball is more than the sum of its mathematics, its mechanics, its physical graces, and the emotional investment of its fans in any given contest.

More than any other sporting endeavor, with the possible exception of golf, it exists within a historical context. Recollections of its former greats are passed from parent to child, and meticulously kept statistics allow comparisons between eras, the placing of one star's accomplishments beside another's.

It has also been there in the bad times, easing the burden of economic deprivation and helping alleviate the horror of war. So ingrained is it in the national psyche that players' names were used to distinguish friend from foe during the conquest of Nazi Germany; if you couldn't recite at least part of the lineup of the Brooklyn Dodgers, you were presumed to be the enemy.

A lot changed between the end of World War II and the competition between the Reds and Red Sox. Just not in baseball. So turn back the clock to '75. Settle in, grab a brew or whatever your favorite baseball-watching drink might be, and enjoy the Series.

The boys of October have taken their places. The games are about to begin.

We come up out of the gloom beneath, Oscar and I, and enter Fenway Park, tucked between bustling Kenmore Square and the soggy fens for which it was named. It's the eleventh day of the month. Game 1.

A corpulent geezer and a lithe young stud are making their warm-up pitches as we settle into our seats in the distant bleachers, three rows removed from the back wall, over which no human being has ever hit a baseball.

Though the temperature at game time is sixty degrees, it's a raw sixty and falling. Low clouds hover, dripping a light drizzle onto the field. Colorful umbrellas dot the stands, and they'll remain open until the first inning, when the rain lets up for good. The day, however, will remain damp and overcast throughout. And the wind will blow continuously, from right toward the left-field grandstands. It's a pitcher's wind, as we shall see.

The teams are introduced, player by player, coach by coach. Cincinnati manager Sparky Anderson playfully sticks out his tongue and points at someone in the stands. He seems in a fine humor, as do most of the Reds. They're joking and laughing, quite in contrast to their image as baseball's most straitlaced outfit. Sparky may have his fun-loving side, but he's a strict disciplinarian and old school when it comes to his players' appearance. They wear coats and ties off the field, and there is no long hair or mustaches here. The only concession to fashion is the occasional pair of sideburns, but even these are trimmed to the nub and razor-edged.

The Sox, on the other hand, are downright scruffy. Lots of mustaches and long, bushy hairdos. Yet, perhaps taking their cue from their dour manager, Darrell Johnson, they're the ones who appear tight. Their expressions are uniformly set, even grim. Carl Yastrzemski looks almost morose. (Later he will tell me that that's his game face, that what I'm seeing is utmost concentration.)

After everyone else has tipped his cap, a solitary figure jogs in from the right-field bullpen. It's Jim Rice, and the crowd cheers loudly for him.

Rice will become The Man Who Was Not There in this series, the subject of an endless "what if . . . ?" He has had a monster rookie season in which he hit .309, with 22 home runs and 102 runs batted in. Then, on September 21, Detroit's Vern Ruhle hit him with a pitch and broke his left wrist. He won't play. Though it's reported that at one point he will beg Johnson to put him in, the manager will refuse.

With Rice out, the thirty-six-year-old Yastrzemski—who has played 140 games at first base this year—moves to left. Young Cecil Cooper takes his place in the infield.

This is a defensive upgrade for the Sox, since Yaz, even at his age, is one of the premier leftfielders in the game, and he knows the Fenway turf like no one else. Offensively, the team should get about as many hits as they would have with Rice; Cooper hit .311 on the season and is a budding star.

But . . . there's no question that the team will miss Jim Rice's power, his intensity, and his consistent ability to drive runners in (102 is a *lot* of RBI for someone with "only" 22 homers). And then there's this: Rice is right-handed. His replacement hits from the other side, and the Reds' best pitcher, Don Gullett, is a hard-throwing left-hander who turns lefty batters into jelly.

There is not likely to be a single knowledgeable fan who thinks this is going to be a good trade-off. Injuries are, however, an inevitable part of the game, and the great teams shrug them off. It is hoped that the rest of the Red Sox will raise their games in the absence of their cleanup hitter.

Treasury Secretary William Simon throws out the first ball. He's roundly booed, undoubtedly catching the blame for New England having the highest oil prices in the country.

The Sox take the field.

Strolling out to the pitcher's mound is the aforementioned geezer, a portly thirty-four-year-old Cuban who looks older. (And according to speculation in the media, may *be* older; no one has ever seen a birth certificate.) This is Luis Tiant, aka *Señor*, aka *El Tiante*. He is one of the most beloved players ever to appear in a Sox uniform. If he says he's thirty-four, then he's thirty-four.

Today, no one gives a damn about his age. He is simply the man on the mound, the focus of everyone's undivided attention, the pitcher who must succeed if the Red Sox are to have a prayer of taking the championship. The chant begins: "Loo-ie, Loo-ie," though not as boisterously as during the regular season.

There's a reason for this. Many of the butts in these seats belong to people entrenched within Boston's labyrinthine political patronage system. For such folks, the postseason likely marks their first visit to the park this year, and they consider it rather undignified to behave like the raucous, in-your-face July regulars.

Looie bobs and spins and throws ball one to the Reds' first batter, Pete Rose, and as he does, it is probably only the few Cincinnati fans in attendance who don't believe something magical may happen here today, with Tiant in the role of the mage.

By his high standards, Looie has had an off year. He went 18–14, with an earned run average of 4.02. Not bad, but nothing like the previous three seasons, when he was one of the most dominant pitchers in the game.

Nevertheless, Bostonians believe Tiant to be the best there is when the rent money is on the line. Better even than his opposite number, Reds' ace Don Gullett, a baby-faced twenty-four-year-old who's already in his sixth season in the Show. He mopped up the National League in '75, leading it in winning percentage and posting a 2.42 ERA.

Gullett has youth and strength and a hellacious fastball. Tiant's heater isn't bad—the Oakland A's, whom he's just beaten, have described it as "better than average"—but at his age he relies more on experience and guile. Gullett can overpower; Looie, at his best, makes major league hitters, even as awesome a group as Cincinnati has, flail away as foolishly as if they belong back in Single A.

That's what Sox fans are not only hoping for but expecting.

And not in vain.

For Looie dazzles.

Boston sports fans are notorious for being savvy, dedicated to their teams, highly opinionated, and extraordinarily hard on players who have displeased them. The local media also tend to be quick to judge, and to condemn. They have exceedingly long memories. It's a tough town for any professional athlete.

Over the years, the city has been blessed with some great ones: Ted Williams, Roger Clemens, Wade Boggs, Bill Russell, Larry Bird. These men were revered for what they could do. Yet for all their consummate skills, all the adulation heaped upon them, none ever earned a place in the fans' heart of hearts. They were admired, but never *loved*. That distinction has been reserved for only the very, very few.

Bobby Orr, certainly.

John Havlicek.

Yaz, perhaps, at the end.

And Luis Tiant.

It's difficult to convey to someone who never had the pleasure of watching Tiant at work how extraordinarily entertaining he was. He was a pitcher unlike any other, a man once called by Reggie Jackson "the Fred Astaire of baseball."

Baseball gospel has forever held that a pitcher in the act of throwing should never take his eye off the batter, and over the years this inherited wisdom has gone relatively unquestioned. One exception, Juan Marichal, bent far backward and looked straight up at the sky, and Fernando Valenzuela sometimes closed his eyes.

Then there was Tiant.

Luis took conventional thought and simply stood it on its head. When he went into his windup, he would completely turn his back to the batter. He would bend and twist and pivot, rolling his eyes, as though dancing to some herky-jerky beat only he could hear. Then, finally, he'd come all the way around and throw the ball.

Maybe overhand, maybe sidearm or three-quarter arm. You never knew. The hitter never knew. It's probable that even Luis didn't know until the second he put his arm in motion. There was also no tip-off as to whether the pitch coming was a fastball or breaking ball, nor at what speed it was being delivered.

All of this had a very disconcerting effect on batters, naturally enough. They were always having to guess, and more often than not they guessed wrong.

But that wasn't Tiant's only advantage.

Twenty-five years later, he was the first of the boys of October I met. When I finally nailed down the interview, I had to settle for an hour and a half in a motel coffee shop in the Boston suburbs. I didn't want to waste a minute of it, and the first thing I asked Luis was about his unorthodox delivery, particularly the part about turning his back to the hitter. He didn't hesitate to offer his opinion.

"Point of release," he said in a soft, thickly Spanish-accented voice that seemed way too high for someone of his size. "That's all that matters. Point of release. Let's say you want to hit me on the chin."

"Actually, I don't."

He chortled. It was a gentle, almost musical sound, and it happened frequently.

"But if you do," he said, "there's a point at which you know you're going to do that. You aim for it, and you do it. That's the point of release. It's the only time you have to look at my chin. Same with pitching."

So much for the standard book of baseball. It might have been a different matter if Tiant hadn't gotten results—all those managers who implored him to change would've nodded their heads sagely—but he did.

"When did you start?" I asked.

"When I was a teenager. I was looking for something different to do, that nobody else was doing. So I started turning my back to the batter. And it worked for me. After that, I just kept doing it."

He paused, stroking the thick black mustache that still curls around the edges of his mouth. It draws attention to his face and de-emphasizes that otherwise he's almost entirely bald. As well as even more rotund than he was in his playing days.

Yet the years have not been especially unkind to someone who would turn sixty in a couple of months. He looked healthy (despite complaints about his aching back and sore knees); his brown eyes twinkled— embarrassing to use the cliché, but they really did; and his skin was as smooth and unlined as a baby's.

For just a moment I envisioned him with his legs crossed underneath him, like a smiling, seated Buddha. And who's to say that isn't what he's become?

"Besides," he added, "it's a better way. To tell you the truth, I'm surprised no one else picked it up."

"Explain."

"Keeps your balance better. More power. Use your body more."

I thought I saw what he meant. "Like golf," I said. I knew he was going to play a round after the interview. "Tiger Woods generates all that power by the way he torques his hips."

"Right."

I nodded. I never thought about applying the same mechanical principle to baseball. But why not?

Certainly on that day in 1975, Tiant was proving his point, right from the start.

To the very first batter, Pete Rose, Looie serves up a hesitation curve on a 2–2 count. The pitch seems to float toward the plate at about twenty miles an hour. Pete can do nothing but stare at the ball in disbelief. There he stares—crazy Pete, tragically flawed Pete, Pete who never in his adult life had a good hair day—and you can almost see him thinking, *You insult me like this? Me? The best contact hitter in baseball?* Lucky for him, it's a couple of inches high, and he's spared the embarrassment of being called out on a pitch you or I or any Little Leaguer could hit. He steps out of the batter's box to compose himself, still shaking his head, then steps back in.

Looie has gone 3 and 2 to leadoff man Rose, the player upon whose sour expression is most clearly stamped the grim and utter desperation to succeed. He doesn't. After a couple of fouls, he slaps a grounder to second. Denny Doyle fields it, flips it to Cecil Cooper at first, and the initial out of the '75 World Series is recorded.

The crowd cheers. Tiant is 26 outs away from a no-hitter.

Of course, no one is thinking in those terms just a single out into the game. In fact, there has been only one no-hitter in Series history, when the Yankees' Don Larsen beat the Dodgers back in '56 (Larsen pitched a perfect game as well). But this *is* Boston, anticipation is keen, and . . . anything might be possible.

The crowd settles down as Tiant goes to the rosin bag, preparing to work his wiles on Reds' second baseman Joe Morgan.

Little Joe is coming off a monster year, in which all he did was hit .327, with a .508 slugging average. He led the league in walks (132), and on-base percentage (.470). In addition, he scored 107 runs, batted in 94, and stole 67 bases. He made but 11 errors in the field. He's a shoo-in for

National League Most Valuable Player, which he will win both this year and next.

Morgan takes a big cut at the first pitch offered him and lines it hard, but right at Doyle. Two down.

Up third is slugger Johnny Bench, certainly the greatest defensive—and arguably the best all-around—catcher in baseball history.

Tiant goes to 3 and 2 once again, then fires a fastball that catches Bench off balance. He swings late and lofts a fly to right field. Dwight Evans gathers it in easily, and the first half-inning is in the books.

The no-hitter is still 24 outs distant, but Tiant looks masterful, and the crowd is pumping him up with every pitch. As he walks back to the dugout, more than one fan is dreaming . . .

There is no doubt that Luis Tiant was a consummate entertainer. No one ever asked for his or her money back when Tiant was out there. Or, as Reggie Jackson once said about himself, Luis "put the asses in the seats."

He also garnered affection and respect for who he was. That's not always easy to discern when you're talking about public figures. But with Luis, what you saw was what you got. He was, and is, a decent, hardworking man with integrity, a prankish sense of humor, and a kind word for everyone.

But he was also a baseball player, after all. And they don't win the fans' love simply because they're nice guys. So, the question might reasonably be asked, just how *good* was he? Not as a neighbor, or a performer. As a pitcher.

Well, the answer is simple. Tiant was extraordinarily good. So good that, ironically, most people have forgotten just how dominating he was.

Let me say this: there's not the slightest doubt that Luis Tiant is the greatest player in the history of the game who is eligible for the Hall of Fame and is not already elected to it. Tiant being denied entry into Cooperstown was completely inexplicable, and now that his window of opportunity for making it via the normal voting process has closed, he'll have to go in through the Old-Timers committee. He will, though that's a crime.

I've said it. Now let me defend it.

Sure, every longtime fan has a favorite player with marginal Hall of Fame credentials that maybe, kinda, sorta, *oughtta* be enough to get him in. But that is simply not the case here. This is not a guy on the margin;

it's someone whose induction should've been a moral certainty. All considerations of art and style aside (and that should be worth *something*), there are the cold, hard statistics. They don't lie.

Luis Tiant won 229 major league games. No record, but quite respectable. It's more wins than Hall of Famers Bob Lemon (207), Catfish Hunter (224), or Don Drysdale (209) could muster. Sandy Koufax (with no argument being offered that *he* doesn't belong in the Hall) won only 165.

His lifetime winning percentage was .571. Again, that's better than Drysdale, Ferguson Jenkins, Early Wynn, and many others.

According to baseball's leading statistical analyst, Bill James, of even greater significance is a pitcher's winning percentage vs. that of the teams he played for. In other words, how much better was he than those teams in general?

Here again, Tiant shines. His career winning percentage exceeded that of his teams' by .033. That might not sound like a lot, but it's quite high. About the same as Hunter's. *Much* better than Drysdale, Wynn, or Nolan Ryan's.

Bill James, in fact, rates Tiant as the fifty-second greatest pitcher of all time. A highly subjective assessment, to be sure, even though James makes it as fact-backed as humanly possible. But his calls are pretty much in line with the Hall of Fame. Of those ranked ahead of Luis, thirty-nine are already there. Five are not yet eligible—Roger Clemens, Greg Maddux, Dennis Eckersley, Pedro Martinez, Randy Johnson—and all are locks. One, Eddie Cicotte, was stained by the Black Sox scandal and won't get in until baseball forgives. Two, Bert Blyleven and Goose Gossage, are close and will likely make it someday. That leaves four who probably won't. None of them has two hundred wins.

Among those who rate *lower* than Tiant, *eleven* are already enshrined.

Another consideration is that, especially in the modern era, an ERA of less than 2.00 is vanishingly rare among starting pitchers. Jim Palmer never accomplished it, nor did Drysdale, Hunter, or Wynn. Steve Carlton did it once, as did Ryan and Tom Seaver. Luis Tiant did it *twice*, and one of those times was in the heat of a pennant race with the Red Sox.

Though the Sox eventually lost that year, Luis did get his chances in the postseason, and he took advantage of them as well as anyone would have. With the big money on the line—in League Championship and World Series games, against the best the opposition could muster—he went 3–0, with three complete games, one shutout, and an earned run average of 2.71. Pretty damn good.

Finally, take a close look at Tiant's greatest campaign, 1968.

It was an epochal year, in more ways than one. Beyond the ballparks, the country was disintegrating. Martin Luther King Jr. was assassinated, and I watched from the roof of my apartment building as Washington, D.C., burned in response. Late that night, I ventured down into the city. The streets were empty of cars; there were National Guardsmen on the corners speaking into walkie-talkies; tear gas hung in the still air. It was difficult to believe that I was walking around in the nation's capital.

Then Bobby Kennedy, the man with the best chance of ending the war in Vietnam, was also gunned down. The Democratic Convention in Chicago degenerated into chaos as the police rioted and clubbed anyone within arm's reach, and inside the hall the Democrats rejected the people's choice, Gene McCarthy, in order to nominate party hack Hubert Humphrey, thereby ensuring the election of the ultimate night ghoul, Richard Nixon.

Small wonder that even the most rabid fans' minds might not have been on baseball. I know mine wasn't.

But, as it almost always has, baseball did go on. So did Luis Tiant, and, sadly, along with many others I missed what he did. His performance in that cursed year bears close examination, because Luis in '68 turned in one of the most brilliant season-long efforts ever recorded.

Unfortunately, if typically for this man so often undervalued, the effort went almost unnoticed, and not only because of the strife in the streets of America. It just happened to occur in a year to remember for pitchers, the year Bob Gibson had an ERA of 1.12 while pitching the Cardinals into the World Series, where he won two more games to go with the three he'd notched against the Red Sox in '67.

Tiant, to his detriment, was toiling for Cleveland, which wound up a distant third to the Tigers in the American League. His team finished a decent 11 games over .500; Tiant by himself was plus-12. His record was 21–9, his ERA 1.60, which was the American League's lowest since Walter Johnson in 1919. It would have been considered sensational but for Gibson.

And, wouldn't you know, he didn't even win the league's Cy Young Award. Voters for that honor tend to reward victories, and nobody was going to deny Denny McLain after he notched 31 wins and led Detroit into the Series against Gibson and the Cards.

Luis won "only" 21. He pitched nine shutouts and completed 19 games out of 32 starts.

His most astonishing achievement, though, wasn't the superlative won/ loss record or ERA. It wasn't the shutouts or the 264 strikeouts in 258 innings. It wasn't the superb 3.6 strikeout/walk ratio.

It was hits per nine innings. Luis yielded a mere 5.3. Consider: opposing batters connected for a base hit against him *fewer than five and a half times a game.* He threw a five-hitter virtually every time out! *That* is dominance. Even Gibson, stellar as he was, couldn't match it; he gave up 5.8.

Other Hall of Famers, at their very finest, aren't even close. Drysdale's *best ever* was a distant 6.78, behind Hunter (6.1) and comparable to Lemon (6.87). Forget about Palmer (7.05), Jenkins (7.16), and Wynn (7.52). Koufax's best? 5.79. Walter Johnson's? 5.98. Bob Feller's? 6.89. Not even in the ballpark.

It is, actually, the lowest hits-per-game average ever recorded for someone who pitched as many as 250 innings, with two exceptions. Pedro Martinez matched it in 2000, and Nolan Ryan averaged a marginally more impressive 5.26 in 1972. That's it. No one else ever did better. No one.

One great season, of course, does not make for Hall of Fame credentials, no matter how extraordinary it might be. Yet if you place '68 in the context of Tiant's full career, you have to wonder how this guy could possibly not be in the Hall, twenty years after he retired. What on earth could be going on?

I asked Bill Lee, Tiant's teammate in '75, and all he said was, "There aren't many Latin voters." But that was Lee, sometimes known as the Spaceman. He loves conspiracies.

I floated the charge of racism past Dick Bresciani, the Red Sox' vice president for public relations, a man who started his career with the ball club just prior to 1975. He disagreed. "No," he said, "I think it's mostly that he just played in small markets." But then, Dick is just a flat-out nice guy. He never says anything unpleasant about anyone.

Seeking a more definitive opinion, I talked with Larry Whiteside, a longtime *Boston Globe* sportswriter, member of the Baseball Writers of America (BBWA), and one of those determining who will be elected to the

Hall. I asked Larry to fill me in on the selection process. Who are the voters, for example?

"Every major league city has a local chapter of the BBWA," he told me. "But you have to have ten years' service to join. They only want really knowledgeable people. The Association works up a list of eligible players each year, passes it on to us, then we vote on them."

Were there meetings where members from different cities got together?

"Two scheduled meetings, at the All-Star Game and the World Series."

And did they talk about candidates?

Only informally, he told me. "It's not considered proper to take up a particular player's cause. Except in the newspaper."

All right, then, what about Luis Tiant? What was keeping him out? Racism, lack of exposure, what?

"I think it's a combination of things," he said. "Bill Lee is right, Latin players do have a hard time. There are few if any Latin voters, and in fact I was the only nonwhite voter until about five years ago. This makes it difficult for Latin players to get access to the media. Then there's the question of, does he measure up?"

Ludicrous, I said, rattling off the relevant statistics.

"I agree," Whiteside said. "But then, I've voted for him every year since he was first eligible. The Association also takes into account character."

Luis should pass that test with ease, I said.

"Yes. As far as the small market argument goes, I believe there's something in that. Tiant had some of his best years with Cleveland and, back then, even Boston was considered a small market. He has no recognition at all out West.

"Another thing that's been working against him is the campaign to get Tony Perez in the Hall. Tony had a lot of very vocal support, both in the Midwest and down in Florida. People wanted him to be the first Cuban to make it into Cooperstown, and that helped cut Luis out. It doesn't matter that they were both deserving. Somebody had to be first, and it was Tony."

Was there anything else?

"Yeah," Whiteside said, "there have been some higher-profile players recently who pushed ahead of him in line. And as the years go by, and someone doesn't make it, he's given less and less consideration. People forget. There's also been a big turnover among writers. Older guys have retired and younger guys who never saw Tiant play have joined."

This was depressing. But as Tom Hanks once said, "There's no crying in baseball."

I thanked Larry Whiteside for his insights and sat back, recalling my interview with Luis. Although he's the perfect gentleman and refuses to play guessing games about the voters' motivations, it's clear that having been left out of the Hall is distressing to him. He's very aware of the injustice.

"Twenty-nine," he had informed me, a bit wistfully. That's how many pitchers are in the Hall who don't have records as good as his.

He was quiet for a long moment, then added, "I don't want to get elected by the Old-Timers committee."

It's the backdoor into Cooperstown, being voted in by a committee that feels an old-timer has been unfairly passed over. I told Luis that I hoped that didn't happen, too. (Now, however, because twenty years have passed since his retirement, that's the way it'll have to be. But it's no disgrace. I'm certain Tiant will accept with the equanimity that seems an essential part of his character.)

In any case, Tiant never again put up the phenomenal numbers he did in '68. It's doubtful that anyone could. The very next season, with the woeful, even more punchless 62–99 Indians, his won/loss record ballooned to a horrendous 9–20, despite his maintaining a perfectly competent 3.71 ERA.

He was beginning to have the arm troubles—brought on in no small part by having to pitch so damn hard all the time—that would plague him in 1970, when he threw 97 innings and won only 7 games. In 1971, he worked 72 innings and won once. For all practical purposes, with back-to-back years like that, he was out of baseball at the age of thirty.

He'd had a similar career (despite '68) to many flash-in-the-pans—one great season and several good ones. He'd won 83 major league ball games—more than most who claw their way up to the Show, but nothing to suggest any future stardom. And the Hall of Fame? Well . . .

The Indians—who were very, very bad—had let him go after '69. The Twins, a much better team, could find no use for him and cut him after 1970. Tiant, just about everyone agreed, was washed up.

Then, over that long, painful winter of '70–'71, something miraculous happened.

Luis rehabilitated himself. No surgery, just rest and an unwavering faith that there wasn't anything serious wrong with his arm. Nobody else believed it, with the possible exception of Mrs. Tiant, but the man was not through. Beyond all reason, the guy on the major league trash heap had 146 more wins left in him.

The brilliant, youthful Don Gullett takes the mound in Game 1 with impeccable credentials: his .661 lifetime winning percentage is tops among active pitchers with at least 100 decisions. But this is the World Series, and the kid looks nervous out there.

Dwight Evans, certainly not your prototypical leadoff hitter, bats first. Evans is slow (3 stolen bases in '75), doesn't run the bases particularly well, and seldom draws a walk (47 times in 459 at-bats). On the other hand, he puts the ball in play; he's struck out only 60 times.

More important, he's one of the Sox' hottest hitters. After losing his starting job to Bernie Carbo, due to a horrendous early-season slump, he's come back with a vengeance, hitting .327 after the All-Star break. (Both Carbo and Evans will wind up authoring some dramatic moments in the days to come.) Darrell Johnson obviously feels that Dwight represents his best chance of putting on a base runner ahead of the big guns in the heart of the order.

Evans is still young, at twenty-four just beginning a career that will span twenty years, all but one of them spent in Boston. He will be the premier defensive rightfielder of his era and finish with offensive numbers that either leave him just short of the Hall of Fame or will eventually get him in.

Dwight Evans a HOFer? Sounds odd. But Bill Mazeroski made it almost entirely on the strength of his Gold Gloves (eight), as did Ozzie Smith (thirteen) and Brooks Robinson (an unimaginable sixteen). Well, Evans won eight, too, while patrolling one of the toughest right fields in baseball. Fenway features tricky wall angles, a very short foul line, great distance straightaway, and a murderous afternoon sun. And this should also be considered: infielders compete for Gold Gloves only with others at their position. Outfielders must compete with all other outfielders, despite the fact that right is the most difficult field to play.

Beyond that, the three players' lifetime hitting stats are lopsided. Evans's exceed Robinson's by a little in every category and Smith and Mazeroski's by a *lot*. Yet Brooks, Maz, and the Wizard of Oz are in Cooperstown, while Dwight is seldom if ever mentioned as a candidate.

Such thoughts are a long way away in 1975. On this October afternoon, Evans is just one young man facing another who's a mere ten months older. At first, Gullett looks like he owns Evans, as he brings high heat that Evans can only wave at. But then, unaccountably, Gullett tries for the punch-out with a forkball. Dwight gets his bat on it and grounds a single through the left side of the infield.

He's followed by Denny Doyle, a short, fiery sparkplug type of player who was picked up in midseason by the Sox, from California. Doyle has been a most fortuitous acquisition. He's stabilized the infield, a .298 hitter and a rock on defense. He lays down a perfect bunt and sacrifices Evans to second.

Carl Yastrzemski comes to the plate.

This is it for the thirty-six-year-old team captain. While he'll have a couple more good seasons (.296 with 28 homers in '77, 21 more home runs in '79, when he turns forty)—and, astonishingly, will still be swinging the bat reasonably well at forty-four—he's on the downside of his career. Time is running out, and more than anything else in life he wants a World Series ring.

In '67, he had his only previous shot at it, and he performed magnificently. He carried his team into the Series with a superlative September performance, then batted .400 against the Cardinals, with 10 hits, 3 homers, and 5 RBI. He had three of the paltry 14 hits Boston managed off Bob Gibson in Gibbie's three outings.

All for naught. The Cards, with Gibson picking up three wins, beat the Red Sox in seven.

Eight years later, Yaz knows the Sox have a nucleus of players that would seem good for at least another two or three pennants. But baseball is fickle in many ways, and he also knows that it may not happen. As things turn out, it won't. This will be his last chance, and he will play as though it is. But then, Carl was always hard-nosed, and he played virtually every game of his career as if it were his last.

In '75, struggling with injuries, he's had an off year, hitting .269 with only 14 homers and 60 RBI. But he's still Yaz, and Gullett is perhaps just a little fearful of him. He walks Yaz on four pitches. Now there are two on, one out. The atmosphere sizzles with anticipation, even after the hometown favorite, native New Englander Carlton Fisk, pops out to second.

Because Fred Lynn now stands in.

Steady Freddie has had a season of such consistency that it'd be remarkable in a veteran. For a rookie, it's beyond belief. From day one to the end of the regular season, his batting average has never risen above .350 nor dipped below .330. He finishes at .331, with 21 homers (not a lot by today's standards, but pretty good in pitching-rich 1975, when only four players in the American League connected for more than 30), and 105 runs batted in. He leads the league in slugging average, doubles, and runs scored; is fourth in total bases; and is third in RBI. And as if all that weren't enough, he wins a Gold Glove for his defensive work.

Lynn is a five-tool player, one of the most promising in the majors. He's won the Rookie of the Year Award and will soon add the MVP. (He'll be the only player in history to accomplish that particular sweep until Ichiro Suzuki matches him in 2001.) Delighted Boston fans envision him in center for the next twenty years and then on to Cooperstown.

Though I love the guy, I'm not quite so optimistic. For one thing, Lynn plays the field with reckless abandon, which makes him injury prone. For another, his power figures for 1975 were highly inflated by a single night in Detroit in June, when in hitter-friendly Tiger Stadium he slugged three homers, barely missed a fourth (settling instead for a triple), and drove in 10 runs. Thus he got 9½ percent of his RBI and nearly 14 percent of his home runs for the year in 1 game out of 160. The performance made the baseball world sit up and take notice of this kid, but it also skewed the stats.

As it turns out, Lynn will become an outstanding player who falls a bit short of superstar status. Only once again will he have a year like '75; in 1979 he'll lead the league with a .333 batting average and a slugging average of .637. He'll conk 39 homers and exceed 100 RBI (122) and 100 runs (116) for the last time. He'll win one of his two remaining Gold Gloves.

Otherwise, he'll remain Steady Freddie, good for 20-some homers and 60 to 80 RBI a year. He'll play in 297 games in 1978–79, then average 113 a year for the rest of his playing days, as the injuries take their toll. His seventeen-year career totals will feature a lifetime BA of .283, 306 home runs, and 1,111 RBI. Pretty damn good, but short of Hall of Fame numbers.

In 1975, however, Lynn is charmed, a stone hitter, one of the best. Even batting lefty against a murderous southpaw like Gullett. He hits the ball sharply, and right into the first controversy of the Series, one that will be eerily recapitulated two games hence.

It's a ground ball up the middle, but right at Joe Morgan, who has positioned himself perfectly. When a power lefty faces a left-handed hitter, you anticipate that the batter will not be able to pull the ball, and you shade him toward second. Morgan sets himself to make the play. At the last second, Yastrzemski, running hard from first, cuts in front of him and obscures his vision. The ball bounces off his glove and out into shallow center field.

Morgan screams and points at Yaz, claiming interference. Rose starts yelling, too, and they're correct. According to the rules, the fielder has a right to an unobstructed view of any ball put into play, and it's the runner's responsibility to stay out of his way.

Second-base umpire Larry Barnett, like his five counterparts, is working his first World Series. He fails to make the interference call, when he clearly should have. As things turn out, it's of no consequence. But it will be an entirely different matter with the next call Barnett blows, three days later. It will vastly alter the complexion, and perhaps change the outcome, of the game. If not the entire Series.

Here, though, Davy Concepcion is backing up Morgan, and he sees that Evans has been waved around by third-base coach Don Zimmer. It's a calculated risk, with Zim perhaps figuring that all the commotion at second will distract the fielders. Not these guys. Concepcion guns the ball to Johnny Bench. It's very close. Evans would beat the throw with a perfect slide, but he fails to execute. He comes in too high, so that his lead leg misses the top of the plate, allowing Bench to tag him on the trailing knee just before it reaches home. He's out, no argument.

Afterward, Zimmer will be unrepentant. It's part of the Sox' overall strategy, to be aggressive on the base paths, trying to force Cincinnati miscues. Darrell Johnson feels as if they must manufacture some runs.

Yet this is a dreadful way to start any game, let alone a World Series, having a runner erased at home, wasting a golden opportunity to jump on top early. There are mutterings among the crowd; New Englanders are always looking for evidence that they're about to witness yet another installment in the Curse of the Bambino.

Luis, though, is unperturbed.

He's never bothered, never nervous, he tells me later. "I just go out there and do my best," he says. "I always do that. Why be nervous?"

Well, he could ask Don Gullett. But he doesn't. He merely walks out to the mound and dispatches the Reds in order again. Tony Perez flies to right. George Foster rips a liner down the first-base line, but Cooper snags it with an excellent leaping catch. Concepcion flies to left.

Nothing to it. The Reds have hit the ball pretty hard but have nothing to show for it, possibly a sign that luck is on the pitcher's side today. Six down, twenty-one to go.

Meanwhile, Gullett continues to struggle. The first man he faces in the second is Rico Petrocelli. A nice Italian boy who hails from Brooklyn and has long been popular in Boston, Rico once held the American League record for home runs by a shortstop, with 40. This year, playing third and fighting a nasty inner-ear infection, he's batted .239 with a scant 7 homers—though he did clock one during the playoff against Oakland.

Rico walks on four pitches.

Next up is a second-year man, Rick Burleson, aka the Rooster. Though Burleson carries only 165 pounds on his five ten frame, Bill Lee describes him as the team's number one "red ass," meaning he's hot-tempered and completely fearless, willing to fight anyone, anytime. True or not, there's no question that the Rooster has brought a much-needed scrappiness to the ball club, along with some timely hitting and a rifle arm at short. Burleson waits on a breaking ball, gets it, and rips a grounder under Pete Rose's glove.

Petrocelli, hardly a racehorse, motors all the way around to third. This must take George Foster by surprise, because left field in Fenway is so shallow. Nobody tries for the extra base on a ground ball to left. But as noted, it's the Sox' strategy to challenge the Reds' fielders, particularly Foster, who they feel is slow getting rid of the ball. This time, it works. Rico slides in safely.

Runners at the corners, nobody out.

Once again, there's anticipation, and once again, it comes to nothing. Gullett bears down, coaxing maximum smoke out of his long, over-the-top delivery.

Twenty-five-year-old Cecil Cooper, who will hit just shy of .300 for his seventeen-year career, begins what will be a long, frustrating Series for him by hacking futilely at Gullett's fastballs. He fans on a high hard one well outside the strike zone. Tiant, who hasn't batted in a game situation in three years, looks it. He whiffs, too. And Evans flies out to short right.

For the second straight inning, Boston has had two base runners with fewer than two out. But no runs have crossed the plate. The fans' mood darkens some more.

Fortunately, Looie continues to delight. The visitors' third is a breeze for Boston. Ken Griffey (Junior's dad), who's been timed going home to first in 3.5 seconds, grounds one of Tiant's lob change-ups to second. Doyle makes a great play, going hard to his right, turning in the air, and making the throw on the money to Cooper. Griffey's out by a skinny half-step. César Geronimo follows with a long fly to center that's held up by the wind and caught by Lynn. Then Gullett—a decent hitter who whacked his first major league home run in the playoff against Pittsburgh—flies out to left. It's taken Tiant four pitches to work his third perfect inning. He looks unhittable.

Gullett settles down and gets the side in order for the first time. Doyle and Yaz ground out routinely. Fisk, though, lofts a high fly to left. When it leaves the bat, it seems like a sure homer, Fenway-style. But, once again, the wind intrudes, blowing the ball back just enough so that Foster can make the catch right at the base of the Green Monster.

To open the fourth, Tiant retires Pete Rose on another easy ground ball to second base. He throws a strike past Morgan. Little Joe assumes his distinctive stance, bat held high, back elbow flapping up and down. On the 0–1 pitch, he slaps a single to center.

The Reds have their main man on—Morgan has stolen 67 bases, second in the league, in 77 attempts. Will he go? Well, of course he will. The only real question is, how quickly will he challenge Fisk's throwing arm? He immediately grabs a big lead, threatening to take off as Tiant faces Johnny Bench. His hands dangle at his sides, shaking slightly.

But Morgan is wary. Luis has an excellent move to first for a right-hander. He stands on the rubber, bringing his hands from his chest to his waist in a series of tiny, time-consuming jiggles. He pauses. Suddenly, in a blur, he throws to first. And again, and again. Once he nearly nails Morgan. And then . . . first-base umpire Nick Colosi calls a balk.

Morgan trots triumphantly to second. Looie is livid. In the days leading up to the Series, Reds' manager Anderson has been setting up the umpires, letting it be known that Tiant's move is illegal, that in the stricter National League he'd frequently be hit with a balk.

For the record, the rule states that the pitcher must step off the rubber and take a step toward first before throwing. He can't throw first, step afterward. In practice it all happens so fast, though, that separating the two is pretty much in the eye of the beholder, a pure judgment call. While the TV replay is inconclusive, even in slo mo, announcers Curt Gowdy and Tony Kubek both believe Tiant's move is legit.

Doesn't matter. Morgan has his extra base without having to steal it, and the Reds have their first runner in scoring position.

Still steaming, Luis goes to work on Johnny Bench. The Cincinnati catcher is nursing a pulled muscle and not his normal self, but he's always dangerous. Can Tiant stifle his anger, settle down, and retire Bench? He surely doesn't want two runners on with Perez coming up next.

The relationship between batter and pitcher is all about timing. The hitter tries his best to time his swing to the individual pitch, so that he gets the meat of the bat on it; the pitcher does everything he can to throw that timing off.

With a great pitcher and batter, it can be an epic struggle, as it is here for these two stars. Everything Luis does is to confuse the hitter. He changes speeds, varies his pitch selection and angle of release, hides the ball until the last possible moment, throws to different locations. He's been working the weather, challenging the Cincinnati sluggers to try jacking one of the slow breaking balls he lobs up there, knowing that with the wind blowing in hard from right they aren't likely to reach the fences.

The struggle between them goes back and forth, with Tiant making one good pitch after another. But Bench is a tough, tough out, and he keeps fouling them off, taking advantage of Fenway's short distance to the stands, patiently waiting for something he can drive, or a walk. 3 and 2, 3 and 2, as if it will never end. The pitch count goes to 10, 11, 12, a very long at-bat. Finally, on the 13th pitch, Bench fouls back one too many. The pop-up stays within the playing field and drops into Fisk's glove. Perez follows by striking out.

The no-hitter may be gone, but the shutout is intact.

Gullet is cruising now, aided by the high strikes called by National League umpire Art Frantz behind the plate. Lynn pops to short to open the fourth. Petrocelli scorches one to deep center, but nothing is going out of the park in that direction today, and it's just a long out.

But Burleson slices a low liner to right for a single and then, wonder of wonders, takes off for second. Talk about aggressiveness. The Rooster is not particularly fast—he's stolen 8 bases this year—and he's challenging only the finest defensive catcher in the history of the game.

Johnny Bench has revolutionized his position. He didn't originate the single-handed method of catching a pitch. Randy Hundley preceded him by a couple of years. But he has refined it to such perfection that most fans will think of it as his innovation.

Prior to these two men's arrival on the scene, catchers presented both hands to the incoming pitch, using their bare hand to secure the ball once it reached the mitt. This helped prevent passed balls and also meant that catchers had their dominant hand on the ball, ready to throw it to a base if necessary. The technique was effective enough, but it constantly exposed the bare hand to injury.

Why take the risk? Bench wondered. So he tried putting his right hand behind his back and gloving the pitch one-handed. The only problem to be solved was how to get the ball efficiently into his throwing hand, so that no time was wasted fishing for it before a quick throw to second. He practiced, over and over, thousands upon thousands of repetitions.

Now, he's so good that his throws are effortless, beautiful to watch. The ball pops out of his glove and into his bare hand in an instant. He even manages to position the seams perfectly for his preferred grip, every time.

Bench fires to second and it's no contest. Burleson is out by an embarrassing six feet.

Foster opens the Cincinnati fifth with a liner to the left-field corner. It's a certain double. But Yaz, old Mr. Experience out there, contributes his first outstanding defensive play of the game. Tracking the ball perfectly, and making an excellent throw to the infield, he holds George to a single.

Concepcion fans, then Griffey hits a slow, checked swing grounder to third. Petrocelli throws him out as Foster moves to second. With first base open, there's a conference at the mound. Unlike today, when the pitching coach would handle the job, manager Darrell Johnson makes the trip out there himself. It's decided to intentionally walk Geronimo, which Tiant does, and the strategy works when Gullett fouls to third for the final out.

Those watching on TV are now switched to what, in retrospect, was a rather special treat. After a pair of ads for Dodge ("Once you look, you're hooked!" "A new Daytona for under four thousand dollars!") and Sony, the network does a little self-promotion, urging viewers to return that evening for the very first installment of a hot new live comedy show, called *NBC Saturday Night*.

In the Sox half, Gullett has control problems again. He strikes out Cooper for the second time but then commits the cardinal sin of walking the opposing pitcher. Luis looks a little forlorn out there. He stays rooted to the bag as Evans pops out and moves to second when Doyle bloops a single to right. Two more base runners, stranded when Yaz grounds to first to end it.

Tiant has a spot of trouble in the sixth. Pete Rose lays into his first pitch and slams a sinking liner to right that Evans turns into a fine catch, running straight in. Good thing, because Joe Morgan, the only Reds batter who seems to have Luis figured, lines one just inside the first-base bag. It's a routine double for Little Joe most of the time, but most of the time Dwight Evans isn't out there. Evans fields the ball and gets off an absolute rope to second. Morgan just barely beats the throw.

But that's it. Bench grounds to third and Perez—normally an excellent breaking-ball hitter—fans on the big, slushy curve.

The Red Sox then squander their best scoring opportunity of the day. After Fisk is out, short to first, Lynn grounds a single up the middle. Petrocelli doubles to right, but this time Zimmer, with only one out, holds Freddie at third. Now Rick Burleson is up, to be followed by Cooper, who's struck out twice, and Tiant. Gullett walks Burleson intentionally.

This time Cooper at least manages to get his bat on the ball, and he lofts a fly to center. Geronimo gets a late jump and appears to stumble slightly as he catches it, so Zimmer turns aggressive again. He sends Lynn. But César recovers admirably and wings a strike to Bench. Lynn is out at the plate. Déjà vu all over again. The fans groan.

The seventh is tougher for Tiant. Foster leads off with a ground single that Burleson can't quite reach. Then Concepcion bloops a fly to left that drops in—*not*. Because there's that man again. Yaz gets a good jump, races in at top speed, dives, rolls, and . . . comes up with the ball. It's the defensive gem of the day.

Foster, perhaps feeling that he's owed second, tries to steal it, and Fisk throws him out. The two potential runners erased loom large when Griffey follows with a double to the right-field corner. Both would probably have scored. But now it's just a matter of walking Geronimo intentionally again and retiring Gullett, which Tiant does on a soft liner to second that Doyle secures with a fine running catch.

Luis leaves with, still, nothing but zeros on the scoreboard. As he walks off the field, it must feel like the dog days of '68, battling to keep a team in the game when they refuse to score any runs for him.

But he's about to take matters into his own hands.

Of all the boys of this October, Luis Tiant is probably the one for whom there is the most poignancy in Bart Giamatti's meditation on home: "how hard it is to get there, and how driven is our need."

Tiant doesn't deal much in metaphor. His difficulties and desires are present every minute of every day. He may not be the farthest away in miles, but the emotional gulf between him and his home is immeasurable. He has been living in exile for forty years.

Born in Cuba, the son of a professional baseball player, Luis was one of many victims of the preposterous political posturings that have gone down between his adopted land and its nearest noncontiguous neighbor since 1962, the year of the embargo. Americans have essentially been prohibited from traveling to Cuba; Fidel Castro has responded by placing nearly insurmountable difficulties in the way of Cubans who want to go to the United States. The situation would be laughable if it didn't cause so much pain.

Like many who were young, impressionable, and quasi-liberal in the sixties, I was enthusiastic about Castro at first. He had, after all, deposed Batista, a vicious and hated dictator, and established a government that was dedicated to sweeping change for the benefit of all the people.

Except those who felt forced out, of course. Those who had their land and homes and businesses expropriated. Those who streamed across the Straits of Florida to the land of plenty.

We didn't care about the involuntary expatriates. They were the pigs, after all. Batista's running dogs. The oppressors of the poor. And probably they were, many of them. But they also included decent, honorable men such as Luis Tiant.

Four decades later, Fidel's defenders might just about fill some unrepentant left-wing professor's classroom. Virtually everyone else has concluded that Castro blew it. Instead of holding onto his principles while working with his wealthy near neighbor, he chose to cast his lot with a creaky empire that was plodding the path to extinction. Instead of leavening his Communism with a little private enterprise, he presided over an economy that worsened with every passing year. Instead of imagining his way into the future, he kept one foot planted firmly in the nineteenth century.

Give him his due. He greatly improved health care and instituted universal public education. But the time is long past when that might be enough.

Luis Tiant should know. He hasn't been back since 1961.

In September of that year, newly married, living in Mexico City, he was planning a trip there, as a honeymoon and so his bride could meet her new in-laws. But when he called his father, to let his parents know when he and Maria were coming, he got a shock.

"Stay in Mexico," Luis Sr. said. "There's nothing for you here now. Stay where you are and make a good life for your family."

The Castro regime was still relatively new, and the twenty-year-old, apolitical ballplayer was taken aback. He had little idea what was happening on the island. He protested, but his dad was firm. If the younger man returned at that time, there was no telling if he'd be allowed to leave again. His hopes of a career in the American major leagues could well be over for good.

Things might change, though. Who could predict? So Luis Sr. added, "I'll let you know when you can come."

Luis Jr. deferred, as he always did, to his parents' wishes. He is a man for whom family loyalties are the most important things in the world. But it would be a costly decision. Though he'd see his mom once, in 1968, nearly fifteen years would pass before he saw his beloved father again.

During that time, Tiant would make his way through the minor leagues to Cleveland, would have a fine career seemingly ended with arm troubles, and would be resurrected in Boston. Though he'd gain a reputation as one of the most easygoing guys in the game—funny, even tempered, uncritical of others, imperturbable in adversity—there was always a sadness at his core, that his parents were unable to share in his success except via beat-up old radios and TVs with antennas made from kitchen implements.

But 1975 would, finally, be a magical year for him. Not only would he pitch the opening game of the World Series, he would be reunited with his dad.

Luis Sr. had been a helluva ballplayer in his own right. A left-handed pitcher with a great fastball and screwball and a devastating pickoff move, he dominated the Cuban League during his playing years, 1926–1948. He also barnstormed the United States with the New York Cubans, playing in major ballparks (including Yankee Stadium), but always against Negro League teams.

Would he have made it in the bigs?

Unquestionably, recalled former Giants' outfielder Monte Irvin, whose own career was truncated by segregation and who played against him. "He would have been a great, great star. He really knew how to pitch, and he had the greatest move to first base I've ever seen."

Most Americans never got to see him play, though, and at forty-two the greatest Cuban athlete of his day retired from baseball and became a furniture mover.

Luis and Isabel Tiant settled in the Havana suburb of Nicanor del Campo. They weren't wealthy, but they both worked hard and by Cuban standards did all right. From the beginning, all the Tiants wanted was for Luis Jr. to have a better life than they'd had. They forced him to learn English and, partly because he was an only child, were able to send him to private school.

But the academic life wasn't for little Luis. What fascinated him was baseball, even though he'd been only eight when his dad retired and thus could barely remember his career. He turned out to have God-given (and probably genetic) talents as well. He could always throw a ball faster and more accurately than anyone else his age.

Luis Sr. helped his son learn the game, and the ins and outs of pitching, but he didn't encourage the boy to think of baseball as a vocation. Education was the key to success, he believed. Otherwise you were likely to end up as an old man schlepping furniture for a living.

There was no holding Luis Jr. back, however. As he grew, he moved through Little League and Juvenile League and was poised to enter the bigtime Cuban League in 1959 when he got an offer to join the Mexico City Kings of the Mexican League, from which many players eventually were plucked to play in the States.

Luis Sr. didn't want his son to go, and no doubt the nineteen-year-old would have stayed at home but for his mother. Isabel, who didn't know or care much about baseball, nevertheless urged her husband to let the kid seize the opportunity. It might be his only chance to see what he could do. Luis Sr. sadly agreed.

A year later, Luis met Maria, who would become his lifelong mate.

The year after that, 1961, his Mexico City contract would be purchased by the Cleveland Indians. And a disheartened Luis Sr. would tell his only child not to return home.

By 1975, Luis, now a major league star and himself a father, was wondering whether he would ever see his own dad again. He would, due to a remarkable and unexpected sequence of events that came about because Tiant happened to play for the Boston Red Sox.

In May, Senator George McGovern announced that he was going to make a trip to Cuba, a nonofficial visit, yet one that might mark the beginning of a thaw in relations between the two countries. When fellow senator Ed Brooke of Massachusetts heard of McGovern's plans, he had an idea. Knowing of the Boston pitcher's powerful desire to see his parents again, he asked if McGovern would be willing to carry a personal letter to Fidel Castro.

He would.

Luis, Brooke wrote to the Cuban leader, "has not had the chance to spend any significant time with his parents for many years. Naturally, he has a great desire to do so. . . . Therefore, with your help, I am confident that a reunion of Luis and his parents is possible this summer. Such a reunion would be a significant indication that better understanding between our peoples is achievable."

The night of May 6, during a dinner with Castro, McGovern started talking baseball as a conversational icebreaker. He knew Fidel was a big fan. After bantering in general terms for a while, he brought up the Tiant matter and passed along Brooke's letter.

Castro knew of the Tiants, both father and son, of course. He studied the letter, then said, "I think that can be done. Let me see."

The following afternoon, it was one of the first things on Castro's agenda.

"I've checked on your request about Mr. Tiant's parents," he said, "and they've been advised that they can go to Boston and stay as long as they wish."

Hours later, when Luis got the news, all he would say was that he'd been praying for this and that when he finally saw them again, "it will be the

greatest day of my life." It would also mark the elder Tiant's first introduction to his daughter-in-law and the first time he had ever seen his
three grandchildren: one-year-old Danny, seven-year-old Isabel, and
twelve-year-old Luis III.

The greatest day was August 20.

The Sox were in the thick of a pennant race, and Tiant's parents' arrival
was the sporting community's human-interest story of the year. When
Luis got to Logan Airport, he was horrified. It was mobbed. All he wanted
was to be alone, yet there was a sea of writers and TV reporters, all fling-
ing questions at him at once.

Once the plane arrived, though, the crowd had the decency to stand
back and then, finally, the family was reunited. Luis Jr., a great bear of a
man, began to cry. As did nearly everyone else in the place.

While Luis embraced his mother, Granddad kissed his daughter-in-law
and his grandchildren. Then after Luis Sr., by now ill with emphysema,
fielded a couple of questions about his readiness to join the Sox, the Tiants
went home.

Tuesday, August 26, was Looie's next start and the first opportunity for
a proud Luis Sr. to see his son play in the major leagues. The Red Sox
wanted to commemorate the occasion in some way but didn't want to be
pushy about it. They offered Luis the option of doing anything he wanted.

No, Luis thought. This whole time was a private, family occasion. But
the more he considered it, the more appropriate it seemed that his father
should stand on the mound that had been denied him because of his color
when he was in his prime. He agreed to a small ceremony.

Small, indeed.

As soon as the public-address announcer began his introduction of "one
of the greatest pitchers of the New York Cubans," the crowd of thirty-two
thousand stood cheering as one, screaming "Loo-*ie*, Loo-*ie*," and the
younger Tiant, almost too happy to catch his breath, knew that he'd made
the right decision.

It was a wondrous scene, timeless and moving beyond words, that
couldn't have been scripted without drawing charges of excessive senti-
mentality. Father and son—the latter one of the most popular athletes in
the city's history, the former a frail but spry shadow of his former self—
made their way slowly to the mound. Luis in his uniform, Dad in a Red
Sox cap. There wasn't a dry eye in the place.

Luis Sr. peeled off his suit jacket, handed it to Jr. to hold, and took a baseball from his boy. The roar intensified. Then, with the younger man grinning like a kid and the fans laughing and screaming their appreciation, the old southpaw launched into a picture-perfect caricature of his son's herky-jerky windup.

Finally, he threw a pitch to catcher Tim Blackwell. Low and outside. He shook his head in displeasure, called for the ball again. This time, he reared back and, as the crowd went wild, smoked one right down the middle.

It was almost impossible to hear as the two walked back to the dugout, but somehow over the din, the elder Tiant was able to pass a message along to the younger.

Later, Luis would recall the moment. "I'll never forget how these fans treated my father," he said.

And Luis Sr.'s words?

Tiant smiled at the memory. "He said: 'Tell 'em I can still go five if they need me.'"

Papa has been allowed one more visit and is in the stands today, sitting expectantly with his wife and grandson as the bottom of the seventh unfolds. Considering that there have been nothing but zeros on the scoreboard so far, and that his weak-hitting son will be leading off, he could hardly be expecting that the biggest offensive explosion of the entire Series is about to happen. And in the most unlikely manner.

El Tiante the Younger hasn't batted in a ball game since the American League decided to institute the designated hitter on a three-year trial basis in 1973. Now he must. The more traditionalist National League won't allow the DH in World Series play for another year.

Luis looked woeful in his first at-bat against fireballer Gullett. His swing was more like a chop, and he turned his body completely around with it. The ball was nearly in the catcher's mitt before he attempted to make contact. He sat down with a quick strikeout. Then in the fifth, the Cincinnati left-hander hit one of his periodic streaks of wildness and committed the cardinal sin of walking the opposing pitcher. But he settled down and worked his way out of trouble. Luis was stranded.

Now, however . . .

"It was a fastball," Luis told me with utter certainty twenty-five years later. "I'm sure."

It isn't. After making his opposite number look silly with a steady diet of fastballs—which Luis, and forgive him for thinking he might, couldn't have hit with a tennis racket—Gullett unaccountably tries to sneak a breaking ball by him.

In truth, it's just a hair slower than the heater—to the average spectator, not much difference at all. But remember that Tiant is a professional. Which means that, as dreadful a hitter as he may appear, he's still a helluva lot better than we are. To a professional, that extra microsecond is crucial. It means that Luis has time to get the bat around before the pitch is past him.

He takes his unsightly swing, slashes at the ball, and, wonder of wonders, grounds a seeing-eye single through the left side of the infield. The crowd goes berserk.

Finally, our moment seems to have arrived. If even Tiant can get a hit, Gullett must be tiring and . . . OK, they may have butchered their earlier opportunities. But this time, surely, the Olde Towne Team will score.

First-base coach Johnny Pesky confers with his portly pitcher, perhaps gently to remind him in which direction to proceed. If so, it works, but just barely. Luis Tiant is preparing to embark upon the most comical baserunning adventure I have ever seen.

Dwight Evans, the next hitter, obediently lays down a sacrifice bunt, and, in typical Red Sox fashion, the wheels nearly come off. Evans punches the ball too hard. When Gullett gloves it, he turns, sees he has an easy force play, and whips the ball to second base. Or, to be more precise, this normally fine-fielding pitcher fires it in that general direction. The ball goes flying into center field.

The Sox have caught a break. Immediately, they nearly give it back.

Luis, only dimly aware of what to do on the base paths and having failed to see Gullett's throw whistle past second, executes one of the worst slides in baseball history. He flops onto his belly, then rolls sideways across the bag, looking not unlike a humpback I once saw execute a similar maneuver during a whale-watching cruise on Stellwagen Bank.

Yet he's safe. Looking bewildered, he gets up and takes a half-dozen tentative steps toward third. Then he realizes that centerfielder Geronimo has come rushing in and is about to grab the loose ball; he'll be thrown out by forty feet. Tiant scurries frantically back toward second. Geronimo makes his throw. It's on the mark. Another break: Luis beats it, by inches. He looks well satisfied, standing there. His father is giggling, merry as can be.

Next, Denny Doyle comes up. Gullett, angry with himself for botching the force-out, brings some serious heat. Working quickly, he throws two fastballs right past the batter. Doyle finds himself in an 0–2 hole, with Gullett determined to put him away on the very next pitch. Denny grits his teeth and chokes up on the bat, hoping to at least advance the runners. In comes another vicious fastball, but it's one too many trips to the same well. This time, Doyle has it timed. He slaps a grounder to the right side that just slips through for a single.

A run scores. But . . . actually, no, it doesn't. Tiant, who should have made it to home easily, is gun-shy. After huffing and puffing his way to third, he decides he can't cover the last leg of the journey speedily enough. He declines to challenge Griffey's arm and plants himself ninety feet from the plate.

Oscar and I look at each other uneasily, as only Red Sox fans do when their team has just loaded the bases with nobody out. Anyone else would be whooping it up in expectation of a big inning. Not us. We're excited, sure, but inside we're also fretting away, wondering: will they find a way to screw it up again?

It can only be said that they try their level best to do so.

Not Carl Yastrzemski, though. He keeps the rally alive by chipping a single to right, and Gullett, who hasn't given up a solid hit in the inning, can only watch in frustration as his mound opponent streaks for home.

Well, maybe not "streaks," exactly.

After nailing himself to the bag until he was absolutely, positively certain he wouldn't have to tag up on a caught fly, Luis lumbers home. Lumber, shlumber. The important thing is that the first run of the 1975 World Series is in the books. Isn't it?

As it turns out, not quite. Because Tiant, capping the inning's comedy of errors, has failed to touch the plate.

Sitting out in the far bleachers, we don't know this yet. All we know is that Griffey makes his throw toward home and Tony Perez cuts it off. It's the proper play. It allows the first baseman—who believes the run has already scored—to take a quick look around and relay the ball to any base where the runner may have been incautious. You go with the percentages, the possibility of salvaging an out, instead of letting the ball go through to home, where there's no chance of a play.

Johnny Bench is beside himself, screaming for the ball, but either he can't be heard above the roar of the crowd or Tony can't imagine what he wants it for. Bench doesn't get it. And Tiant? Finally we notice him and realize what has happened. We can't help but laugh.

There is Luis, feigning invisibility in front of thirty-five thousand partisans and nine dedicated enemy soldiers. What is he doing? Tiptoeing back to home plate like a teenager who's late returning the car and is trying to sneak past his dozing dad. Realizing that nobody is fooled, he then breaks into what passes for a mad dash.

Amazingly—considering that the Red Sox inhabit a universe cruelly governed by the principle that whatever can go wrong, will—he makes it. The master now has a precious run to work with. Though the Sox will go on to score five more times, the first is the only one he will need.

Over our breakfast, I asked Tiant if he missed the plate out of nervousness.

Nah, he said. He was never nervous. Not in the biggest games. Never.

Never?

"Well, maybe my first game for Cleveland, a little. But after that . . ." He shrugged. "When it was my turn to pitch, I go out and do it. It's my business."

In someone else it might sound like braggadocio. Not here. I've been talking with a man for whom the bedrock American values have never gone out of style: hard work to achieve what you want, the respect for others that begins with respect of self, devotion to family. A man suffering a four-decade-long exile from his homeland who can say without bitterness that, "I love *my* country, and I love *this* country." It's no surprise that he looked upon his pitching as a job that he just happened to have a talent for and that he labored long and hard to become very, very good at.

I'm prepared to believe that the first game of a World Series was simply another trip to the office.

We talked about his magnificent performance in his Series debut and chuckled as we relived his stroll back to the plate that he hadn't touched. They were clearly joyful memories for someone who has been continually battered by the dictates of international politics.

I'd been a little reluctant to steer us onto the subject of Cuba, though I'm sure it's never far from his mind. But it's one I wanted to explore. True, there's an official travel ban on American citizens visiting there. Yet it's not that difficult to circumvent it. Over the years, I've known a number of people who've gone. Tiant could, presumably, if he wanted to.

We'd talked around it, me hesitant to either cause him pain or to wind up on the receiving end of a lengthy anti-Castro diatribe. The interview had gone so well, so far. He was relaxed. Many people still knew who he was: three or four came up to our table during the interview to pay their respects, some of them too young ever to have seen him play. That clearly pleased him. I didn't want to be the one responsible if things went sour.

Still, it looked as if *he* wasn't going to bring it up. So I took a stab at it. "I spoke with Bill Lee last week," I said. "He goes to Cuba in the winter. He takes balls and bats for the kids, and a bunch of guys who play exhibition games against Cuban teams. What would it take to get you to do something like that?"

There was a long moment of silence. Then, when he spoke, it was with sadness but not rancor. I'd been steeling myself against the diatribe, half expecting it, and I was relieved when it didn't come.

"Bill Lee can do that," he said. "But not me. You don't understand. If he goes, nobody cares. If I go, everybody knows it, and . . ."

He paused, then continued. "I'm not a political person. I got nothing against anybody. I don't know anything about all that. My family in Cuba, they're hardworking people, not political. . . . It's sad. Ninety miles away. I have an aunt there who is very old, and she wants to see me before she dies. I want to see her, and relatives I've never met, kids. I would like to see all my family."

This was beyond my comprehension. "Why can't you?" I said. "Castro wouldn't let you in?"

His answer, when it came, surprised me.

"No, they would let me go back. But the Cubans in Venezuela, in Miami, other places, they wouldn't like it."

"But it's been . . ."

"Thirty-nine years."

"Surely they'd understand that you just want to see your family." I couldn't imagine even the most hardened anticommunist objecting to that.

But he just shook his head, the sense of resignation right there on the surface. Buddha at rest, trying to practice nonattachment.

"When my dad came to see me that year," he said, "somebody said that I was going back to Cuba to play in front of Castro, out of gratitude."

I was stunned, and it showed.

"Crazy, isn't it?" he said. "I would never. But I got letters, a lot of letters. 'You're a pig.' 'You're killing my family, you're killing me.' Stuff like that. They said they would blow up my car, kill me. Others can go, Oliva, Campaneris, I just don't have it inside me."

And I realized he was right, that I didn't understand. I *couldn't* understand. I may have railed against the politics of the cold war, but they never affected me personally. Not like this.

"I'm sorry," I said.

"It's OK," Luis said. "You talk to one side, and it's bad, you talk to the other side, and it's bad. I'll do it when it feels good. And when I go, I don't talk about it."

He smiled, and I changed the subject.

The rest is routine.

Boston scores six times in the seventh, chasing Gullett and reliever Clay Carroll. Will McEnaney mops up.

There will be no more runs in this game, but it's immaterial. El Tiante closes out Cincinnati with a flourish, retiring the side in order in both the eighth and ninth innings. The Red Sox have won Game 1 in classic style, with pitching, great defense, and a cluster of timely hits.

It has taken two hours and twenty-seven minutes from beginning to end, routine at the time though remarkable by today's standards. Reviewing old tapes, it's easy to see why.

Hitters, once they stepped into the box, seldom stepped out until the at-bat was over; there was no pounding of shoes, no endless fiddling with the Velcro on batting gloves, no walking from nowhere to nowhere, none of the rituals that put a drag on today's version of the game.

Likewise, pitchers pitched; they got their sign and they threw, with no meandering around the mound between offerings.

There was also no time taken up with TV reruns of every play, from fourteen different angles. You saw it and it was gone. They did occasionally rewind the tape, for really crucial plays. Those you might view twice, three times at the absolute most. Then it was back to live action.

And, finally, there was the brevity of television ads, all thirty-second spots. Three of them between innings, sometimes only two. Just enough time for a pee break or to grab another beverage from the fridge. You got a half-minute's worth of solicitation to buy Gillette Trac II blades, followed by the same for Kellogg's Corn Flakes, and then you returned to the field, where the teams were already set to resume play.

It was far more pleasant to watch a game under those conditions than it is now. Many who complain about the glacial pace of baseball have probably never seen it when it moved right along.

I couldn't foresee that I'd be writing these somewhat gloomy words twenty-five years later. But back in the moment, I'm ecstatic. All I know is that Luis has thrown a superb 5-hit shutout at the haughty Red Machine. To him, it must seem as if the cheers will never end.

I slap Uncle Oscar on the back.

"We can do this!" I say. "We can beat these guys. Tiant will win two or three, Lee one or two. Maybe Rick Wise one. And that's *all we need!*"

He nods in agreement, but I can see the stoic New England pragmatist in there, staring out from behind the smile.

This is a guy whose ancestors had come to this inhospitable land 338 years earlier. Three generations of Carpenters, all of the males named William, arriving on the *Bevis* in 1637. William the Elder took one look at Massachusetts and must have tossed his lunch, because he fled back to England on the *Bevis*'s return trip. You had to really hate a place to want to suffer a second transatlantic crossing in those days.

The ones who stayed—the ones who bred down the years until the patrilineal Carpenter line finally terminated with a half-dozen sisters, including my grandmother Ethel—they didn't manage to eke a living out of the region's stony soil by being mushy headed.

Oscar is very much one of them. "We'll see," is all he says.

Down on the field, the thought must at least have flitted like a mayfly through Darrell Johnson's mind: *hell, this is a breeze.* His second year in the bigs and he's got a World Series victory without having to make a single managerial move of any consequence.

Little could he know. It will never, ever get this easy again.

Space

[T]his game that I loved with all my heart, not simply for the fun of playing it (fun was secondary, really), but for the mythic and aesthetic dimension it gave to an American boy's life—particularly to one whose grandparents could hardly speak English. For someone whose roots in America were strong but only inches deep, and who had no experience, such as a Catholic child might, of an awesome hierarchy that was real and felt, baseball was a kind of secular church that reached into every class and region of the nation and bound millions upon millions of us together in common concerns, loyalties, rituals, enthusiasms, and antagonisms. Baseball made me understand what patriotism was about, at its best.

—Philip Roth, "My Baseball Years"

Once upon a time, back in the mid-1950s, St. Louis Cardinals outfielder Wally Moon said of his teammate Jackie Brandt, that "ideas just seem to flake off his mind." And thus was born the term *flake*, along with its adjectival form, *flaky*. Or so the story goes.

I have no idea how apocryphal the tale might be, but it's a certainty that the term is applied to baseball players with far greater frequency than to participants in other sports. The fans of the game love their oddballs. Not that that's the only thing "flake" means. It's been stretched to include mild eccentrics, those with out-of-the-mainstream political views, and unfortunates suffering from mental illness. Mostly, though, the tag is put on someone in a friendly way, with good humor, in order to denote a person who thinks, speaks, or acts differently from the majority of his fellow players.

The Red Sox have, over the years, been endowed with at least (some would say *more than*) their share of colorful characters. Yet it seems certain that to no one else in the team's history was the *flake* label as firmly and enduringly fixed as the quirky left-hander entrusted with putting the Red Sox two up in the win column.

For pitcher William Francis Lee, 1975 was a difficult year.

He won 17 games in 1973, 17 again in '74, and got his 17th, again, on August 24 of '75. He was the staff's number two starter, behind Tiant, seemed well on his way to his first 20-win season, and had already established himself as the third winningest left-hander in Red Sox history, after Mel Parnell and Lefty Grove. (Although Babe Ruth would undoubtedly have eclipsed them all, had he remained a pitcher. And had he stayed in Boston. But that's another story.) The 20 wins were, however, not to be. Due to a combination of elbow problems and late-season fatigue, he didn't gain another victory during the regular season.

He missed the playoff series against Oakland, as well. Shortly after his final win in August, he was taking batting practice in anticipation of the World Series, during which there would be no designated hitter. He hadn't swung a bat in years. When he tried, he overdid it, hyperextended his already tender elbow, and suffered a slight tendon tear. He was sidelined until the start of the Series.

To further complicate matters, Lee had alienated a substantial chunk of the team's followers.

Lee nearly always found (or made) himself the center of attention during his career. This was during a time when ballplayers were expected to toe the corporate line. They were there to be seen and not heard; if they had to speak, it was to be about baseball, period.

Bill broke all of the rules. He was intelligent, well educated, articulate, and highly opinionated, and he *loved* the media. He'd answer any question. He'd spout his views at the slightest provocation, or none at all. He carried on about national and world politics, the class struggle, racism, economics, anything. He sometimes seemed to enjoy committing one of the cardinal sins, which was to criticize one's manager or the club's front office. They weren't off-limits if he felt they'd made a mistake.

Reporters on the baseball beat considered him prime copy. They dutifully printed just about every word uttered by the "Spaceman" (sometimes shortened to just "Space"). This was a nickname he'd been saddled with early on. It probably evolved from sportswriters calling him the Ace from Space and the Space Cowboy and was sometimes used affectionately, sometimes not. Either way, it always labeled him as a kook, an outsider, someone different in kind from the other guys.

Lee was "never offended by the appellation," he says in his autobiography, *The Wrong Stuff*, although he "wasn't crazy about it." Typically, he simply found it off the mark. He would have "preferred to be known as Earth Man."

In any case, to the extent that Lee endeared himself to the young and counterculturally inclined, he outraged in equal measure their more conservative parents with his condemnation of the war in Vietnam, his support for Fidel Castro, and wry comments such as, "Do I use drugs? Sure, I sprinkle marijuana on my pancakes in the morning."

But nothing he'd done before prepared him for the outpouring of hatred he brought upon himself in 1975.

That year marked the beginning of Judge Arthur Garrity's court-ordered busing in Boston. It was designed to promote the integration of the public school system, which remained about as racially divided as it was the day the Supreme Court outlawed educational segregation. Because no plan had yet made a dent in the status quo, Garrity decided to take matters into his own hands. The court's decision was applauded in liberal quarters, while it was violently opposed, to say the least, in the city's more ethnic white neighborhoods.

Enter Bill Lee, who insinuated himself right into the middle of the controversy, albeit rather by accident.

It happened on June 23, after an 11–3 drubbing of the Sox by the Cleveland Indians. The hometown fans had booed unmercifully, almost as if it was a critical game in September. Carl Yastrzemski, who'd had a bad game, was on the receiving end of much of the abuse.

Afterward, in the locker room, the media had hounded Yaz, trying to get him to admit that this might be the beginning of the end of the season. Yaz, frustrated by his poor performance, didn't want to talk about it. He finally locked himself away from them.

Lee witnessed the badgering of the team captain, and it angered him. So, as he puts it: "I decided to create a diversion."

And what a diversion.

He heaved a trash can across the clubhouse and popped off with the first words that came into his head: "Boston is a horseshit city, a racist city with horseshit fans and horseshit writers. The fans boo Yaz when he's playing his heart out, and they boo Fisk who always gives his all. They are all afraid we're going to lose their precious little pennant! If the writers and fans in this city want to quit on us, fine. Then they're quitters. But what can you expect? The only guy with any guts in this town is Judge Arthur Garrity!"

Now, that particular dog was not gonna hunt down in Southie and other parts of the area that were right on the firing line. Yet, though it may seem unlikely, Lee claims that he knew exactly what he was doing.

"Garrity was being burned in effigy throughout the city," he wrote after the fact. "I thought he had done the right thing. But I also knew that by making an issue out of it at this precise moment, I would take the media spotlight off whatever was temporarily ailing us and goad most of the writers into forgetting about Yaz so they could take it out on me."

Not many would have chosen such an incendiary way to deflect criticism of the ball club. But it worked. Lee's words were duly published and, for many, they were the last straw. His hate mail went through the roof. He got death threats. "Four Irish guys came to my house in Stoughton," he recalled to me, "and beat the shit out of me. But—" he grinned, "later on we ended up in a bar, drinking together."

Lee shrugged it off, the fights, the catcalls, the personal abuse, all of it. He believed that if the game of baseball wasn't fun, it was nothing. He was playing in the big leagues and, even though he was causing a ton of trouble, he was having a hell of a time.

At least until late August. Then, with his elbow blown out at the height of the pennant race, a mere three games short of the magical 20th win that he'd never gotten, he was forced to sit and watch. Bill Lee, whatever else might be said about him, was as intense a competitor as you'd ever want to meet. He didn't like to sit.

The Red Sox won the division with one of their three best pitchers on the shelf. They won the playoff against Oakland without him, as well. By the time the World Series began, Lee hadn't played in more than a month. He was stale. His arm wasn't yet 100 percent. But he wanted to pitch, as badly as he'd wanted anything in his life.

Would he get the opportunity to go against the mighty Reds? He couldn't have liked his chances.

The odds, if anyone had wanted to bet, seemed to be dead against it. Lee was in the doghouse for his outspokenness. He was also tired—he'd pitched 260 innings already in '75, after more than 280 in each of the previous two seasons, and those were long innings; Bill always put a lot of runners on and liked to joke that he was the master of the 12-hit shutout. He was rusty, and perhaps still injured. He'd never been a favorite of manager Darrell Johnson, anyway. Virtually everyone—including the entire Boston press corps—believed there was no way in hell he could be effective. The consensus was that he was behind Rick Wise (who'd won 19) in the rotation, and maybe Reggie Cleveland, and possibly Roger Moret. Mop-up duty was probably all he was going to get.

Until someone stepped up and spoke for him, someone who would have to be considered his unlikeliest supporter of all.

Don Zimmer was the Sox' third-base coach and future manager. He and Bill Lee, to put it mildly, hated each other's guts. Lee saw Zimmer as a narrow-minded buffoon and publicly likened Don to a gerbil because of his puffy cheeks (later, Lee's way of apologizing was to say he actually meant "hamster"). Zimmer, in his memoir, *Zim*, paints his adversary as a mean-spirited troublemaker and states that Lee is the only man he's met in his fifty-year baseball career whom he wouldn't allow in his house. (It's possible that he never actually *met* Billy Martin.)

"And I don't care who knows it," he adds.

Nevertheless, according to his book, Zimmer's baseball instincts overcame his personal distastes. He wanted to win, and he went to bat for the left-hander. On the eve of the World Series, he approached Darrell Johnson, knowing that the manager had not penciled Lee into the planned rotation. He suggested that he was of a different opinion.

The Cincinnati Reds, Zim pointed out, were a free-swinging team, excellent fastball hitters. A pitcher like Bill Lee, who threw mostly off-speed stuff, would give them fits, he believed. Especially in Fenway, where the natural surface benefits a sinkerballer and where the Reds would be sorely tempted to try jerking his junk out of the park.

Fenway has, throughout its long history, been considered a graveyard for left-handers because of the Wall. The left-field wall is officially listed as 315 feet from home plate, very short by major league standards, but it isn't even that far. Best guess is that it's more like 300, and some have claimed that it's a shade under. The *Boston Globe*, after analyzing aerial photos, once proclaimed on its front page that the distance measures exactly 304.779 feet. For its part, Red Sox management has always been coy on the subject, preferring to let fans engage in a perpetual guessing game.

Whatever the case, mesmerized right-handed hitters are continually attempting to pop one over the Green Monster, and left-handed hurlers throwing to them fear leaving a pitch anywhere in the danger zone, from the inside corner out over the middle of the plate. And weak flies *can* sometimes clear the wall. Just ask Bucky Dent.

Thus most lefties don't like pitching in Fenway at all, and over the years southpaws have been continually underrepresented on the staff. This, according to Bill Lee, is a shame. A number of left-handers have flourished in Boston, including himself. In actuality, Lee says, Fenway is ideally suited to him and others like him.

True, strict fastballers don't do well. You can't force the issue. There is simply too little margin for error when a pop-up with the wind at its back can turn into a home run.

But the good pitcher adapts.

As Lee put it in his book, "A lefthander's first good look at the leftfield wall, the Green Monster . . . is an automatic reason for massive depression. . . . From the vantage point of the mound . . . I felt like I was scraping my knuckles against it every time I went into my motion, and I was always afraid that it would fall down and kill Rico at short.

"The key to pitching at Fenway, whether you are righthanded or left-handed but especially if you're a lefty, is to keep the ball outside and away on righthanders and down and in on lefthanders. Make that ball sink to lefthanders. Your lefty hitter is going to try to shoot your pitch the other way so he can jack it against or over the wall. If he can't get the ball up he's going to hit a two-hopper to the second baseman. You can make the temptation of the wall work for you. The Monster giveth, but the Monster can also taketh away. You just have to know what to feed it."

Lee practiced what he preached. Though he always gave up a lot of hits, not many of them were homers. (In 1974, for instance, he was reached for a mind-boggling 320 hits in 282 innings! That's more than 10 for each full game, and it led the league. Yet he won 17 games, and his overall ERA of 3.51 meant that opponents could translate each of their 10-hit barrages into a measly 3½ runs.)

Don Zimmer thought that Lee could entice the Reds' hitters to over-reach, that they would end up either beating the ball into the dirt or loft-ing weak flies to the outfield, and that they'd ground into a lot of double plays when they did get base runners. Which was exactly what was wanted. He swallowed his pride and recommended that Johnson give the Spaceman a start.

Johnson said he'd think about it.

The following day, the manager announced his pitching rotation for the 1975 World Series. Bill Lee, despite his long layoff, was going to start the second game. There were howls of disbelief from the press. Some even accused Johnson of quitting before he'd begun, of simply rolling over for the Big Red Machine.

But he, as it turns out, and Zim, and Bill Lee are about to show a skep-tical world that they know exactly what they're doing.

I've had my moment in the sun . . . or, rather, the rain. I've gotten to attend the first game of a World Series for what is almost certainly the only time in my life. For the rest of the games, I'll be like any other fan, watching on television. Which in my case means Uncle Oscar's venerable seventeen-inch black-and-white set; it'll be another couple of years before this frugal New Englander moves up to color. Fuzzy as the reception is, I can't do any better. On what I make driving for Town Taxi, I can't afford any kind of TV at all.

Still, I'm pumped. I love Bill Lee and I'm convinced he's going to make all of the doubters proud of him today. Oscar just sits there placidly, in his favorite chair, hands folded over his paunch.

October 12 is another damp, chilly day, with the temperature fifty-four degrees at game time and the sky threatening to burst open at any moment. It's rained overnight and now, though the rain has stopped, low-lying clouds hang over the city. The infield, covered until game time by a tarp, is in OK shape. The outfield is soggy and treacherous; there'll be some slip-pin' and slidin' out there before this one is over. Neither team has taken batting practice.

The wind is blowing in hard for the second straight day. Once again, home runs will be at a premium, which should favor the Sox.

Lee, you can see it, is really hyped up—this is the culmination of years of hard work for him—as are the rest of the Red Sox. They have a game in hand, and if they can prevail here today, they'll head for Cincinnati up 2–0 and in control of the Series. Even if they were then to lose all three on the opponents' field, they would still be coming back home to friendly Fenway for the final two games.

They want this one.

Darrell Johnson, after managing by remote control a day earlier, has made the first of many moves that will be subject to second-guessing in this Series. In a pregame interview, he defends his selection of Bill Lee to start this important game. He mouths the same words Zimmer claims to have used with him, that the Cincinnati hitters are vulnerable to off-speed pitches (certainly shown to be true in Game 1), and adds that Lee also has a good pickoff move that will help hold the running Reds on. He attributes his decision to "scouting reports" and doesn't mention his third-base coach.

(Zimmer didn't feel slighted, he told me when I met him. To him, it's the manager's job to take both the credit and the heat. And he added that never, before or since, had he pulled so hard for a pitcher as he did that day for his mortal adversary.)

Lee, trotting in from the bullpen after warming up, is the last player on the field before the opening ceremonies. He makes his way to the dugout amid a mixed chorus of cheers and boos, with the former outnumbering the latter. Announcer Ned Martin, in what has to rank as one of broadcasting's all-time great euphemisms, describes him as a "blithe spirit." He relates that when Lee was asked if, considering his long layoff, he was ready, the pitcher replied, "Johnson came to me and said I'm ready." And so it would prove.

Today is the two hundredth anniversary of the founding of the U.S. Navy. A naval officer sings the national anthem, and a young navy recruit throws in the first ball, after taking it from Secretary of State Henry Kissinger. Kissinger, too, is subjected to a substantial number of boos among the cheers.

Kissinger is seated with baseball commissioner Bowie Kuhn. Nearby are House Speaker Tip O'Neill, former Sox great Joe Cronin, and, his long hair just flecked with gray, the last standing brother, Senator Ted Kennedy.

Out come the Sox. Rick Burleson leads the way, running hard. He's always the first to his position. Lee takes his time. He may or may not be as flaky as the press has made him out to be, but on the mound he's all business. He presents an intense, unchanging, open-mouthed stare to every batter. He works fast and has been known to yell at hitters who step out on him in an attempt to disrupt his rhythm.

Pete Rose leads off. The Cincinnati lineup is unchanged. It's what got them here, and Sparky doesn't believe in tinkering with success. Lefty, righty, no matter.

Lee, probably to show the Reds at the outset that he has one, fires a first-pitch fastball right down the middle. It catches Pete by surprise, and he takes it. Then Lee settles back into his game plan: a lot of slow breaking stuff, hit the corners, stay outside on right-handed hitters, go for a lot of ground balls, make sure that anything over the heart of the plate lacks the velocity needed for the batter to drive one for distance through the wind.

He works Rose to perfection. His third pitch is a wicked screwball that tails away from the hitter and drops low over the outside corner. Pete doesn't come close to hitting it. Strikeout. Morgan follows by grounding another breaking ball to second. It takes a bad hop, but Denny Doyle stays with it and throws him out. Then up comes Johnny Bench.

And Johnson makes a risky move. Given that Bench is such a dangerous pull hitter, the manager overshifts his infielders, so that there are three of them on the left side and a huge, beckoning hole between first and second. There will be no seeing-eye ground singles to the left; anything hit there is a sure out. The gamble is that Bench won't be able to go the opposite way. If he does, he's on.

He doesn't. He flies weakly to left and the inning is over. Three up, three down. Just like yesterday. These guys are very mortal, I'm thinking.

As the teams change sides, it's worth considering that from a manager's viewpoint, playing the game of baseball, especially at the major league level, involves a continuous game of cat and mouse. It is highly cerebral. Players, other than pitchers and catchers deciding what to throw next, rarely have to think. Everything is physical, instinctual, with rational thought being counterproductive. Even defensive positioning, which does require some cogitation, is usually done from the bench.

Managers are a different breed. They have to use their brains, as well as their intuition, all the time. They must have a bucketful of statistics at their fingertips. They must know the strengths and weaknesses of both their own players and their opponents. They must be attuned to enemy pitchers' tendencies in certain situations and pass those along to their hitters. They must be aware of percentages, know when to go strictly "by the book" and when it makes sense to take a chance. And with many decisions, especially the most difficult of all, they must trust their hunches.

It is a baseball truism that great players almost never make great managers. There are undoubtedly many reasons for this: stars are used to being in the limelight, not the perpetual dark of the dugout; they may be inept at communicating what they know; they're not likely to have the patience to work out sticky personnel problems; they can be impatient with players less skilled than themselves; and so on. But a very important reason is surely that there's a delicate transition to be made from *doing* to *thinking*, and the one skill does not necessarily translate well to the other.

Sparky Anderson did not play in the big leagues. Darrell Johnson did, but only briefly and not very notably—320 at-bats spread over six years. Both are thinking men. Both are successful, or they wouldn't be here. Johnson has already made the first big moves of the day, selecting Bill Lee as his starter and overshifting his infield on Bench. Now it's Sparky's turn.

For one thing, there's the pitching choice, Jack Billingham. Billingham has had a decent year—though that's pretty much a given, considering the team has won 111 games. But the natural number two starter is probably Fred Norman. He has a better record and ERA than Billingham, as does Gary Nolan. Like Johnson's choice for this game, Bill Lee, Jack didn't pitch at all in the League Championship Series.

Norman, though, is a left-hander and will be spared a Fenway start. He's also old, having first come up in '62, and is the very definition of a journeyman: his fourteen-year record is 52–57. This is the first season he's ever been more than mediocre. Nolan is a righty, but a finesse pitcher better suited to Cincinnati and will get his start there.

Billingham throws right and is, like Lee, a sinkerballer, ideal for Fenway. In addition, it is Sparky's job to be cognizant of Jack's postseason record. In the 1972 World Series against Oakland, he pitched 13⅔ innings, giving up a total of 6 hits and 1 run. That's excellence under pressure. So Billingham gets the nod.

Darrell Johnson counters by making a lineup change. He moves the left-handed-hitting Cecil Cooper to the top of the order and drops Dwight

Evans (not a good breaking-ball hitter) to seventh and Rick Burleson to eighth.

Defensively, too, Anderson has made some subtle adjustments. Joe Morgan said, in a pregame interview, that he felt the Red Sox outfielders played the park and the weather better than the Reds in Game 1. The Sox took more shallow positions, allowing them to catch short flies pushed backward by the wind, balls that were dropping in front of the Reds' outfielders.

In response, Griffey and Geronimo are now playing farther in. In treacherous left, though, George Foster has gone the opposite way. He's standing almost on the warning track. Sparky's thinking is that he's willing to concede the bloop single in order to keep the batted ball in front of his outfielder. What he doesn't want is Foster having to track down flies hit over his head. A Fenway-knowledgeable defensive genius like Yastrzemski can do it. For an average fielder like Foster—confronted with the horror of sharp wall angles, inset doorways, and scoreboard windows—it just means too many extra bases.

How all of these moves and countermoves play out is about to be seen. Cooper leads off.

And immediately, the field condition comes into play. Cecil hits a catchable liner to left. Foster runs to his right and, just as he's about to leap for the ball, slips on the wet grass and stumbles. He misses it, and Cooper is into second with a stand-up double. As was the case yesterday, the Red Sox have put their first batter of the game on base.

I'm excited and become even more so a moment later. Denny Doyle, a great contact hitter (he's struck out only 12 times in 97 games), has one purpose here, to move the runner along to third. He's very good at it. So, dutifully, he slaps a hard ground ball to the right side. Unfortunately for Billingham, the pitcher tries to spear it rather than letting it go through to Morgan or Perez. He winds up just getting his glove on the ball, slowing it down enough that there's no play. Doyle is safe and now, instead of a man on third with one out, there are runners at the corners, nobody out. Once again, the Sox have a golden opportunity to break it open early.

I grin over at Oscar, who merely nods and says, "Good start." He's such a damn fatalist, but then, he's been here many, many more times than I have. And, of course, he's right.

Because what happens next is a nightmare. Yastrzemski hits a screaming one-hopper right back to Billingham. Jack redeems himself by fielding it cleanly. Cooper is trapped off third, and the proper play, by the book, is to nail him; you eschew the double play in return for preventing the run from scoring. But no. Billingham doesn't hesitate; he whirls and fires to second to force Doyle.

Cooper, as it turns out, is the hesitant one. Had he broken for the plate as soon as Billingham turned, he'd have made it easily. As it is, he's taken a step toward home, then one back toward third, and now, belatedly, has made his move down the line. Too bad for him. There's a Gold Glove shortstop out there, Davy Concepcion, who takes Billingham's throw. Though the normal thing for Concepcion would be to make the relay to first, completing the sure double play, he sees what's happening with Cooper and fires to Bench. Cecil is caught in a rundown and tagged out to complete the unorthodox double play.

It is a baseball axiom that you should never, ever run yourself out of a big inning. Yet, for the second day in a row, that's exactly what the Sox have potentially done. Cooper's assignment was to score—or, if he couldn't do that, to bluff toward the plate enticingly enough to draw the throw, but without committing himself so much that he couldn't retreat to the bag, thereby ensuring that there would still be two runners on for the next batter. He did neither.

Poor baserunning will plague the Red Sox throughout the Series, and never more so than here, as Fisk keeps the rally alive by following with a single to right. Yaz scores from second, but the inning ends when Lynn grounds out. The Sox have a run. As always, they coulda shoulda mighta oughtta had more.

The second is a breeze for Lee, who strikes out the two sluggers, Perez and Foster, and gets Concepcion on a grounder to short. Six in a row.

For the Sox, it's another inning of trouble. First off, Petrocelli hits a long fly down the right-field line, directly at the Pesky Pole.

The Pole, which separates fair territory from foul out in right, is less celebrated than the Wall in left, but it is in fact a shade closer to home plate, at 302 feet. It's a tempting chip shot, and countless batters have turned routine flies into home runs by curving them (or having the wind blow them) around the Pole. The margin of error is small, however, because right field drops off precipitously thereafter. To clear the bullpen wall in straightaway right, you have to hammer the ball 380 feet, a pretty good poke.

In one of those endearing bits of Fenway lore, the Pole is named for Sox legend—infielder, coach, manager—Johnny Pesky. Former pitcher Mel Parnell coined the term around 1950, according to John, and you might think that's because Pesky, a slightly built left-hander, hooked so many home runs around it. Wrong. In his ten-year major league career, Johnny hit 17 homers *total*, with all of six down the right-field line in Boston.

One of those, however, happened to be a game winner, and Parnell, providing color commentary for that night's radio broadcast, quipped that the batter had curled one around Pesky's Pole for the victory. The name stuck.

On a calm day, or with a left-to-right breeze, Petrocelli's drive probably drops behind the pole for a home run. Not today, as the wind pushes it back toward the playing field. OK, but it's at least a double, maybe a triple after Griffey runs into the wall trying to catch it. There's no way it should be anything else, because there are only about six inches between the foul line and the stands at that point. Which, of course, is precisely where the ball lands. No homer, no extra-base hit, nothing. Rico, perhaps deflated, proceeds to strike out.

Dwight Evans crowds the plate, so Billingham throws at him to move him off. He can't get out of the way in time and is hit by the pitch. Down to first he goes. Burleson (who, despite his .252 BA, was second on the team in game-winning hits) then grounds a single to center, which would have scored Rico if. . . . Bringing up the pitcher.

Bill Lee is not a bad hitter, and he handles the bat very well. So Darrell Johnson makes another move here. With Pete Rose creeping in from third, he has Lee bluff a bunt and try to ground one past the third baseman into left. He swings and misses. Bench comes up throwing, trying to pick Evans off second. Uncharacteristic of the Cincinnati catcher, it's a bad throw. It hits the ground and caroms into center field. But, luck of the Sox, not quite far enough for Dwight to advance.

Johnson rolls the dice again. On the next pitch, Lee squares around to bunt for real. At the same time, Evans makes a move toward third. When Lee misses the ball, Bench obligingly pegs it down to second again. Evans, once Bench is committed, takes off for third. Well, *hellooo* . . . Bad idea, guys, these are *great* defensive ballplayers here. I know the strategy is to be aggressive, but this, this is suicide. Concepcion guns it to Rose, and Evans is out.

Burleson moves to second on the play but dies there when Lee strikes out swinging. Two base runners with one out. No runs. Those innings'll come back to haunt you.

Space, though, is pitching as though the one run they have managed to put across is all he'll need. In the third, Griffey grounds to first, Geronimo strikes out swinging, and Billingham grounds to short. Nine up, nine down. Strikeouts, groundouts, and a single lazy fly. A picture-perfect Bill Lee performance. So far.

"One-nothing?" I say to Oscar, as if there's a chance in hell that will be the final score. He shakes his head. Uh-uh.

Billingham has an easy third, giving up a walk to Yaz but otherwise retiring the side on two grounders and a strikeout.

There are very few sports that even attempt to deal with the concept of perfection. There's gymnastics, where some limber preadolescent may be awarded a "perfect ten." Or an ice skater's freestyle routine may be scored as "perfect." But these are individual activities, and they involve the highly subjective pronouncements of judges. Only baseball, among team sports, recognizes perfection, and only baseball, among all pastimes, has a completely objective yardstick by which to measure it.

Imagine a quarterback who reared back and completed a pass every time he handled the ball, a basketball player who scored off every dribble, a soccer star who beat both the defense and the goalkeeper every time down the field. Impossible. Nor, for that matter, can a baseball hitter succeed on every pitch.

A pitcher, however, can be perfect. He can deny the batter first base each and every time he throws the ball. He'll need some help from his teammates, of course, but if he does his primary job—preventing base runners—through twenty-seven consecutive hitters, then he has hurled what is called a perfect game.

It's a feat that demands not only brilliance in a pitcher but flawless execution by the defense behind him, as well as a healthy dose of luck. Each bounce of the ball must be to his advantage.

All of these things make it an occurrence of extreme scarcity. In all of major league history, it has happened a microscopic sixteen times. (Or seventeen, if we count, as we should, Harvey Haddix's extraordinary performance on May 26, 1959, when he pitched a nearly unimaginable 12 perfect innings, only to give up a hit—and lose the game—in the 13th.) The perfect game is no respecter of talent; most of the game's greatest pitchers never accomplished it, while a number of journeymen have. No one has done it twice.

There is also a higher level of perfection, if that is not a contradiction in terms. "Superperfect" games, ones in which the pitcher strikes out everyone he faces, have occurred. But never in the majors (where 20 strikeouts is the record, and none of those three games was otherwise perfect). In fact, not above the Little League level, to the best of my knowledge.

It is not recorded whether, in any of the "superperfect" games, the hitters completely failed even to get the bat on the ball. If that has happened, then we would have to coin a yet higher superlative.

Because we can at least envision such a "super-superperfect" game, it seems natural to me to want to speculate a little further on the delicate balance that baseball strikes between batter and pitcher. We agree that some measure of perfection has already, if infrequently, been attained. But what about absolute and, more important, repetitive perfection?

What would it look like? Simple. It would arrive in the form of a pitcher who threw a perfect game every time. Impossible right now, yes. However, suppose something happened to upset the aforementioned balance. Suppose future genetic manipulations produced a human capable of throwing a baseball 110 miles per hour instead of 100. Would the batter then have sufficient time to react? Maybe not. Or suppose that some tinkerer with the mechanics of pitching came up with a truly unhittable pitch.

Baseball is unique in that, within its traditional framework, we can theorize about such things. We can predict that they may, in fact, come to pass. And what if they did, what would happen then?

Thomas Klise explores this intriguing question in his classic novel *The Last Western*, which is a meditation on various kinds of perfection. The novel's protagonist is Willie, a poor, uneducated kid from the American Southwest who as a young adult discovers that he has something extraordinary: a fastball that is not only faster than everyone else's but that hops sharply as it enters the strike zone. It's the theoretical unhittable pitch come to life, at least in fiction.

Every professional ball club wants this kid, of course. Unsurprisingly, Willie is signed by the man with the deepest pockets, the owner of the New York team. (In a supreme example of art prefiguring reality, that fictitious owner is a dead-on depiction of George Steinbrenner, imagined years before the actual Steinbrenner took control of the Yankees.)

Willie is rushed into the big leagues and, at first, is the toast of the town. Capacity crowds jam the stadium every time he pitches. The hometown fans are nuts about him. He goes out there and, no matter what team he's facing, no matter how good their players are, he strikes everybody out. New York wins all of his games.

But as his success continues, something happens. First his teammates, the seven guys supposedly playing defense behind him, begin to resent him. They now have nothing to do. They become sullen, or bored at best. And then, slowly but surely, the crowds turn on him, too. Not just the fans of the opposition, either. His own, as well.

Willie is reviled. Because, as it turns out, this simple soul has ruined the game of baseball. The game, in the form in which it is loved, depends on drama, unpredictability, the duel between pitcher and batter, offensive explosions and defensive lapses, the possibility that a team losing by eight runs in the ninth inning can still come back and win. Those elements are what bring the fans out to the park. Take them away, and the essence of the sport departs with them.

Klise brilliantly illuminates the ambiguity of our relationship with perfection. Like an incandescent love affair, we want it, crave it, will kill for it in the short run. Yet it cannot be sustained. Having it day in and day out destroys it.

Willie is a good, kind fellow. All that he's guilty of is doing, impossibly well, what he's supposed to do. For that, he is booed mercilessly. The New York team, finally recognizing that one must be careful what one wishes for, cuts him loose. No other team picks him up and, inexplicably to him, he's out of baseball. (All is not lost, however—Willie will go on to become the pope, but that's another story.)

In the real world, the occasional perfect game is cherished by the spectator, and every time a pitcher strings together a series of one-two-three innings from the outset, a sense of excitement begins to build. As each retired batter heads back to the dugout, it grows. It crests after eight, and as the pitcher comes out to try to seal it, the crowd will be on its feet, cheering regardless of team affiliation. Everybody wants to be, even vicariously, a part of something that happens, on average, about once every eight years.

When perfection is spoiled before the end, as it nearly always is, then there is disappointment, in direct proportion to how far into the game it happens.

Bill Lee, like Tiant in Game 1, has retired the first nine batters he's faced. So there is some anticipation, some minute hope that we might be witnessing the beginning of what would be only the second perfect game in World Series history. I'm not optimistic, though. Lee is not that kind of pitcher. He is neither overpowering nor baffling. He makes mistakes. And the Reds are a well-oiled hitting machine that takes advantage of mistakes.

Thus it's hardly surprising when, in the fourth, the balloon is punctured. Bill doesn't pitch at all badly, but he doesn't get the kind of breaks he'd need if he aspired to perfection on this day.

It begins innocently enough, with Lee going after Rose with a screwball again. Pete reaches out and tries to go to right with the pitch but hits a routine grounder to second. Rose, the tenth consecutive Cincinnati batter set down, precedes Lee's first mistake, and it's a big one. He walks Joe Morgan. End of perfect game. Morgan trots down to first and nonchalantly digs the mud out of his spikes. The message is sent: *I don't care about your damn move to first; I'm running.*

Except, surprisingly, that Johnny Bench won't let him. Bench swings at the first pitch and lines a single to center. There goes the no-hitter, as well. Morgan reaches third with ease.

Perez up. Lee works him carefully, keeping the ball low, trying for the ground ball that—Bench and Perez both being slow runners—will yield an inning-ending double play. He gets almost exactly what he wants. Almost. Perez reaches for a pitch low and away and gets just enough bat on it to rap a slow grounder between short and second. In retrospect, the moment stands out as important in and of itself, but also as the precursor of a nearly identical, even more significant play that will occur later on today.

Baseball is a game of inches, and of good and bad fortune. Burleson charges the ball, fields it cleanly, and flips it to Doyle, who pivots and rifles the relay to Cooper. They've executed the double play to perfection. Yet they don't get it. The ball was hit just slowly enough that Tony Perez can beat the throw to first. The run scores. The game is tied.

The TV announcers question whether even Bench should be out, because Doyle was only "in the neighborhood" of the bag at second when he should have been tagging it. But it's just normal major league umpiring and that, as former Yankee shortstop Tony Kubek points out, is quite as it should be. "When they enforce the rule that the runner has to slide at the base and not at the fielder," he says, "then they can enforce the rule that the fielder has to be on the bag."

Lee follows up by trying to lob a blooper curve by George Foster, but this one stays up in the strike zone just enough that Foster can pop it into left field for a single. Two on, two out, a run in, and Lee still hasn't been hit hard. Concepcion then lofts a fly to short, straightaway center. If the otherwise nonpareil Fred Lynn has a weakness, this is it: the inability to quickly judge the trajectory of balls hit at him. Later in the Series, this flaw may prove costly. In this instance, Lynn gets a late jump on the ball and has to run in at top speed to make the awkward, lunging catch that finally bails his pitcher out of the inning.

One run, which Cincinnati had to really scratch for, yet that could easily have been more. On the whole, I'm relieved.

In the home fourth, Lynn tries to bunt his way on. The ball rolls foul and Lynn, seeing how incredibly fast Bench comes out from behind the plate, isn't about to try it again. He hits a fly to left. Foster, who must be spooked at the amount of work he's getting out there, is playing perfectly, though. He retreats to the Wall, then makes the catch coming back in. Just the way Sparky planned it.

It begins to rain as Petrocelli grounds to short and Evans strikes out swinging on—you guessed it—a hard breaking ball. The rain is steady but not too hard, and this is the World Series. Play on.

Lee recovers from the lapses of the previous inning and gets Griffey on a ground ball to first and Geronimo on a fly to right. Billingham hits a grounder to second that takes a nasty hop, but Doyle stays with it and throws him out.

Burleson leads off the bottom of the inning. It's chilly and now raining harder. The batboy comes out and wipes off home plate. Play on.

Announcer Ned Martin says that Rick was tagged with his nickname, the Rooster, because of the way his hair sticks up when he takes his hat off. That's the sanitized, TV version. Alternatively, he got it because he behaves like a fighting cock. Take your pick. Whatever the case, the Rooster is perfect in the series (4 for 4) until this at-bat. He strikes out swinging.

Bill Lee, an excellent bunter, then casually drops his bat and lays down a perfect one along the third-base line. With anyone else behind the plate, he beats it out. Not with Johnny B. Bench shoots up out of his crouch as if a cherry bomb had exploded beneath his butt. He chases down the ball and fires a rocket to first while still in the midst of turning his body. It's a wonder to behold. The throw beats Lee by a mere half step, but it beats him. Cooper raps back to the pitcher for the third out.

Between innings, the ads are, as usual, all male-oriented. Mercury marine engines and Quaker State motor oil, to go along with earlier pitches for Prestone with silicone silicate, Owens-Corning fiberglass, Gillette Foamy (a "symphony for shaving"), the Max for Men hair dryer, and the U.S. Navy ("get your diploma and join up," says Pete Rose warmly).

In keeping with the manly theme, when the live camera returns it zeros in on Carlton Fisk, who's pulling at his crotch. He does it more than any player I've ever seen. I wonder, *what's going on in there, Pudge?* Whatever it is, it's apparently resolved, because Fisk settles in comfortably behind the plate, feeling good enough that he'll shortly be half of a great defensive play.

Lee opens up with a mistake. He's gotten Pete Rose with screwballs the previous two at-bats, but this time he elects to go with a slow curve. Rose smacks it into left for a single.

Joe Morgan then tries to reach base by claiming that an inside fastball hit him on the uniform. No way, says home-plate umpire Colosi. Morgan even appeals to the second-base ump, to no avail. So, instead of two on and none out, it's one on and one out when Morgan grounds sharply to Cooper, who makes a great play. He dives to snare the ball, comes up on his knees, and manages to get the ball to second in time to force Rose who, typically, is trying to sever Burleson's legs at the knee. There's no attempt to turn a double play against the fleet Morgan.

Morgan immediately goes into I'm-gonna-steal-on-you mode. He's been successful on all four steals he's attempted in the postseason. He takes a major, five-and-a-half-step lead, daring Lee to pick him off. Lee makes a couple of perfunctory throws over. He doesn't show the good move, this time. Instead, he goes to the plate and Little Joe takes off. He has a good jump.

Now, Pudge Fisk isn't Johnny Bench. No one is. Yet he's begun staking out a spot as the next best guy around. He pops up and makes a perfect throw to Denny Doyle, just to the first-base side of second, right where you want it. For his part, Doyle blocks the bag brilliantly. There is nowhere for Morgan to go but into the tag. The master base stealer is out. By maybe three inches, tops.

The batter, Bench, is an anticlimax. Or should be. He hits a routine fly to center. Fred Lynn, however, slips on the wet grass as he breaks in toward the ball and again has to make a mad rush for it. He dives, his face plowing into the soggy turf, his arm bent at the elbow, glove held slightly aloft. The ball is in it and amazingly stays there. Another superb fielding play in a Series that's fast becoming noted for them.

The rain stops, but the sky remains very dark and threatening. As the camera pans around the crowd, it's easy to tell it's the seventies. There's as yet no ordinance against smoking pipes or cigars in the stands, and many of the men are doing so.

Doyle, batting first, grounds out, but Yaz singles to right. Billingham calls time in order to clean his cleats. It's getting very muddy out on the mound.

When he's finished he induces Fisk to bounce to short on a 3–2 count. Yastrzemski, running with the pitch, can't be forced at second. Maybe Concepcion takes his eye off the ball for a moment to note where Yaz is, maybe not. Whatever the case, the sure-handed shortstop improbably bobbles the grounder and everyone is safe. Both teams have been playing so well, even under trying conditions, that this is the first error of the Series for either of them.

It couldn't come at a more opportune moment for Boston fans. "If we can get a run here," I say to Oscar, "then if the game is called on account of rain, we win." No one wants a rain-shortened victory. Of course. On the other hand . . .

"Could be," Oscar says.

It's the perfect situation for Fred Lynn. His job is to work the pitcher here, to force him to come up with good pitches or risk walking the bases loaded, to wait patiently for a fastball and then, when he's sure one is coming, to really drive it. But Lynn, for all his wonderful attributes, is still a rookie. If either Johnson or Zimmer shoots him a sign to stretch out the at-bat, he misses it. He's been told by the manager to be aggressive at the plate, and aggressive he remains, even when he shouldn't. He swings at the first pitch and flies out to short right.

Now it's up to Rico and, despite his veteran status and the two hits in Game 1, he's not the man we want there in the clutch. He was 2 for 12 against Oakland and has struggled all season with a variety of physical ailments. He's still not 100 percent.

While we may wish someone else was at the plate at this critical juncture, in so doing we underestimate Mr. Petrocelli. He's a fighter, a street kid from Brooklyn, always the first out of the dugout to aid a teammate in trouble. He singles to left, and Yaz scores. Sox on top, 2–1. It's the third RBI for Rico, who will wind up hitting .308 in the seven games and play flawlessly in the field.

In the World Series, you never know who will stand and deliver.

And the inning is not yet over. Evans runs the count to 3–2 and then checks his swing on the final pitch. The replay shows that he clearly went around, as Bench argues, but it's immaterial. Ball four was called, and that's not going to change.

Billingham has hardly been pounded, but Sparky Anderson has had enough. He has a strong, deep bullpen, and he yanks his pitcher in favor of Pedro Borbon. While Borbon makes his way in, a groundskeeper comes and spreads a layer of something that looks like sawdust on the mound. Ned Martin, who calls games for the Sox during the season, claims that it's actually what he calls "dried fertilizer." Whatever the case, Borbon and his nose must find the conditions to their liking. He retires Burleson on a soft fly ball to center.

The network finally gives us a family ad, a large Italian family—appropriately enough, since Rico has just come through—that gathers around their table to sing operatically in praise of Kentucky Fried Chicken.

Play-by-play resumes with the information that the O. J. Simpson–led Buffalo Bills are losing to the underdog Baltimore Colts. This is preface to a quick inning in which Lee makes the Reds look foolish. He walks Perez right off the bat. But then Foster swings mightily at an off-speed pitch, trying against reason to jack it out, and flies to left. Concepcion hits a fly that Evans catches coming in, almost at the infield dirt. And Griffey strikes out.

The Spaceman is in the zone.

It's a place he's quite fond of, one that he's apt to wax a bit, um, rhapsodic about, as he does in this passage from *The Wrong Stuff*: "When your arm, mind and body are in sync, you are able to work at peak performance level, while your brain remains relaxed. It's Zen-like when you're going good. You are the ball and the ball is you. It can do you no harm. A common bond forms between you and this white sphere, a bond based on mutual trust. The ball promises not to fly over too many walls after you have politely served it up to enemy hitters, and you assure it that you will not allow those same batters to treat the ball in a harsh or violent manner. Out of this trust comes a power that allows the pitcher to take control of what otherwise might be an uncontrollable situation. During those moments on the pitching rubber, when you have every pitch at your command working to its highest potential, you are your own universe. For hours after the game, this sense of completeness lingers. Then you sink back to what we humorously refer to as reality. Your body aches and your muscles cry out. You feel your mortality. That can be a difficult thing to handle. I believe pitchers come in touch with death a lot sooner than other players. We are more aware of the subtle changes taking place in our body and are unable to overlook the tell-tale hints that we are not going to last on this planet forever. Every pitcher has to be a little in love with death."

Bill will now have an indefinite period in which to contemplate Zen, death, his pal the ball, and whatever else might be on his mind. Because at this moment, out comes the tarp. A rain delay is announced.

The game is, however, official. Should the precip now force a cancellation, the Sox will win. Given the Curse, it's probable that more than a few are praying fervently for a deluge.

The suspension of play will, however, be brief. Just twenty-seven minutes. During that time, the network has some space to fill, and they do it with interviews. Tony Kubek, who looks years younger, is working on the afternoon of his thirty-ninth birthday. He draws the Man Who Is Not There.

Jim Ed Rice is not camera-friendly. He's shy, awkward, and ill at ease, and he doesn't articulate well. In October of '75, I'm sure that I watched the interview with frustration that the guy who led the team in game-winning hits wasn't going to play in the World Series. I probably noticed little else.

Two and a half decades later, what I see on videotape is a twenty-two-year-old kid from the Appalachian South. A soft-spoken kid with youthful enthusiasm and a bashful, winning, and, yes, sweet smile. A kid whose heart has been broken but who realizes that he's still got all the world ahead of him.

Jimmy hails from Anderson, South Carolina (the "Electric City"), an old textile town that claims to be "the first city in the South to have an unlimited supply of electric power." When he was a child, it was probably booming. Now the population, at around twenty-five thousand, hasn't changed in more than ten years.

He may be the only major leaguer ever to have had a school district line temporarily redrawn because of his athletic talents.

It happened his senior year, when the Anderson schools were in the process of implementing desegregation and Rice was a superstar in basketball, football, and track (he once ran a 9.9 hundred), as well as baseball. Previously, he had gone to Westside High, the all-black school, and that's where he should have continued going because he lived just on one side of the new line demarcating attendance on the basis of residence rather than race. But Hanna was the town's favored, formerly all-white school, and that's where Jim went for that one year. Because authorities had added a little indentation to his district that just happened to be drawn around his block. The following year it was gone.

Sox scouts watched him through high school and American Legion ball, and they sure liked what they saw: a self-effacing kid with enormous natural talents, a rock-solid work ethic, and a prodigious physical strength that never needed a boost from the weight room. The team made him a number one draft choice.

It was clearly justified after he won back-to-back minor league MVP awards in Triple A, as well as being named the Sporting News Minor League Player of the Year. He was brought up as the heir apparent to Boston's left-field superstar tradition, a virtually unbroken line that extended from Ted Williams down through Carl Yastrzemski to him.

He was also a retiring young black man with a subpar education, thrust into the spotlight in perhaps the most difficult possible market: a city of high intellectual orientation that had nevertheless drawn the most savage racial divide in the country.

Rice immediately, and throughout his career, felt underappreciated. And rightly so. While he was unquestionably one of the most feared hitters of his era, while he gave his all on the field, he constantly played in the shadow of his white teammates. Fred Lynn. Carlton Fisk. Even Rick Burleson, who somehow edged him out for the team MVP award in 1979, a genuine monster year in which Rice hit .325 with 39 home runs and 130 RBI.

Sportswriters, radio men, TV commentators—who in Boston were overwhelmingly white—went to the other guys first for stories. And when the writers did publish what he said, Jimmy felt that they twisted or misquoted his words. They made things up, as reporters will do, and that both perplexed and hurt him. So he withdrew from them and, never very comfortable as a public person, from the fans, as well.

"I don't know what [the media] wants from me," he once complained in frustration. "I'm not going to kiss writers' butts just to get better hype, and while the good writers have had a very good relationship with me, the lousy ones think a player's performance is somehow linked to the volume of stupid statements one gives out. I don't know what the public wants, either. I go out there and play every day, whether I'm hurt or feeling great."

Rice worked *hard*. He studied Ted Williams's *Science of Hitting* and spent long hours in the batting cage, making himself a pure hitter, not just a slugger. Although he was a mediocre fielder when he first came up, he pushed himself to improve. Don Zimmer recalled that either he or Johnny Pesky would be pestered to hit fungoes out to Rice in left, over and over until their fingers blistered. Every day. In time, Jimmy mastered the nuances of the field. According to Pesky and Zim, who should know, he matured into a defensive asset only slightly less valuable than the fabled Yaz.

At the plate, he produced. He hit over .300 seven times, posted a lifetime slugging percentage of .502, averaged 27 home runs a season (back when 20 was a lot), and drove in over a hundred runs eight times.

Yet he and Boston remained a classic mismatch. The Hub wasn't really ready for a black superstar, not in the days of Southie vs. Roxbury, Arthur Garrity vs. Louise Day Hicks. And Rice, tragically, was never ready for Boston—though it's difficult to imagine *any* high-profile African-American athlete who would have welcomed the role of lightning rod for the city's torment over race. Had Jimmy played for the Yankees, the Dodgers, virtually anyone but the last major league team to integrate, who knows what kind of career he might have had, and in what esteem he might now be held.

My own most indelible memory of Jim Rice is of the night I watched him check his swing and break his bat in half. I couldn't believe what I had just seen. There was no contact between bat and ball; it had shattered entirely because of the arrested force in his swing. Ken Harrelson, a member of the 1967 Red Sox Impossible Dream team, was color man for the broadcast at the time, and he was flabbergasted. "I . . . I've never seen that before," I recall Harrelson stammering. No one had. Harrelson, a Rice golfing buddy, also related that Jim was longer off the tee than anyone then on the PGA tour and that he'd seen Jimmy similarly snap a driver on an aborted downswing.

Rice was that kind of strong. Some said, though there was no way to measure, that he was the strongest man in the major leagues. So strong, and yet, as the interview clearly reveals, oh so vulnerable, too.

In 2000, he told the *Boston Herald*, "I knew I could have played [in the Series]. I'd played with pain before. But I was on the DL [disabled list] and they said they were not going to take me off it." Fewer than three weeks into the normal six- to eight-week healing period, he'd cut the cast off himself. "I [did that] because I wanted to play. I knew I was taking a chance, but it was to play in the World Series. They said it would jeopardize my career if I were to play." So he didn't.

Back in '75, he says all the right things. How he wishes he were playing but isn't disappointed that he's not. Sure. Like the pain doesn't show. He says he has to be careful, that he agrees the best thing to do is rest it over the winter, that he shouldn't take the chance of reinjuring it. Sure. He's proud of the contribution he made to get the team here and wishes them continuing success. Well, that at least seems true.

The Jimmy Rice in the Kubek interview wants to play so bad you can slice the desire coming out of the TV set and eat it for bread. And the amazing thing is, you also get the feeling that he's not being insincere. Yeah, he says, he wasn't voted onto the All-Star team this year, and he's missing the World Series, but he'll be there in the future, no problem. He's surrounded with burgeoning talent and has the boundless optimism of youth. He will excel, and so will his teammates. There are so many All-Star Games, so much postseason play, to come. His eyes shine with his vision of the future.

In reality, yes, he will become a perennial (eight-time) All-Star. He'll win the league MVP award in '78. He'll amass statistics that many feel are Hall of Fame–worthy. But when the Red Sox finally make it back to the World Series, in 1986, the only members of this group still with the team will be Dwight Evans and himself.

Today, Jim Rice remains media-averse. I left countless messages for him, and he didn't answer them. I tried to get the Red Sox to pin down his whereabouts for me—he did work for them, after all, and I was prepared to drive wherever he was on the chance he'd talk to me—but they told me they didn't know, that he moved around a lot, on his own schedule. Regrettably, I never did connect with him.

Watching his youthful self, I can't help but think how the years will take this kid and, like most of the rest of us, beat him down. Is he bitter? It wouldn't surprise me; he was, after all, recently fired as the Sox' hitting coach after a four-year tenure during which the team's collective batting average was twenty points higher than during the previous four years. But then, there's not much point in speculation, considering that I've never met the man.

Mostly, I'm sad. When Kubek says, "I wish you were out there," and Rice replies quietly, "I do, too," my heart crumbles as well, all these years later.

Kubek signs off and there follows a short interview with Sparky Anderson.

Sparky laments his team's lack of offensive production, which is why they're in the hole they're in, and notes, rather quaintly, that "we haven't been able to 'do our thing,' as the kids say." And "the Red Machine is gonna wake up," wait and see.

Almost wistfully, he adds "and this one isn't over yet." But they're more like brave words, with no sense of conviction behind them. This is not the Reds' kind of day, with the weather essentially denying the long ball and a junkman on the mound. You can see it in his face and body language. Sparky's accepted defeat already and is priming himself to put an optimistic face on a return to Riverfront Stadium down 2–0.

It's a remarkable thing to see, especially since his team is behind by only a run and there are still two innings to go.

Cut to Johnny Bench, who flogs the obvious by saying that Bill Lee is "pitching smart." Then there's a promo for NBC's *NFL Grandstand*, a "new concept in sports coverage, with news, scores, features, and much more." And then the rain delay is over, and it's back to live action.

Right away, Darrell Johnson has a decision to make, because his pitcher is due to lead off. Lee is pitching a "smart" 3-hitter, yes. But by the end of the inning he will have been sitting for well over half an hour, plenty long enough for muscles to tighten up in this kind of weather. Johnson has plenty of fresh arms in the bullpen, including sinkerballer Jim Willoughby, well suited to the present conditions. And there's also the possibility that a pinch hitter could start a rally that pads the lead by a crucial run or two. The way Lee is swinging the bat, he's not likely to do it, not with reliever Will McEnaney, a lefty, now on the mound.

The tough decisions, as it turns out, are just beginning. On this one, Darrell weighs his options and sends Lee up to bat. Lee strikes out. Cooper grounds to short. And Doyle strikes out, too, on a pitch that looks out of the strike zone.

On to the eighth. Johnson has Dick Drago and Jim Burton warming up. Sparky has his ace, Rawley Eastwick, getting ready.

But Lee has little trouble. Rose does get Cincinnati's fourth hit, a fisted single to right on a tough 1–2 pitch. It comes with two out, though, and Morgan follows by grounding to second. Just three outs to go. I'm beginning to feel this one is in the bag, and even phlegmatic Uncle Oscar is optimistic. Lee continues to pitch masterfully, and Morgan, the Reds' most dangerous base runner, has just made the last out in the eighth. It won't be Little Joe who beats them. True, the 3-4-5 hitters will open the ninth, but who cares?

Between innings, Whitey Ford and Mickey Mantle playfully reminisce that they were known to have a beer or two in their playing days and that "it's too bad Miller Lite wasn't around then." If it had been, they'd be "in the beer drinkers' Hall of Fame." Given what we now know about Mantle's alcohol problem, the ad is depressing.

Now Sparky Anderson makes a move. He pulls McEnaney and puts in Eastwick. It's an odd move, considering that Rawley is a right-hander and there will be two lefties—Yaz and Lynn—coming up. But Eastwick, a rookie, has been dominating this year, tying for the league lead in saves with 22 (a pretty fair total in the days before top closers pitched in every close game and were expected to get 40 or more). He's rested, and Anderson obviously hopes he can shut the Sox down the rest of the way while his team scratches out enough offense to get them back in the game.

The strategy almost blows up in his face immediately. Yaz, the first batter, takes Eastwick deep to left center. It's a drive that on an ordinary day would at least be off the wall. Not today. It's too far out there, and the wind is too strong. The ball stays up long enough for Geronimo to run it down and gather it in.

Fisk walks. Lynn golfs at a pitch and flies to short right. Petrocelli, continuing to deliver in the clutch, singles to the opposite field. Two on, two out. It's a scoring chance. Anderson has his outfielders move in, so that they'll have a chance to hold Fisk at third on a single. But Sparky is playing psychologist, too, daring batter Dwight Evans to play the fool and try hitting it over their heads. Evans strikes out looking, and the rally fizzles.

Of all the boys of October, Bill Lee has taken the longest, strangest journey, both physically and spiritually, in his quest for home. Or perhaps it's not so strange, if we think of these fellows as overgrown teenagers, playing at a kid's game far into adulthood. Because what do teenagers do? Rebel against their parents.

Parlor psychology, yeah. But it just might help explain why a fair-haired, sun-loving West Coast boy, from good Republican Catholic stock, would want to recast himself as a tree-hugging, Buddhist Socialist living in Vermont's Northeast Kingdom.

Lee was born in Burbank and spent his childhood in southern California before moving to Marin County for his high school years. His family was, in his words, "the middle of the middle class." He never did take well to authority or organized religion. As a kid, he once handcuffed himself to the bed and hid the key, in order to avoid catechism. His mother had to free him with a hacksaw.

There wasn't much in the way of early athletic prowess, either. The other kids made merciless fun of him when he unknowingly ran around the bases backward in an early game of kickball. He was shunted into adaptive PE because of his gawky body.

He grew into the body, though, and soon found that he excelled at baseball. Not so much that he thought he'd make a career out of it, but he could hit and he could throw. He remained unscouted out of high school, partly due to missing his senior year with an injury. All in all, he just loved to play and decided to continue in college at the University of Southern California.

At USC, Lee played under legendary coach Rod Dedeaux and came into his own as he helped the Trojans win a national college championship. They didn't have much hitting in his era, Lee recalls, but always-great defense and, Lord, what a gang of arms. Tom Seaver for a year. And then, during the championship season, there was Lee, Brent Strom, and Jim Barr, who all eventually made it to the Show. There was also a hulking young, wild, flamethrowing freshman named Dave Kingman (later to be known as Kong), who was converted into an everyday player when it was discovered just how far he could hit a baseball.

Though he'd gone 24–8 his last two years and pitched well in the College World Series, Lee still wasn't sure he could make the bigs. He "didn't have a major league fastball," as a couple of scouts told him. But the Red Sox decided to take a chance, picking him "around three hundredth," in the secondary phase of the free-agent draft. He was given, essentially, no bonus, which was his only choice if he wanted to start working in the minors. At this point, he'd decided baseball was worth a shot, and he signed.

He was a professional ballplayer. He was also well on his way to becoming the character who would later be the darling of one segment of the baseball-watching public and the anti-Christ to another.

The SC years were pivotal. Other than being an important member of that championship team, the best part of them for Lee was hanging at his uncle's place in Malibu. Unc might have been a humble locksmith by trade, but Lee says he was the "locksmith to the stars," forever getting calls from "wives who were throwing their husbands out of houses."

That old locksmith was also shrewd. He got in early on the Malibu boom, grabbing an oceanfront house for fifty grand that he later sold for two million dollars. But young Bill Lee didn't care anything about property values. All he knew was that his dorm was back in Watts, with government snipers patrolling the rooftop during the riots, while his uncle's pad was over at the beach, with fun-loving neighbors like Don Henley, Glenn Frey, Neil Young, and the Turtles.

Where to pass his free time was a no-brainer. It was the tail end of the sixties, and Malibu was the place. Party Central. A perfect spot for an impressionable kid to feel the first stirrings of a political consciousness, as well as to develop an initial taste for recreational chemicals. The era, it turned out, was made for the man. Bill Lee, he of the uncapped mouth and nontraditional ways, the soon-to-be Spaceman, was off and running.

Despite the brushes with notoriety that still make Lee proud—such as gracing the cover of *High Times* magazine and claiming to have once shared marijuana with fellow baseball nut George W. Bush, back in the days the current president doesn't like to talk about—there is a lot more to him than pot and middle-class rebellion, as I found out when I visited him at his home in rural Craftsbury, Vermont.

To reach Craftsbury, you have to drive nearly to Canada, deep into the heart of the Northeast Kingdom. It's an area with such short summers and brutal winters that most of the countercultural types who flee there to escape American city life find themselves quickly fleeing home again. A few have stayed, starting eateries with names like the Egress and the Deli Lama, and staging an annual reggae festival.

But for the most part, the Black River Valley—a table of land at eighteen hundred feet above sea level—is a landscape of small dairy farms, creameries and sugarhouses, cornfields, double wides, and wheel-shaped bales of hay shrink-wrapped in blue plastic. It's beautiful in a semicivilized, back-of-beyond way. Half of the names on the mailboxes are French.

I drove up to Lee's property and could see immediately why he fell in love with the site when a friend first showed it to him. His house, an idiosyncratic handmade wood structure that would not be out of place in *Hippie Homes and Gardens*, sits on a hill overlooking the valley, with an unobstructed two-mile view to Craftsbury Common. The Common, looking like a toy village at this distance, is as picturesque as New England gets. There are white clapboard houses, sugar maple trees, and a white-steepled church. You expect there to be a little Lionel train, running round and round the town. When the church bell tolls, a deep, rich musical note rolls across the fields and seems as if it comes from nearby and the far distance at the same time.

Bill Lee was out front, between his flower garden and the ancient BMW parked next to his garage. It's a good thing the place is a half-continent north of Miami, because the Cuban flag flies on a pole in the front yard. Lee travels to the island every winter, bringing groups of amateur American baseballers to the country to take on the locals in friendly games. He also distributes balls, bats, and other equipment to kids for whom they are a luxury.

The first thing I noticed about Bill was his size. Being familiar with professional ballplayers primarily from TV, I tend to think of them in terms of their shrunken small-screen images. Like most fans, I suppose, I'm inclined to underestimate their true stature, to think of these guys as average. This is the kind of mistaken perception that produces thoughts like: *He's about my size. Hell, I could do that.*

Well, he's not, and I couldn't. I'm a bit above average at five feet, eleven and a half inches, and 175 pounds and have always tended to think that Lee is similarly built. Uh-uh. He is way bigger than I am. He stands a good six feet three inches, though the years have bent him just a little, and his playing weight of 205 has grown to perhaps 230. It's also been redistributed here and there, as whose hasn't?

If I'd been paying better attention to the dynamics of baseball, I wouldn't have been at all surprised. Because with major league pitchers, all other things being equal, the number one predictor of success is height. These guys are *tall*, and tall is good. It is in fact so good that among all pitchers born since 1900 and subsequently elected to the Hall of Fame, precisely *two* toed the rubber at less than six feet: the Yankees' Whitey Ford and Ted Lyons of the White Sox. (And Lyons, with his December 1900 birth date, barely makes the cut.)

Which tells us what? Well, presumably, the ability to effectively throw a baseball past a hitter has something to do with leverage, and the taller fellows have more of it. Randy Johnson—all six feet ten inches of him— has the most verticality of anyone, and he's headed for Cooperstown.

But there's also the matter of endurance. Though there are plenty of shorter, lean, whippet-type pitchers who can throw just as hard as the big guys, they tend to be less strong, to burn out earlier. Ron Guidry would be a good example. And of the two best pitchers of the nineties, Pedro Martinez (five eleven, 165), who should be entering his prime, is already racking up long months on the disabled list, while the taller (six four), stronger, and, yes, pudgier Roger Clemens cruises toward his three hundredth win.

Election to the Hall is not just about excellence. It also depends in large part on sustaining that excellence through a long career, and that seems to be where the more imposing physical specimens have a clear-cut edge.

Bill Lee won't make the Hall, of course. But neither will Sparky Anderson's favorite man-child. Don Gullett, at barely six feet, will burn out after nine years, an abbreviated career that leaves him well short—no pun intended—of Hall consideration. Let it also be noted that the guy Sparky once touted as a Cooperstown shoo-in will total 109 lifetime major league wins, leaving him with exactly ten fewer victories than will be posted by the man purportedly from space. But who's counting?

As for Lee, OK, let's say it: a lot of people can't stand him, and it's not difficult to understand why. There are those with major lifestyle differences, who object to his left-wing politics and cavalier attitude toward illegal drugs. He also has a king-sized ego and, backing it up, a highly articulate mouth that is rarely closed. He loves controversy and courts publicity. His sense of humor strikes some as nasty. *Boston Herald* reporter Tim Horgan, who covered the Red Sox in those years, told me he was a divisive influence in the clubhouse, always creating friction in one way or another, always trying (in Horgan's opinion) to set the players against the manager.

'Nuff said. (Though none of the teammates I asked backed Horgan up.)

The other side of Lee is a person who was always a tireless promoter of the game of baseball. He's been deeply involved in charity work in his community, wherever that happened to be, never turning down a request for his help. You won't find Bernie Carbo bad-mouthing his old pal. As I'll detail later in the book, when Bernie desperately needed some friends to help salvage his life, he called on a few key people to come through for him. Bill was one of them.

And with regard to me, he couldn't have been more hospitable. He invited a complete stranger to his home, put me up, and made sure there was plenty of good Canadian beer to drink. We even went for a ride in that rickety Beamer, looking for stray moose. All this at a most inopportune time for him, because he was right in the midst of a painful separation from his second wife.

For a day and a night, Lee and I talked about economics, philosophy, U.S. foreign policy, women and kids, politics and life. Bill is personable, smart, educated, and very well read. On the other hand, he's highly opinionated, is a bit self-centered, and can be overbearing at times. He has a wit that's often quite acidic. But flaky? Nah, I don't think so. What I found was a pretty decent fellow with two great loves: baseball and the center stage. Given his superior athletic talent, plus an unerring instinct for controversy, he realized he had a unique ability to merge the two, and he went for it.

Whatever the case, the man knows a great deal about baseball. At one point we were half-watching a game on TV and Bill opined that the pitcher had terrible mechanics and was going to have arm trouble; within two months, the guy went on the disabled list for just that reason. So baseball is mostly what we talked about. We talked in general terms about the game within the game and specifically about 1975 and the Series—what happened on the field and what was happening in the locker room.

By the time I left, I felt as though I'd lived with the '75 team for a while. I just needed a few second opinions.

After having stymied the Red Machine for eight innings, Bill Lee heads to the mound to get the final three outs.

And falls right into trouble. His first pitch to Johnny Bench is a dandy, a slider just off the outside corner at the knees. Most batters simply take it. If they do swing, they dribble it foul or fail to make contact entirely. Bench, though, is not most batters; he's a future Hall of Famer who does what HOFers do. He's got Lee timed now, and he attacks the pitch, going the opposite way, and slices a double into the right-field corner.

Later, writing in *The Wrong Stuff*, Lee will refer to Bench's rain-delay TV interview, lamenting that "John said he was going to try to hit me to the opposite field. He had been trying to pull me all afternoon, and I had gotten him out by pitching him away. Bench was now telling sixty-five million Americans that he was going to take the ball to right, and not one of them thought to call me with a warning."

Tough break for Lee. Big-league decision time for Darrell Johnson. On the one hand, Bill doesn't seem particularly tired. He's still yielded only five hits and shows no sign of wanting to leave the game. Bench did nail him, but on a very tough pitch. He could definitely work his way out of this jam.

On the other hand, the entire bullpen is well rested. The Oakland series ended five days ago, and Tiant went the route yesterday.

Burton and Moret are ready, but both are left-handers and, as Johnson will point out after the game, "There were three right-handed batters coming up and that was right down Drago's alley."

Willoughby apparently wasn't factored into the mix, which seems more than a little strange, as he's a sidearming sinker specialist who generates a lot of ground ball outs. Which is exactly what's wanted here, and which he is even more likely to get on a day when the weather makes the ball "heavier" than normal. On the other hand, two grounders to the right spots will get the run home. So at least one strikeout could be needed.

Lee departs. There are no boos now, just a standing ovation for a guy who, whatever his politics, has just pitched his heart out and totally flummoxed the most potent offense in baseball. He leaves with his lead intact. As he sits down in the dugout, he is no doubt thinking of how it will feel to get his first World Series victory.

Johnson replaces him with his primary stopper, the longhaired, bristly mustached, fierce-visaged Dick Drago. A strikeout man.

In all of sports, there is nothing else quite like the job of baseball closer. It's as if a basketball player were required to decide a game with a last-second three-pointer, a placekicker to boot a forty-yard field goal with no time on the clock, a golfer to sink a twenty-foot birdie putt on 18, not just now and then, but every single time he steps into the arena.

A closer is not summoned when the opponent is winning, or when his own team is comfortably ahead. No, it's only when the game is on the line, the ninth inning, the lead at a run or two, with one, two, or three outs needed to secure the victory. Everything he does is magnified. The failures of his teammates may be of greater or lesser importance, or none at all, depending on the situation. But if *he* fails, then by definition the game is lost. And even when he succeeds, all he gets is a save, the preservation of a win for somebody else.

It is among the most nerve-racking of occupations, the perpetual pressure cooker, and not only must the closer embrace it but he must convert something like 80 percent of his save opportunities, or he'll be replaced. Few are up to the task, and those who *can* hack it are highly prized.

Considering the many and varied paths a baseball game can take to its conclusion, it's surprising how often the closer is needed, how often the game comes down to getting the last out or even just one more strike, when to not get it will alter the outcome of the contest. Or perhaps it just seems that way, because we remember those highly charged moments in which the last strike was *not* gotten and the game slipped away.

That kind of failure, if it happens in the crucible of postseason play, can have enduring effects on the man responsible.

In Game 1 of the 1988 World Series, Dennis Eckersley, the best closer in baseball (and perhaps in history), had two strikes on Kirk Gibson with two out in the ninth, a runner on, and his A's ahead by a run. Gibson was in terrible pain from leg injuries. He had hobbled to the plate for what would be his only at-bat in the Series, after taking some cuts in the training room and reportedly telling his manager that if he were called upon to pinch hit, "I think I have one good swing." He did, but not right away. He fouled off three fastballs, looking woeful each time, then worked the count to 3–2. Eckersley wound up and threw his best pitch, a slider low and away. And Gibson, by whatever force of will or magic, found the swing that would deposit the ball in the right-field stands, turn a certain defeat into a Dodger victory, and help propel his team to the title.

The Eck was lucky. He admits to having suffered nightmares for months after that one unlucky pitch. But he fought through the angst. He was both talented and steel-nerved enough to come back the following year, post 33 saves in the regular season, and close out a World Series championship for his team. He persevered, pitching effectively for nearly another decade.

Others who failed to get that final out were not so fortunate.

The Sox' own Calvin Schiraldi, for example, was a rising star who had performed brilliantly in the team's march to the 1986 pennant. In Game 6 of the World Series against the New York Mets, with Boston up three games to two, he'd relieved Roger Clemens in the eighth inning. He yielded the tying run but recovered, finishing the eighth with no further damage, pitching a scoreless ninth, and getting the first two outs in the tenth. Meanwhile, the Sox had scored twice. They were one out away from their first Series win in sixty-eight long years when Schiraldi came unglued.

First he challenged Gary Carter with a fastball right down the middle. Carter ripped it for a single. Kevin Mitchell followed and, because he was a dead fastball hitter, Schiraldi threw him a curve. It hung, and Mitchell singled to center. Then Ray Knight came up and Calvin battled him as gamely as he possibly could. He threw good pitch after good pitch. Knight barely fouled them off, all but the last, which he fisted just over the infield for a bloop RBI single that brought the Mets to within a run. Schiraldi looked like a ghost, and manager John McNamara took him out.

Everyone knows what happened next. Bob Stanley relieved and allowed the tying run to score on a wild pitch. The winning run came home on Bill Buckner's error. The Mets went on to take Game 7, and the Sox, one strike away from clinching, had lost another Series.

Schiraldi had left Game 6 with the lead. The final two runs, though he was no longer on the mound, were nevertheless charged to him, and he took the loss. Worse, he never recovered from the experience. The promising career went down the tubes. He posted a record of 26–34 over the next five years, was traded three times, and dropped out of the game at the age of twenty-nine.

It was tragic, but nothing compared to what befell Donnie Moore following the 1986 American League Championship Series against the Red Sox.

Moore, the Angels' outstanding closer, was summoned from the bullpen with two out in the ninth inning, his team up 5–4 in the game and 3–1 in this Series. He faced pinch hitter Dave Henderson, righty against righty, and blew two fastballs right by him. One strike to go, and the Angels were in the World Series. Moore tried to throw one of his nasty split-finger fastballs, but this one wasn't as nasty as it had to be. It stayed up in the strike zone and Henderson hit it out. Though the Angels rallied to tie in their half of the ninth, Boston scored the winning run in the eleventh on a sacrifice fly by the same Dave Henderson. Off Moore, who was still in there.

Asked about the home-run pitch six months later, Moore said, "More than likely, I'll think about that until the day I die."

Perhaps he did. After '86, his career went into a steep nosedive, and by 1988 he couldn't get anybody out. His playing days were over. To make matters worse, he ended up broke, with a marriage that had gone on the rocks.

In July 1989, after an argument with his wife over the custody of their children, he shot her three times with a .45 handgun (amazingly, she survived), then put the pistol to his head and killed himself.

"Henderson's homer did it," his agent said in the aftermath of the violence. "Donnie blamed himself for the Angels not going to the World Series, and he couldn't get over it."

It's only a game. Sometimes.

Dick Drago, however, is still alive and well, as I found out during my travels, although in 1975 he is about to receive some rude and largely undeserved instruction in just how damnably elusive that final out can be.

On the face of it, Johnson's choice has the look of danger to it. Drago is strictly a fastball pitcher who challenges batters to hit his best heat. Cincinnati eats guys like that for lunch, dinner, and afternoon snack.

Yet it's hard to quarrel with the manager's decision. In a year in which the closer's role was not strictly defined—Drago led the team with 15 saves, but Willoughby had 8, and creaky 38-year-old Diego Segui had 6—Drago emerged as the Man. In addition, he was nothing short of magnificent in the League Championship Series, going four and two-thirds innings against Oakland, another excellent fastball-hitting club; giving up two hits and no runs; and saving both games not started (and finished) by the peerless El Tiante.

Perez is first to face Drago, and all he can manage is a weak grounder to short. He's thrown out, but, more important, the ball wasn't hit sharply enough to hold Bench. The Cincinnati catcher moves to third, raising the possibility of a squeeze bunt. The infielders gather at the mound to discuss what each of their roles will be if Sparky tries it.

One down, two outs to go.

George Foster turns in a courageous at-bat. He fouls off two pitches, then takes one just off the outside corner that could easily have been called strike three. He fouls off another outside pitch, then a tough heater inside, before finally flying out to shallow left. Bench bluffs for home, but he's not going to challenge Yastrzemski's arm.

Cincinnati is down to their final out. Dave Concepcion takes a hard fastball inside for strike one, then another that is just barely high, for a ball. This is a time before radar guns recorded the velocity of every pitch, but Drago is clearly throwing in the midnineties. Concepcion looks over-matched. And then the baseball gods decide to intervene. Drago offers a great pitch, a sinking fastball that tails away over the outside corner, impossible to hit squarely. It should be a picture-perfect strike two, allowing Drago to then either waste a pitch or, more likely, reach back for all he's got and try to blow the third strike past the hitter.

Doesn't happen. Concepcion reaches out and—all he can do—hacks at the ball. He tops it, of course. It slams into the ground, bounces high over the mound, beyond the reach of Drago, and continues up the middle. Shortstop Burleson can't cut it off. Doyle races to his right, as fast as he possibly can, stretches, somehow gloves the ball. But his momentum is propelling him toward left, one step, two, past second base. He whirls toward first in the middle of the third step, now on the outfield grass, wanting to make even an off-balance throw as much as he's ever wanted anything in his life and . . . his hand, still clutching the ball, settles slowly back to his side. Sadly for the Sox, the runner happens to be one of the fastest men on the Cincinnati team. Doyle has no play.

"I still think about that last out a lot," Drago told me later. "I thought I was out of the inning after I got the big guys, Perez and Foster. I knew Concepcion was a good high-ball hitter, so I made sure to keep the ball down. In hindsight, maybe I shouldn't have. I was throwing really well, and the high fastball was my best pitch that day. It's what I used to get the other two. Maybe I should have just stayed with it."

He didn't, and the Reds, one out from defeat, have tied the game on the cheapest kind of infield hit, a Baltimore chop. The great crowd goes silent. Doyle looks like an inflatable doll that's just met up with a hatpin. Burleson stares in dismay. Bill Lee, undoubtedly, is burying his face in his hands. It's one of those moments that make baseball such an excruciating experience for both player and partisan fan. Lee, having pitched the game of his life, can no longer win it. Doyle and Drago have both done their jobs surpassingly well, and for naught.

In 2001, I met Denny at the headquarters of Doyle Baseball, an organization dedicated to the development of young players. It's in a one-story metal shed-type building in Lake Hamilton, Florida. The conference room where we talked was festooned with placards bearing passages from scripture, but Doyle, as positive and upbeat a guy as you'd ever want to meet, doesn't otherwise preach his faith. He loves to talk baseball, straight up, without it coming back to Jesus.

He was fifty-seven and didn't have the impish, leprechaun, baby fat kind of look I remembered from '75. He had thinning, gray hair and metal-rimmed spectacles that made him look very like the middle-aged Buck Henry of *The Man Who Fell to Earth*. He dressed casually, in a sleeveless blue nylon shirt and slacks. And he was still a bundle of energy—very friendly, very chatty, and impossible to interrupt when he got riffing. He spoke passionately of the things he cared about: the game of baseball and his work with kids. He had a great sense of humor and laughed a lot. He tightened up only when we got on a subject he wasn't comfortable with, which was anything that he felt might be detrimental to the game.

Denny remembered Game 2, all right. And he told me I was on the money about how deflated he felt at the moment he was forced to hold the ball. But then he smiled and his eyes lit up as he offered me a postscript.

"You know," he said, "the ironical thing is that my friend Larry Bowa [the Phillies' shortstop at the time] called me after the game and said, 'Oh yeah, I forgot to tell you, we always play Concepcion to pull, especially under pressure.' So if I'd been playing him that way, I get to the ball in time to throw him out."

If only. The truth, though, is that Darrell Johnson would probably never have let Doyle shade Concepcion those couple of steps toward second base, which is what you do with a right-handed pull hitter. No, with the tying run on third, the book of baseball says not to let the batter beat you with a ground ball through the right side. That's what they would have risked by opening up the hole between first and second. And Johnson was a by-the-book man.

Still, Doyle thought, if he'd at least been leaning that way . . .

He grinned. "Thanks a lot, Larry," he said.

Oscar and I, ready to high-five each other when Concepcion beat the ball into the dirt, are staring at the TV screen, stunned, unable to speak. The pall has dropped over us, or at least me; Oscar's had more time in which to refine his fatalism. Though all we have at the moment is a game tied in the top of the ninth, I'm overcome with dread. Had they closed it out, I have no doubt the Sox would take the Series, maybe even in Cincinnati, no question. But lose here, after having it in hand, and . . . well, there might be no bouncing back from such a blow.

Still, I remind myself, it's only tied, it's only tied. I speak to the team as if they are in the room with us, imploring them to suck it up and turn this thing back in their favor. Get that last out. Beat them in the bottom of the ninth, or let it go to extra innings, where Boston would gain the advantage over Cincinnati's depleted bullpen.

Meanwhile, Darrell Johnson now has another agonizing decision. Griffey, a left-hander and dangerous fastball hitter, is up. Should he let the right-handed Drago try to punch out Ken, or intentionally walk him and let his pitcher face the much weaker-hitting César Geronimo?

It's a psychological duel that's not for the fainthearted, but with first base occupied Johnson elects to go after Griffey. Most managers would.

Looks like it might work. Drago throws a fastball down the middle that Griffey watches for strike one. Then he turns his attention to Concepcion. The pipe-stem-thin twenty-seven-year-old just might be the Reds' premier base stealer. Sure, Joe Morgan has the flashy 67 thefts. But Davy had 33 on the season, none too shabby, and . . . he's been thrown out at second only four times in the past two years.

Drago rifles the ball over there three times. Good moves that have Concepcion diving back. Then he teases Griffey with a ball just off the outside corner, followed immediately by a quick pitch, the heater again, with no attempt to hold Concepcion this time. Probably hoping to catch him flat-footed.

Griffey waves at the pitch for strike two, but . . . Concepcion is not fooled. Or maybe it was a hit-and-run all the way. In any event, he lights out for second. Fisk comes up out of his squat and throws. Burleson sets himself, crouching by the bag. The throw is low, as it should be, and right on line. If it arrives direct, they've got him by three feet. It doesn't. The baseball gods speak again, and the throw bounces once on the grass before arriving at second. It doesn't bounce very high—Burleson never leaves his crouch—but high enough that the shortstop has to raise his glove to catch it. This takes just enough time that Concepcion can slip his leg under the tag.

Burleson argues heatedly because, he will say later, umpire Dick Stello told him he didn't tag the runner, which is untrue. But it doesn't matter; the TV replay shows that Concepcion is clearly safe, tagged or not. There's a runner in scoring position.

I groan. "They're gonna blow it," I say out loud.

The dynamics of the situation have been drastically altered by Concepcion's steal. And Darrell Johnson, looking out at the now-vacant first base, is faced with the same strategy decision he had before—walk Griffey intentionally, or pitch to him? Or, if he's grown a whole gang of guts today, he could conceivably walk *both* Griffey and Geronimo. That'd be off-the-chart daring, because it'd load the bases on purpose. But it would bring pitcher Eastwick to the plate, thereby forcing Sparky to choose between taking an almost certain out and pinch hitting for his stopper with Clay Carroll (ineffective in Game 1) his only short reliever left in the pen.

First base *is* open, so the percentages would probably say to walk Griffey. Yet Johnson, normally an immovable percentage player, stubbornly refuses. After the game, grim-faced, he will snap, "There were two strikes on Griffey at the time. We don't walk a man with two strikes on him."

When I interviewed Darrell in 2002, I tried to talk to him about the process by which he arrived at certain key decisions, including this one, but he was having none of it. Though I was more interested in what was going through his mind than I was in whether his moves worked or not, he refused to discuss anything that even remotely smacked of second-guessing. He doesn't engage in that, he told me, and added tersely, "Anything I did, if I was sitting in the same spot, I'd do again."

Wow, I thought. That was a level of certitude I wasn't familiar with. There sure were plenty of things in *my* life that I wished had come with a do-over option. But maybe that was one of those elements you needed built into your character if you expected to make it as a big-league manager in the first place.

So I never did get to ask him whether he perhaps considered instructing Drago to pitch around Griffey. Don Zimmer did tell me that he doubted Darrell would have done so.

"He was more like me, I think," Zim told me. "As a manager, I never told a pitcher to work around a guy. To me, that just takes everything off you and puts it on the pitcher, which isn't fair. You're the manager; make the decision. Either pitch to him or walk him. The pitcher knows not to give a guy something good to hit. That's his job."

Johnson eschews the intentional pass and, in this instance, it looks as though he will be vindicated. Drago continues to bring some smoke. Griffey nearly goes down on the 1–2 pitch, but he just barely gets a piece of it, fouling it off to stay alive. The next pitch is an instant replay, another chintzy foul. Ken is hanging tough. Then Drago goes to the well once too often. A final fastball and Griffey, his timing set, is all over it, smashing it on a line to left center for a double.

The Reds have their first lead of the 1975 World Series, and I have a migraine.

I met Drago in 2001, in a restaurant near Tampa, Florida, where he runs a printing supply business. I asked him if he remembers the sequence of events. Yes. Did they consider walking Griffey? Nope.

Dick was a big guy who looked in reasonable shape for his age. His face was relatively unlined. He had a wonderful, deep basso voice. The old mustache was still there, but not as big and bushy as it was in '75. The hair that was so long and flowing was close-cropped now, gray from what I could see of it, which wasn't much. He wore a Diamond Dreams Fantasy Camp shirt and an NYPD cap (this was post-9/11) that he didn't take off the whole time. From his comments about hair, I suspected he was largely if not entirely bald on top.

"Darrell never suggested a free pass," Drago mused, "though I could've pitched around him, of course. We sometimes do that on our own. But to tell you the truth, I was so focused in that I didn't even know who was coming up next. Who was it, anyway?"

Geronimo, I told him.

He shrugged. "Well," he said, "maybe I should've."

When Geronimo does finally get to the plate, the Reds are up a run and now, at last, comes the intentional walk. Perhaps Anderson then toys with the idea of hitting for his pitcher; if so, he decides he's better off with a one-run lead and his best guy out there. Eastwick takes his turn and grounds to second, forcing Geronimo. But the damage is done.

The crowd remains subdued. If it's going to take vocal fan support to initiate a Red Sox rally, it ain't gonna happen.

Burleson leads off. Though the Rooster rarely bunts for a hit, Rose creeps in on him from third, all but saying, *come on, sucker, hit it by me.* Rick fouls out to short right.

Bernie Carbo bats for Drago. Bernie is another of the "blithe spirits" on this team. He's also the ideal pinch hitter in this situation. A lefty with a sweet inside-out stroke, he often takes right-handers the opposite way, to the Wall. Which is a much better option today than trying to pull something into the teeth of the wind.

But what's happening out there in left is also important. Critical, as it turns out. For George Foster, whether by instruction of his manager or on his own or by direction of the baseball gods, has *moved in.* There's no rhyme or reason to it. The last thing Sparky could want in this situation is a double over George's head. Yet there Foster is, positioned precisely to be in the right place at the right time.

The fans come to their feet when Carbo hits one of his patented slices to left. The ball spins away from Foster, toward the foul line. Had he been playing at the warning track, as he was earlier, he would have had no chance and Bernie would be at least on second. But Foster was where he was. He's able to spear the line drive on the run.

All excitement drains from the crowd. No one believes any longer that the Sox can pull it out. And they don't. Cecil Cooper, now fully mired in the slump that will dog him for the rest of the Series, pops to short, and it's over.

For the forty-eighth time this year, the Reds have come from behind to win. It's the twenty-fifth time they notched the victory in their last at-bat.

The following morning's *Boston Globe* op-ed page will carry a piece by U.S. Congressman Augustus Hawkins, in which he opines that "Most communities in America, facing the busing issue, have done it head-on, and with a great deal of honesty and valor. To their enormous credit, even under tremendous anxiety and stress, they have realized that adjustments can be made and that the major goal is providing all youngsters with maximum opportunities in this multi-racial, multi-ethnic society."

The sports pages will feature Game 2's postmortems. Darrell Johnson, no surprise, defends his managerial moves. He passes along a reminder to everyone that, despite the previous game's bitter ending, "It still takes four to win this thing." And he downplays any potential psychological aftereffects. "A loss is a loss," he shrugs.

It is. Despite how well they played, the Red Sox have come up short in this one. One may say that the breaks went against them or that the Reds took maximum advantage of their opportunities. Neither view is quite right or quite wrong. They are, perhaps, equally true, and that's baseball.

Bill Lee, who had to watch his World Series victory turn into a no-decision, just like that, is understandably crestfallen. When the man of a thousand words on any subject under the sun is asked how he would characterize the Series so far, this is all he has to say:

"Tied."

DAY THREE

Irreversible Error

An umpire must have agility, stamina and be able to run. He's also got to be willing to umpire with pain, because men working the plate often get hit with foul tips going 100 miles per hour. That's the physical side of it. An umpire is constantly being tested by managers, coaches and players, so he can't have rabbit ears. Quick decisions aren't that hard if the man is in position. What's hard is making sure they are based on reason.

—FORMER UMPIRE BILL KINNAMON

One of the pleasures of the 1975 World Series was that each team made it through its league championship playoffs in the minimum number of games. Both the Reds and Red Sox were, therefore, well rested, their ideal pitching rotations set.

With the proliferation of teams in the past two decades, and the continual realignments, this has become increasingly rare.

For most of its history, baseball had two leagues, and the teams with the best records won their respective pennants (a term that has been rendered essentially meaningless) and met in the Series. Then each league split into two divisions and the division winners had to play off, as in '75. Today the divisions have further subdivided into thirds, so that there are two sets of playoffs: best of five to get into the League Championship Series, then best of seven to make it to the big stage.

This is bad in that it has sent some very mediocre teams into the play-offs, ball clubs that managed to win weak divisions.

It's also introduced the repugnant concept of the wild card, a team that failed to win its division but qualified for the playoffs because its record was the next best. This was "necessary" in order to ensure that there'd be four teams from each league involved in postseason play. The greater the number of playoff series, the higher the profits, seems to be the reasoning.

In order to appreciate how this structure has changed the game, one need only recall the 1951 game between the Dodgers and Giants to determine the National League champ. That was the one in which Bobby Thompson hit the dramatic ninth-inning home run and radio announcer Russ Hodges went crazy, screaming, "The Giants win the pennant! The Giants win the pennant!"

Today, Russ would have to say (with considerably less emotion, one assumes): "The Giants win the division, the Dodgers win the wild card." Just doesn't have the same impact, does it?

Beyond these indignities, the present system has wreaked havoc with a manager's ability to plan out his pitching rotation. Ideally, a team's number one starter should pitch the first game, followed by the number two man and the number three. This makes the staff ace available for games four and seven, as well.

Now, however, a manager may have to work so hard to win a qualifying series that his best is unavailable until the second or even third game of the next series, which follows close on the heels of the previous one in order to get everything in before it begins to sleet. This confers a distinct advantage on the opponent, should that team have breezed through its own playoff in the minimum number of games. Which, some would argue, is just. Excellence is rewarded.

But from the point of view of the fan, it's a rip-off. What we want to see is a marquee matchup. The best going against the best. Anything less demeans the game, especially in the World Series.

The powers that be could deal with this, of course, by allotting enough time between series that the teams could reset their pitching rotations. But that would mean shortening the regular season, and there's never been much support for that.

Fortunately, in 1975 everything worked out as it should. Tiant vs. Gullett in Game 1. The two aces matched up at the outset, with the delicious prospect of them meeting three times over the course of seven games.

Then a couple of instinctive choices—Lee against Billingham in Game 2, which produced the first nail-biter of the Series.

Now, it's time for the managers to consult their guts again. Both have more than one third starter well rested and ready to go. It's time to decide whom to send to the mound in Cincinnati for Game 3.

As noted before, Riverfront Stadium is, um, aesthetically unpleasing. But it was home, very sweet home to the Cincinnati Reds. In 1975, they were 64–17 down by the Ohio, for a gaudy .790 winning percentage.

Had the Sox—as they might well have—taken a 2–0 lead into Riverfront, they could have afforded to lose two out of three there, then come home needing to win only once in two games to claim the title. At 1–1, they could still stay alive with a pair of losses, but in that case they would need to sweep the final two.

The Reds, of course, were looking to close out the Series in five.

On paper, their chances looked good. Not only did they sport a near-invincible home record, but they were back on the artificial surface that so favored their style of play. Many National League parks in addition to Cincinnati had it, whereas in the American League it was virtually unknown. The Red Sox had played on fake turf a total of six times all year.

Sparky Anderson was cocky. "The Sox will have more trouble adjusting to our park than we did there," he said. "Fenway Park is an easy place to play in." Guess that was why his team managed to total three runs in two games.

Boston, though, is not likely to be intimidated. In 1975, the team went 48–31 away from home, to lead the league with a .608 road winning percentage. Which was actually a shade better than they did at home (47–34, .580). The Red Sox are a consistent team. As are the Reds, for that matter: they led the NL in *both* home and road winning percentages.

So the teams are set. And now the pitchers are, too.

Sparky Anderson tosses a coin between Gary Nolan and Fred Norman. Fred has had a very good year and is probably the titular number two starter after Gullett. His regular-season record is 12–4, with an ERA of 3.73. He pitched six innings in Game 2 of the LCS against Pittsburgh, gave up only one run, and got the win.

Nolan—a former power pitcher who missed nearly all of 1973–74 with arm troubles—has reinvented himself as a control artist and has come back on fire. He's gone 15–9 in the regular season, with a 3.16 ERA. He went six innings against Pittsburgh in Game 3 and gave up two runs in a no-decision.

Two guys with similar names and virtually identical records. The coin is tossed and it comes up Nolan.

Darrell Johnson has more options. The logical choice is Rick Wise. Though only thirty, Wise is a ten-year veteran. He's had a good year (regular season: 19–12, 3.95 ERA), knows National League teams and parks because he came over from the NL in '74, and has already won more than 125 games in the major leagues. In 1971, he pitched a no-hitter against a Reds team that featured many of these same players.

Of course, Johnson could confound the prognosticators, as he did with the choice of Lee in Game 2. Reggie Cleveland (13–9, 4.43) is available. So is brilliant but unpredictable twenty-six-year-old Puerto Rican native Roger Moret. Moret had a sensational year in his first regular season, 1973, tailed off in '74, but came back very strong in '75 (14–3, 3.60).

It's likely a no-brainer for Johnson. He goes with experience. He goes with the guy who really got him here. He goes with Wise.

And so begins Game 3, one that will ultimately go down in the cursed history of the Boston Red Sox as the Game of the Blown Call. It's a game so tainted by frustration that—as with Bucky Dent and Bill Buckner—it can be reduced to a single proper name, and every fan will know exactly what you're talking about. Only in this instance the mere surname will suffice: *Armbrister*.

But that's many innings down the road. Before the game's fateful conclusion there is a lot of very exciting baseball to be played.

It all begins quietly enough, with Gary Nolan going out to face the same Red Sox lineup they fielded in Game 2.

Nolan is a feel-good story. When he first came up, he was an excellent fastball pitcher, striking out nearly a man an inning in his rookie season. That was eight years ago, when he was all of nineteen.

He was an effective pitcher for six years before blowing his arm out, appearing in two games in 1973 and none in '74. Now, amazingly, he's back and as good as ever. Even though he can no longer bring his serious heat and depends instead on an outstanding change-up, he's still only twenty-seven. He hopes to fashion a long major league career as a finesse pitcher. It won't happen. He'll have more arm troubles and will be out of baseball before his thirtieth birthday.

But for now, he's a formidable opponent, and a workhorse. He comes in with 211 innings pitched on the year. Though he's struck out a mere seventy-four batters over that span, he's walked only twenty-nine (five intentional). Twenty-nine. That's barely one per nine innings—phenomenal control. If the Red Sox are going to score runs off this guy, they'll have to earn them. He won't be giving any away.

Boston can take some comfort, however, in Gary Nolan's postseason record. Though he's always performed well in the League Championship Series, his World Series record is less impressive. He's had four starts and has gone 0–2 with an ERA of 5.40.

The Sox come out seeming anxious to get off to a good start. Or perhaps the proper expression would be *overly anxious*. The top of the lineup is Cooper, Doyle, and Yastrzemski, all lefties stacked against the right-hander. All three swing at the first pitch. All three ground to the right side. Three pitches. Three up, three down—as quick a half-inning as you can have.

Rick Wise is a tall, stocky, bespectacled veteran who is the answer to three wonderful baseball trivia questions, two of which are: What pitcher once hurled a perfect game and homered twice in the same contest? And, for whom was Steve Carlton once traded, straight up? Wise and Wise. (The third we shall encounter three games hence. Remind me.)

Like Nolan, Wise came up early, first reaching the majors in 1964, at the age of eighteen. "I was what they called a bonus baby in those years," he told me. "If you signed for more than eight thousand dollars, the club had to protect you or risk losing you. That's why they called me up to Philadelphia when I was so young."

He became a regular in '67 and has been a very solid if unspectacular performer: good earned run average, but never much better than a .500 winning percentage. He's just turned thirty and has reached what will be his personal high for wins (19), although he also lost 12. Wise is something of an enigma, either a hard-luck guy who never seems to get enough support to be a big winner or someone who finds a way to lose the close ones.

(Rick would go on to have a long and fine career. He's also a nice guy who has overcome a lot of personal adversity, as I found out when I talked with him. Nevertheless, any comparison to Steve Carlton will necessarily be lopsided, and thus a consideration of what the Cardinals were thinking when they traded Carlton for this fellow—Lefty would go on to win 236 games for the Phillies and waltz into the Hall of Fame—must be consigned to that limbo in which folks ponder such imponderables as What possessed Harry Frazee to sell Babe Ruth to the Yankees? and How did Lou Gorman decide that Larry Andersen was adequate compensation for Jeff Bagwell?)

Also like Nolan, Wise was a power pitcher when he arrived and evolved into more of a control man. Another workhorse, he's had 141 strikeouts in 255 innings in '75 and has walked but 72. His best pitch is his slider. If there's a matter of serious concern, it's that Wise has no sinker. He gets a lot of fly ball outs. This could be not so good against the Reds, a premier power-hitting club hungry for its first Series home run.

With a right-hander on the mound, Sparky Anderson has modified his lineup, moving the left-handed Ken Griffey up to second and dropping everyone else a notch. He's also, for whatever mysterious Sparky reasons, flip-flopped Tony Perez and Johnny Bench (both righties); tonight Perez will bat cleanup, Bench fifth.

As Pete Rose leads off, the TV announcer, Curt Gowdy, speculates as to whether Pete will join baseball's exclusive 3,000-hit club. He presently has 2,546 and is thirty-four years old.

"I think so," Gowdy says. "He takes good care of himself. He should have three or four more years."

Well, um, yeah, Curt.

For sure, Rose is not what anyone would call a natural athlete, not a Ken Griffey or Fred Lynn. Yet he is almost certainly the most single-minded player in the game and will prove to be one of the most durable. Here, as has been the case throughout his career, he is being just a tad underestimated. Rose will in fact continue on for another *eleven* years. When he finally retires in '86, he will have amassed not only the requisite 454 hits to make his three grand, but more than *1,200* beyond that, to set the major league standard at 4,256. It's a record that is unlikely ever to be broken.

Contrary to his usual style, Rick Wise retires both Rose and Griffey on ground balls to second. Joe Morgan, who has averaged 111 walks a season for the past seven years, won't get one today. He flies to center. Wise looks good out there.

In Boston's second, Nolan gets hit hard. Fisk leads off and gets one right in his wheelhouse, a mediocre fastball, belt-high, right down the middle. Pudge loses it deep in the left-field seats. After Lynn flies to center, Petrocelli continues his hot hitting with a single to left. It's the Sox' moment to go for the early knockout. They don't get it. Griffey makes a nice catch on an Evans foul fly, and Burleson grounds out. The rally fizzles. More important, Nolan has worked his way out of trouble and can take some time in the dugout to settle himself down.

Wise, though, is looking as though this might be his day. He breezes through the second and third innings, with four more uncharacteristic groundouts. The only blemish is a walk to Foster in the second. Foster is not a skilled base runner; he has a grand total of two stolen bases on the year. But the Cincinnati strategy is to run on Boston in general, and on Wise in particular, because Rick doesn't hold runners all that well. So George lights out for second. And the Dark Cloud appears.

Fisk throws the ball into center field. Foster takes third. It can be said that the error doesn't hurt, because he dies there when Concepcion flies to right. Yet considering what will happen a couple of hours down the road . . . Fisk's errant throw is ominous, to say the least. Fortunately, we have no access to the future at that moment, and thus no inkling of what is to come.

The Boston third is a one-two-three for Nolan, and then, in the visitor's fourth, there is more trouble on the base paths. Yaz grounds out to open it, but Fisk walks and Lynn singles to right, Fisk going to third. Griffey hits Concepcion, the cutoff man, and this bit of basic baseball pays off when Lynn slips rounding first. Concepcion fires the ball to Perez, and Freddie is tagged out. Petrocelli follows by grounding to second, and, once again, a good scoring opportunity has gone by the boards due to faulty baserunning. These mistakes will prove costly. The Reds have too good a bullpen for any team to be giving away early chances like this.

As with Tiant and Lee in Games 1 and 2, Rick Wise takes a no-hitter into the fourth. He's been keeping the ball down, and the Reds have obliged by pounding it into the dirt. Now, his pitches are beginning to rise in the strike zone. Bad idea.

Griffey leads off and flies to center. Morgan follows with another fly to center, this one very deep, that Lynn also tracks down. Two away. But then Wise gets overly cautious with Perez and walks him.

Atanasio Perez is arguably the slog-footedest runner on the Cincinnati roster. Tony has precisely one stolen base in 1975. Over the course of a season, you get one by accident. Wise is locked in on the batter, Johnny Bench, and doesn't bother to hold Perez on. So what does he do but try to steal second. A flabbergasted Fisk makes a decent throw, but Tony has a huge jump and he's safe.

Wise, perhaps a little shaken, now comes in with a meatball to Bench, who poles it into the left-field seats. So long no-hitter; so long shutout. The Reds lead, 2–1. Foster grounds out to end the inning.

Surprisingly, Nolan fails to answer the bell for the fifth. He's developed a stiff neck and takes himself out of the game. It must really hurt. No one leaves a World Series game voluntarily.

Anderson now has to decide how to manage his bullpen. It's still the middle innings, and he likes to hold his four studly short relievers in reserve so that he can make situational substitutions late in the game. This leaves him with, essentially, one long-relief man, a baby-faced twenty-five-year-old rookie named Pat Darcy. Darcy has had a nice year, going 11–5 with an ERA of 3.57. On the other hand, he's yielded 134 hits in 131 innings, and his walk/strikeout ratio of 59/46 is plain awful. He is in fact a marginal major leaguer. He'll appear in eleven games in '76, after which he'll fall out of the bigs forever.

Sparky's nothing if not gutsy, though. Despite it being a tight, one-run game, he brings Darcy in. And the kid does just fine. Evans grounds to short. Burleson singles, but Wise, trying to sacrifice him along, forces him at second. Cooper grounds out.

As things turn out, Darrell Johnson shoulda sent up a pinch hitter for Rick Wise, because in the fifth he comes completely unglued, in a very big hurry. Not to fault Johnson, of course. His starter *was* pitching a one-hitter, after all, with the bottom third of the order coming up. Three guys with eleven homers among them. No punch there.

Uh-huh.

Lest we forget, the great stage that is the World Series has a way of transforming banjo hitters into sluggers, and vice versa. Davy Concepcion, leading off, is already a hero for the hit he got that tied up Game 2 in the ninth. Never mind that it was an ugly infield job and that he's otherwise hitless in nine trips. It was big, and now he gets another.

Wise starts him off with a strike on the inside corner, then leaves the next pitch out over the plate. Concepcion turns on it and drills it on a line to left. Yastrzemski can only look up as it sails into the seats far above his head. Davy claps his hands joyfully as he circles the bases. Cincinnati 3, Boston 1.

Jim Burton and Reggie Cleveland begin loosening up in the Red Sox bullpen.

Two hits off Wise. Two homers. Three earned runs. Has Concepcion's dinger further rattled the Sox starter? Maybe. He misses the strike zone high with his first pitch to César Geronimo, another weak hitter. Then he misses low. His third pitch barely nips the outside corner, then he misses badly high and inside, almost hitting the batter.

Three and one. Considering that Wise is obviously struggling with his control, Anderson may have been tempted to have Geronimo take the following pitch. But, with Pat Darcy due up next, Sparky lets him swing away. Good decision. Wise grooves one down the middle and César launches it into the right-field stands. Evans goes to the wall but has no play.

For the seventh time in the history of the World Series, a team has hit back-to-back home runs. And Rick Wise has to try to figure out what's gone so wrong.

In the modern era, professional baseball players are often seen as a bunch of whining, spoiled millionaires. You'd probably be hard-pressed to find anyone with compassion for those who have fallen on hard times. Yet they do exist, particularly among men who played before the advent of the *really* big bucks.

Baseball careers are relatively short, and a lot can happen once they're over. Many players don't leave with enough to retire on. Many flounder because they don't know what to do with their lives when they can no longer identify themselves as professional athletes. Many fail to find satisfying second vocations. And none is exempt from the financial ills that can befall any other citizen, at any time: fiscal mismanagement, placing trust in the wrong hands, reversals of fortune, a run of bad luck, governmental persecution, bankruptcy.

Two of the boys of October have stories to tell in this regard—very different stories that stand as variations on a common theme.

Dick Drago left the game in 1981, after a thirteen-year career in which he was a decent pitcher, if never a star. In today's market, he'd be worth at least a couple of million a year, but he played before they started handing out that kind of money. His annual salary peaked at $150,000. Not bad, but when he walked away it was with no job, no skills, and not a whole lot put aside.

He also had two ex-wives and three children, and that's where his real problems began. The administration of divorce cases in America is, shall we say, irregular.

In Drago's case, he'd been ordered to pay twenty-five hundred dollars a month in alimony and child support to his first wife and one thousand dollars a month in child support to his second. Those were serious numbers in the best of times. When the major league checks stopped coming, the numbers were crushing.

Still, Dick kept his head above water until the Internal Revenue Service dropped an anvil on it. He'd been making a living in the real estate business in Ft. Myers, Florida, when the government tax collectors suddenly decided to disallow a shelter his financial adviser had set up for him in 1986. By the time the IRS hit him with the bad news, interest and penalties on the $30,000 they claimed he owed had ballooned it to $115,000. He didn't have it, or anything remotely close to it.

The government took everything he had and further garnisheed his earnings, so that he received an allowance of eighty dollars a week on which to live. A Florida court granted his petition to get his child support payments reduced accordingly, and he continued to make his payments in the belief that he was fulfilling his obligations.

Massachusetts disagreed. The state Department of Revenue, claiming he owed thirty-five thousand dollars in back payments, put out a warrant for his arrest. It was a time when state authorities all over the country, under considerable public pressure, had finally decided to get tough on "deadbeat dads." Though Drago was far from the worst offender on the department's list, his former fame gave him something of a high profile and led the agency's head to say that he liked to use cases like Dick's to "send a message."

"That was awful," he told me. "Being branded a 'deadbeat dad' in the papers. Especially since I'd been paying everything I could, following the court's ruling."

Florida authorities arrested him in late 1992. They attached a red band to his wrist, which signified a prisoner at serious risk for flight, and threw him in jail. Three days later, he was returned in handcuffs to face prosecution in Essex County, Massachusetts, just a few miles from Fenway Park, where once he'd stood tall.

In his preliminary hearing, the prosecutor argued before the court that he had concealed assets somewhere and that, as a "fugitive from justice," there was a high likelihood he'd take off if he was released. "Right," he said.

"To where? They claimed they'd had a hard time finding me, even though I'd been living in the same place for seven years. They claimed other people would answer the door for me, even though I lived alone. And they said that every time they got close I'd run to some island called Marco, in the Caribbean."

Marco Island is, of course, a popular retirement destination off the southwest Florida coast, about as American as a place can be. Dick sold real estate there. But what did some bureaucrats fifteen hundred miles away know? A familiarity with U.S. geography was apparently not a hiring prerequisite.

"Nobody would believe I was broke," he said. "They kept insisting I had this secret stash somewhere, when all they ever had to do was ask the federal government. The IRS had control of everything."

Because Drago had no previous criminal record, his lawyer asked for release on personal recognizance, a routine request in cases where the defendant doesn't pose any threat to society. They didn't get it. Instead, bail was set at a ludicrous $350,000. Luckily, his brother came through with the $35,000 needed to post bond, and Drago was able to go home.

When he returned for his trial a month later, he was ready to fight. His lawyer had proof that his client wasn't actually in arrears, including a stack of canceled checks that showed Dick had been faithfully making the payments he owed. As Dick and his lawyer headed for the courtroom, they met up with the plaintiff and prosecutor, who suggested that they all sit down together and see what could be worked out. There, behind closed doors, they hammered out a settlement, and it was over.

Or, at least, the court battle was. Ten years later, Drago was still meticulously maintaining his child support payments, despite the fact that his son turned twenty-two in May of 2002. I'd never heard of support going on for that long, but Dick assured me that, under Massachusetts law, he was required to pay until the boy reached his twenty-third birthday.

"Don't get me wrong," Drago said emphatically. "I believe in child support. But a thousand dollars a month? My ex-wife is remarried, with five kids by her second husband. So you feel like you're paying for your own and three others. And I do think it's unfair at this point, since my son is now legally an adult."

Still, he maintained a good humor about it and looked forward to someday repairing a father/son relationship damaged by years of tension between former husband and wife.

There was no positive spin to put on his brush with the criminal jus-tice system, however. "I was scared to death," he said of jail, calling it "degrading, disgusting, horrifying." He found it beyond belief that anyone who'd once been there would ever again do something that could get him sent back.

"We were all thrown together," he recalled, "chained together when we were moved. You had murderers and other very dangerous people. And then those guilty of nonviolent crimes. And then people like me, who hadn't really done anything wrong. And we're all supposedly high risk.

"The Florida authorities treated me like trash," he went on. "But in Massachusetts, they were decent. They kept me away from the media. The Boston press had gotten word that I was being extradited, and they were waiting for me at Logan Airport, newspaper people, TV, everyone. But my escorts took me out the back way, so I didn't have to walk through the ter-minal. I really appreciated it.

"That's one of the things that's most embarrassing, when you're a for-mer ballplayer and you know that the press can't wait to put your picture all over the papers. And once they do that, you're guilty. I had my life ripped apart for three days, horrible stuff written about me, with no one even bothering to check my side of things."

Fifteen months would pass before George Kimball of the *Boston Her-ald* finally tried to help square the record by giving Drago the space to speak out on his own behalf.

"I was certainly happy about that story," Drago said. "It came long after we'd settled, though, and by then you can't undo the damage to your reputation that's already been done."

Also changed forever were some of Drago's other perceptions. He assured me that he didn't believe in coddling criminals. No way. He thinks that how people in trouble are handled should be based on what they did, and he is for the harshest of punishments for violent offenders. Yet it's the others that concern him. He received some firsthand experience of how those guilty of little or nothing are treated, and he wonders what's gone wrong.

"You watch TV now," he said, "and you see people getting away with murder while somebody else is going to prison for five or ten years for some minor offense. How can this guy be here and that guy there? It's almost like it comes down to what the legal system or the prosecutor think they can get away with. They have to get the notches on their belt. So if they can't get this one because it's too difficult, they put someone else away for twice as long."

Quite an ordeal, I said. I wondered how he'd gotten through it all.

"Well," he said, "I learned you can survive anything if you don't look a week or a month ahead. Each day you wake up and you're OK, and you go on from there."

Which was pretty much the same path followed by another of his teammates.

If, before the fact, you had to pick one of the boys of October as a candidate for future bankruptcy, you might well have selected Dick Drago, who never made a great deal of money during his career and carried the burden of two failed marriages. By the same token, it's a cinch you never would have chosen Rick Wise.

Wise's stay in the Show was longer and more successful. He endured into the big-bucks era, earning millions. Equally important, he had a stable home life. His marriage to wife Susan survived the difficult baseball years, his family stayed intact. When he retired, they moved into their dream home near Portland, Oregon—five thousand square feet of custom-built cedar house on eleven secluded acres with panoramic views of five mountains in the Cascade Range: Jefferson, Hood, Adams, Rainier, and St. Helens. There was a huge deck, spacious kitchen, basketball court, wine cellar, and his-and-her Jacuzzis.

An article by Larry Colton in the *Sunday Oregonian* magazine, published on July 4 of 1982, painted the rosiest of pictures for the future of Rick and Susan Wise and their two preadolescent children. Dad had just received more than a million dollars in severance pay from the San Diego Padres, he owned two condos in California and a second house in Oregon, he had a limited partnership in an apartment complex and an aircraft leasing business, and he was even considering putting his money to work by lending it to other people.

"I'm not quite sure yet [exactly what I want to do]," he told Colton. "My financial adviser is making a list of ideas. He'll figure out what our monthly bills are, then arrange investments to provide for those needs."

Like much of what Colton wrote, this would come to ring with irony. Because the Wises would eventually learn that a sense of security—even in America, even for someone blessed by the baseball gods with talent and longevity—can be the cruelest of illusions, as evanescent as the morning dew. And all that Rick would be guilty of was misplaced trust.

The man in whom Wise put his faith was the aforementioned financial adviser, LaRue Harcourt. Harcourt—a superagent who represented a stable full of star-quality players such as Don Sutton and Bert Blyleven—oversaw everything. He arranged for a living allowance for Rick and his family, with the balance directly deposited to him to invest as he saw fit. This is not as suspicious as it might sound; in fact, it's quite common in player/agent relationships. The players rarely know much about financial planning, nor do they often have the time and interest to devote to learning.

Wise had "total trust" in Harcourt, he told the *Hartford Courant* in a 1991 interview. "He was the expert and that's why you hire people."

In November 1990, Rick Wise emerged from bankruptcy court in Portland. The dream home was gone, his Mercedes was gone, his truck was gone, the condos were gone. He was left with $11,600 in assets. Susan had returned to nursing work after a twenty-two-year absence. And Rick was back in baseball, albeit in rather reduced circumstances.

LaRue Harcourt was not a crook, at least not a prosecutable one. He was, rather, a high roller who was drawn to risky investments and hated the IRS. What brought him down, and a number of ballplayers with him, was a series of legal but unprofitable limited partnerships.

Harcourt typically created partnerships in which his clients put up the actual dollars and he took a free share as compensation for his efforts. His most complicated, and ultimately most damaging, endeavor involved the aircraft leasing business. Harcourt used millions of the players' dollars to make down payments on Learjets and the like. The idea was that the planes would then be leased back to various commercial carriers, thereby generating a steady and substantial cash flow. Perhaps more important, the venture could be a legitimate tax shelter if properly structured.

The airplane deal crashed. Whether it was due primarily to changed conditions in the airline industry, or an overzealous IRS (which Harcourt blames), or his own sloppy bookkeeping and overspeculation (as lawyers involved in the case believe) is immaterial from the point of view of Rick and Susan Wise. All they were certain of was that the hammer fell late in 1984, when Susan took a phone call from a lender who demanded $150,000 by week's end or else he would seize their home.

The next few years were ugly. Creditors lined up. A dozen lawsuits were filed against the Wises. "You'd come home from somewhere," Rick told the *Courant*, "and [a process server would] be sitting in his car in the driveway. And once he saw you, you were served. It was humiliating."

The Wises, however, were not about to be crushed by their misfortunes. As Rick's lawyer David Slaby put it: "They showed remarkable resilience. With two other people, you could easily imagine them turning into alcoholics and maybe reading a sad obituary one day. I've seen it in my work; some people just don't recover. They don't have enough of whatever quality Rick and Susan have, the same quality, I guess, that made Rick a winner."

Slowly, they put their lives back together. The Baseball Assistance Team, an organization dedicated to assisting needy former players and their families, stepped in and helped Susan resume her medical education. And Rick took whatever coaching jobs he could get, in the Oakland A's system, then in the Astros'. After the Astros let him go in 1989, the only team that would hire him was a Canadian semipro outfit in New Brunswick. He went.

"That was a low point," he recalled, "having to leave the country to get a job in baseball."

But the following year he was back with his old World Series team, the Red Sox, as pitching coach for the club's Double-A affiliate in New Britain, Connecticut. He was there for two years, followed by three with its Triple-A Pawtucket outfit. Since then, he's continued to bounce around, as coaches will, and was still instructing minor league pitchers when I caught up with him in 2002.

He admitted that, although he was forced to seek employment when the financial sandstorm hit, he probably would have done it anyway.

"I was stagnating, mentally and physically," he said. "I *had* to go back to work, yes, but it was more than that. I wanted to get back into baseball. I missed baseball. I'm a field man. I love being in the dugout, out on the field. That's where the game is."

Did he want to coach in the big leagues?

"Of course I'd like to," he said. "But that's largely a matter of luck, of being with a manager who gets promoted and takes you with him. I think time's probably running out for me there."

When I interviewed him, Rick Wise's daughter was nearly as old as her dad was when he pitched his final major league innings. A lot had happened since then, but he was still in the game and, more important, his family had toughed out the bad times together. Though no longer wealthy, the Wises were comfortable and counting their blessings.

Rick still firmly believed what he had told the *Courant* eleven years earlier. "I think about the things I do have, and it doesn't matter to me anymore if I don't have the big house or the Mercedes. I didn't flaunt them when I did have them. They're not important, they really aren't. My health, and my family's well-being and my work, which I'm very happy about—that's all that counts."

Well aware that his pitcher is struggling, Darrell Johnson comes to the mound, where he meets with Wise and Fisk. For whatever reasons, he decides that Wise is not through, that he may yet settle down. And it certainly doesn't hurt that opposing pitcher Pat Darcy hits next. Getting an easy out might be just the ticket. Johnson leaves his starter in, and Darcy obliges by striking out on three pitches.

Pete Rose, though, is no Pat Darcy. First he tries a bunt and misses for strike one. Next he takes a borderline pitch on the outside corner for strike two. He fouls one off, then takes ball one outside. Finally, he gets a chest-high fastball, and he's all over it, belting it to deep right center. Lynn takes off and, going flat out, makes a game try at it, but his last-second leap is short of the ball by about six inches. It bounces once and hits the wall and, by the time Evans tracks it down, Rose is into third with a stand-up triple.

Later, Rick Wise will remember that hit as the game breaker. "To tell you the truth," he told me, "I believe Freddie misjudged that fly, just for an instant. But it was hit straightaway, which is the hardest to pick up. I think he hesitated. Ninety-five times out of a hundred, Freddie makes that play."

Misjudged or not, however, that ball was hit *hard*. Rick has given up only four hits, but they've all been creamed. Three homers and a triple. Yet the game is still young. No one can fault the manager for getting the hook. Wise departs, and Darrell Johnson brings in Jim Burton. It's an interesting choice. Burton is a rookie, he didn't play much down the stretch, and he has yet to appear in the postseason. But the Boston manager is playing the percentages all the way. Burton throws left, and lefties Griffey and Morgan are coming up. (Darrell may also think the game is all but lost, who knows?)

The lanky twenty-five-year-old Burton, looking disconcertingly like a deer in the headlights, makes five pitches to Griffey, only one of them a (questionable) strike. Runners at first and third, still only one out, and the National League's Most Valuable Player at the plate.

It's a pretty pressurized situation, and Burton is feeling it. He throws over to first three times in a row. He doesn't have a good pickoff move, and these are not hard throws. Most likely, he's trying to calm himself. He may also know that Griffey is not likely to go. While Ken is the fastest man on the team, at twenty-five he hasn't yet mastered the art of getting a jump on the pitcher, and he stole only sixteen times during the season. In addition, Morgan doesn't like anyone running when he's at bat with fewer than two strikes on him. He claims it impairs his concentration and, because he's Joe Morgan, he's listened to.

Whatever the case, Griffey stays close to the bag as Morgan swings and misses for strike one, takes two balls, then hits a screamer into the right-field corner. Evans has no chance to catch it; he can only wait for it to carom back at him, hoping it goes foul. It does, by an inch or two. Morgan takes ball three on a pitch low and away that could just as easily have been called a strike. Then Burton makes another good pitch, in much the same spot. Morgan gets the end of the bat on it and hits a weak fly to straightaway center. Rose tags and, when Lynn's throw home runs up the first-base side, it's 5–1 Cincinnati.

The rookie has done a creditable job but, with four right-handers in a row following Morgan, Darrell Johnson replaces him with Reggie Cleveland. Tony Perez strikes out to end the inning.

Sparky is now on cruise control. He's got a four-run lead, with all of those bullpen arms ready to go. This is the way the Series was supposed to play out: Cincinnati dominating with power and untouchable relief pitching. No one will give the Sox a chance in hell here. However . . . baseball would never have attracted its millions of devoted fans over the years if the games always (or even usually) went the way the self-appointed sages said they should. There are four innings yet to play. At least.

The Red Sox start to climb back in it during the next inning. Doyle begins by fouling out to Pete Rose, one of whose more remarkable records is that he's the only player ever to appear in more than five hundred games at five different positions (1B, 2B, 3B, LF, and RF). Then, however, the jitters seem to set in, and Darcy (who hasn't pitched in seventeen days) suddenly begins grappling with his control. He walks Yaz on five pitches, the last of which reaches the plate on one hop. He does better with Fisk, but walks him too, on a 3–2 pitch. After getting ahead of Fred Lynn 1–2 (and dodging a bullet when Lynn fouls off a letter-high heater right down the middle), he bounces a curveball in the dirt. This time, it almost hits Bench in the face and rolls away from him. The base runners move up. Now there are two in scoring position, with only one out and no force play available—a golden opportunity for a big inning.

It's not to be. Lynn chases a pitch up around his chin and hits a fly to shallow left center. Fortunately, Foster (with his weaker throwing arm), rather than Geronimo, catches it. Yaz tags and scores standing up. But Petrocelli grounds out, and Boston has to settle for the single run. It's 5–2, Reds.

Cleveland breezes through the Cincinnati half of the inning, fanning Bench and getting Foster on a fly to left and Concepcion on a grounder to first.

In the top of the seventh, Anderson stays with Darcy—somewhat surprising because Sparky normally replaces a struggling pitcher in a heartbeat. And just like that, the Sox threaten again. Leading off, Dwight Evans swings at the first pitch and grounds a single up the middle. It's over for young Pat. Clay Carroll—who faced one batter in Game 1 and walked in a run—relieves him, and the pitching change pays immediate dividends when Rick Burleson raps into a 4-6-3 double play.

Now Bernie Carbo pinch hits for Reggie Cleveland, and Anderson confounds the Sparky-watchers again. He leaves the right-handed Carroll in to pitch to Carbo—a left-handed batter who will be followed by three more lefties—even though his left-handed relief specialist, Will McEnaney, is warmed up and ready to go.

It makes some sense, though, at least with Carbo. Bernie is a dead opposite-field hitter. You want to pitch him in tight, away from his power zone. A right-handed pitcher can jam a lefty more easily than a southpaw can. All of his breaking balls are riding in toward the batter.

In this instance, however, it turns out to be a mistake.

When I met Bernie Carbo at his home near Mobile, Alabama, one of the first things I asked him about was his swing. Although a natural left-handed hitter, Bernie rarely pulled the ball, preferring instead to go the opposite way, to left field.

This is how that came about, he told me: when he was a kid, he used to play every day at a park near his home in Michigan, but they never had enough players to make full teams. So one side of the field was always left open. If you hit it there, you were out. Yeah, that's a shared memory. Just like the eight-man pickup games of my own youth on Cape Cod, I told him. The only difference being that we were more charitable; balls hit the "wrong" way were strikes, not outs.

Because everyone out there except Carbo was a righty and a pull hitter, it was always right field that was out of bounds, which created a problem when Bernie came up. Either the fielders would have to shift to the other side of the diamond and allow him to hit to right, or he would have to hit to left, the way they did. No contest. They weren't gonna walk, and so Bernie learned to hit to the opposite field. And to like it.

He did this by perfecting what is known as the inside-out stroke. I asked him to demonstrate that for me.

Basically, he explained, when a pull hitter swings, his hands move away from his body, leading the bat through the strike zone in a broad convex arc that terminates close to the body once again. Ideally, when the bat meets the ball, the arms are fully extended and the ball is "pulled" in the direction the bat head is moving. Left to right for a left-hander, vice versa for a righty.

With the inside-out swing, it's the reverse. The arc is concave. The hands are first pulled in toward the batter, so that the bat assumes a position more or less parallel to the flight of the ball, rather than perpendicular to it. Then, as the ball crosses the plate, the hands complete the arc so that they're behind the ball and the bat meets it more to the side, instead of head-on. This has the effect of "pushing" the ball the opposite way.

It can be a very effective way to hit, especially when the batter is facing a pitcher who throws very hard. Because you're swinging a little late on the pitch, you have a fraction of a second longer to see it, and that can make all the difference. It did for Bernie. He resisted coaching efforts to get him to become more of a pull hitter and stuck with his childhood swing throughout his career.

Carbo unleashes the inside-out stroke on the first offering from Clay Carroll and slices a perfect liner to left, long and curving toward the foul line. Foster gives chase. It appears that he believes he's going to make the catch all the way. But in the end the ball bounces off the top of the fence and over. Bernie pauses at second, thinking for a moment that he's hit a ground-rule double. Then he realizes it's a home run, and he finishes circling the bases. The previous double play looms even larger.

(The following day, in the locker room, Carbo will find a signed photo that Carroll, an old pal from his days with the Reds, had given him for good luck. It's been torn into a thousand pieces. When he asks a member of the Reds' staff who destroyed it, he's told: Clay Carroll.)

The Cincinnati lead has been cut to two. Sparky isn't worried, though. He still has a lot of arms available out there, and now he goes and gets one. Will McEnaney comes in to pitch to Cooper, who continues not to hit. He pops to short to end the inning.

It's 5–3, and there it remains. Jim Willoughby comes in to pitch for Boston and has little trouble. A one-out infield hit by McEnaney in the seventh is erased when Rose lines into a double play, and the eighth is one-two-three. McEnaney also retires the side in order in the eighth.

Top of the ninth. Last chance for the Sox, down two. Cincinnati doesn't lose in this kind of situation. But then, Game 2 gave us an inkling of what was to come. Reversals of fortune will be the norm rather than the exception.

Fred Lynn takes a called third strike to open the inning. Two outs to go. Rico Petrocelli is up.

That Petrocelli played so well in the Series was a minor miracle, because only a couple of months earlier there was doubt that he'd be able to play at all.

Rico, the son of immigrant parents and one of seven children, grew up in Brooklyn. He didn't even play baseball until he was thirteen—he'd concentrated mostly on basketball and was good enough by high school to receive a scholarship offer from North Carolina State—but once he started it was evident that he was blessed with a lot of natural talent. He could hit with power, and he could throw very hard. Nine professional teams scouted him. Many saw him as a potential major league pitcher.

He signed with the first team to work him out, the Red Sox, and he knew he wanted to be a position player. He loved the Wall. He never even considered the Yankees. "It was 400 feet to the wall in Yankee Stadium," he told me. "That's about as far as I can hit my best shot. So what's a long out there is a home run in Fenway."

And he did thrive once he made the parent club. He was the team's regular shortstop for six seasons, including the World Series year of 1967. For a while, he held the major league record for home runs in a season by a shortstop, at 40 (these were the days when the position was normally filled by light-hitting slick fielders, before the likes of A-Rod and Nomar).

He was eventually moved to third base, a transition he accomplished with relative ease, and that's where he was playing in 1974 when he was hit in the head by Milwaukee pitcher Jim Slaton. The beaning had serious aftereffects. It caused an inner-ear problem that plagued Rico for more than a year.

"I was really struggling," he recalled. "Everything was off. I couldn't see; my balance and timing were screwed up. They kept trying different drugs to treat it, but they didn't get it right until there were about two months left in '75. Then, all of a sudden, I could see again and my swing came around."

He came on strong late in the season and was ready for the Series, where he not only hit well but performed flawlessly in the field.

"Unfortunately," he told me, "the combination of drugs they had me on, you couldn't stay on them for very long. I had to go off them over the winter, and the next year I was right back feeling like a Little Leaguer playing with adults. I couldn't take it."

Petrocelli retired after the '76 season. He went into broadcasting for a while, and still does some, then started his own marketing business. The company handles sports equipment and apparel, and there's a kind of symmetry to that, because his dad had worked in the garment industry back in New York when he was a kid.

The inner-ear problem cleared up with time, and when I spoke with him he had only fond memories of his time with the Red Sox. "We had a really good team in the mid-'70s," he said. "The most professional group I was ever with. Even the rookies were mature. Great players and a great clubhouse atmosphere. We shoulda won a bunch of pennants."

Maybe if Rico hadn't been forced out of the game prematurely, they would have.

Petrocelli continues his hot hitting, jumping on McEnaney's first pitch and ripping a line drive to center for a single. It's his sixth hit of the Series and gives him three consecutive multihit games. Dwight Evans is now the batter, with Burleson to follow. Two righties. Sparky doesn't hesitate. He yanks McEnaney in favor of Rawley Eastwick, a right-hander and his designated closer.

Get those last two outs. Shouldn't be a problem for Eastwick. He's facing the number seven and eight hitters in the Boston lineup. In addition, Rawley has made three appearances in the League Championship and World Series, and he is yet to be scored upon.

That changes just two pitches later. After taking a ball low, Evans gets around on a belt-high fastball and nails it. It just clears the left-field wall, as George Foster buries his face in the padding and the stunned crowd goes silent except for a vocal handful of relocated Red Sox fans. The game is tied. Now, can Boston take the lead?

Eastwick can't believe he made such a crappy pitch, but he pulls himself together in a hurry. He throws serious heat to Burleson, making the batter look overmatched. Then, with the count 1 and 2, he makes an excellent pitch, in on the fists. Rick swings and bloops one straight out over second base. Morgan races out, Geronimo races in, and the ball drops right between them. The rally continues.

Now what? With only one out, Darrell Johnson has three basic choices. First, he can leave in Jim Willoughby—who's handcuffed the Reds so far—and let him hit away. Willow swings the bat well for a pitcher, but perhaps not well enough to hit Eastwick. An inning-ending double play is a distinct possibility.

Second, he can have Jim try to sacrifice Burleson to second. If successful, that'd put the go-ahead run on second with two out and Cecil Cooper up. But Coop is in a horrible slump. In addition, it's tough enough for anyone to bunt on artificial turf—where the ball gets to the fielder in a hurry—much less a guy who hasn't been to the plate all year. You almost have to make sure you go to the right side, or Pete Rose, charging from third, will probably gun the lead runner out at second. Could even wind up a double play.

Third, he could send up a pinch hitter. Hit for Willoughby, who's going great? It's an eerie prefiguring of the identical choice Johnson will face in Game 7, when there is considerably more at stake.

The problem is that he's already used Carbo, his best lefty and only serious home-run threat. So what he has is left-handed defensive specialist

Rick Miller, who hit .194 on the season, and reserve catcher Tim Black-well, a switch hitter who batted .197. Then there are a couple of light-weights, Bob Heise (.214) and Bob Montgomery (.226); Doug Griffin, a pretty good hitter, but nursing a bad back; and Juan Beniquez, another good hitter who also has some speed. These four all swing from the right side.

It's an unappealing set of options, and it probably comes down to a choice between the sacrifice and Beniquez. Johnson goes, as is his tendency, with what looks to be the percentage play. Get Burleson to second. Give the lefty Cooper a chance to break his slump here and drive the run home.

After a lengthy confab with third-base coach Don Zimmer, Willow steps up. He squares to bunt. The first pitch is low. Bench straightens and whips a throw to first, where Morgan has snuck in behind the runner in a set pickoff play. Morgan, though, has overrun the bag and he falls down. He does well just to glove the ball and still almost makes the play. Burleson slides on his belly and just makes it back in time.

In a tight contest filled with improbabilities, this could have been a game-turning play. Burleson could easily have been out. Just as easily, the throw could have gone into right field, moving the runner up. The greater improbability may be that neither happened.

On the next pitch, Willoughby lays down his bunt, and it's a beauty, right down the first-base line, a foot fair. Perez fields it, and his only play is to first. Burleson coasts into second. If they can get him home, the way Willow is pitching, they should win this thing.

Cooper swings at the first pitch, a very hittable inside fastball that he should be able to pull. He fouls it weakly back to the screen. Next he almost swings at a pitch down around his shoetops. He fouls off an out-side fastball. Then, Eastwick brings one in shoulder-high. It'd be ball two, even in an era when the strike zone extended to the letters, yet it's close enough that Coop feels like he has to swing rather than chance taking a called strike three. He loops a fly to center. For a moment, it looks as if it might be a repeat of Burleson's pop. But that would be a lucky break, and the Reds have a monopoly on those. The fleet Geronimo gloves it, and the inning is over.

Nevertheless, the Sox have battled back to a 5–5 tie. They're in position to steal this one.

Willoughby continues his mastery of the Reds in the home ninth, getting Bench, Foster, and Concepcion all to beat his sinker into the dirt. One-two-three. Extra innings, though Cincinnati still has only five hits.

There's a ray of hope for the Sox in the tenth, when Denny Doyle leads off by chopping a 3–2 pitch up the middle for an infield single. He's followed by Yastrzemski, who gets every bit of an Eastwick fastball and rips one to deep center. Looks like a homer, or at least a run-scoring double. But Geronimo plays the ball's flight path perfectly and, at the last minute, jumps and hauls it in at the wall, 405 feet from the plate.

It's a deflating moment, yet another nonbreak, but the Sox are undaunted. If they can't win it with power, they'll try strategy. With Fisk up, they send Doyle on a hit-and-run. Fisk obliges by hitting a slow bouncer that ought to get the runner over. Not in this game. Because, unfortunately, he hits it in the only place where Joe Morgan has a play, directly at him and just to the right of second base. No force is possible, but Morgan tags the sliding Doyle a foot before he reaches the bag. Outstanding fielder that he is, Morgan also takes care to stay clear of the runner, so that he isn't upended before he can flip to Perez to complete the double play. An inning of maddening *almosts* is over, and time is about to run out. We move on to the reviled (by Red Sox fans anyway) home tenth.

What happens in Cincinnati's half of the frame has been hotly debated ever since. The question: *Was it or wasn't it?* And the key word: *interference.*

Geronimo leads off, and home-plate umpire Larry Barnett makes the first of his questionable calls. Willoughby gets two quick strikes on the batter, then lays a beautiful sinker on the outside corner at the knees. Geronimo is frozen by what should be strike three. You look at it on tape, it's not even borderline. But Barnett perversely calls it a ball. The moment takes on a huge significance when Geronimo grounds the next pitch up the middle for a single. Instead of bases empty with one out, it's winning run on, nobody out. And instead of light-hitting Terry Crowley coming up . . .

It's Sparky's turn to play tactician. He's had Crowley in the on-deck circle, waiting to bat for Eastwick. Now, with Geronimo aboard, Anderson has a fateful change of mind. He wants a better bat handler at the plate to move the runner along for Rose and Griffey. So he sends up Ed Armbrister, who serves a dual purpose for his manager. Not only is he an excellent bunter, he allows Sparky to save the left-handed Crowley for later, in case he's needed to face either Willoughby or Boston's other right-hander, closer Dick Drago.

Armbrister is about as marginal a major leaguer as can be. He will wind up with a five-year career during which he totals all of 265 at-bats. None of the others will be as big as this one.

On Willoughby's second pitch comes the famous Blown Call. Armbrister lays down his bunt. Well, *lays down* is probably not the best way to describe it. The pitch is a superlative one, a nasty sinker that poor Ed barely gets the bat on. Then again, Armbrister is an excellent bunter, and it's to his credit that he makes contact at all.

He clips the top of the sinking baseball, which means that it comes off the bat face very fast and straight down. Then it rebounds and bounces straight up, about nine feet into the air. Meanwhile, Armbrister starts toward first. He takes a step and then stops and goes into a kind of crouch, and Fisk runs into him. Barnett raises his right hand, as if to signify that the batter is out. Fisk shoves Armbrister out of his way, fields the bunt, and elects to try for Geronimo at second. He throws the ball into center field.

When the dust has settled, both runners are ruled safe. Geronimo's on third, Armbrister is on second, and Darrell and Fisk are all over Barnett like white on rice.

OK, let it be said at the outset that umpiring is among the world's most thankless jobs, the only one I can think of where the folks you serve never, ever have a kind word for your efforts. Or, as former major league umpire Ron Luciano once put it, "Sometimes, although many people do not believe this, being screamed at by a manager or player standing inches away, and perhaps spitting tobacco juice on you, is not as much fun as it appears to be from a distance."

Nevertheless, the split-second decisions of the men in blue are going to be subject to hindsight analysis; they know this and accept it. So it seems fair to ask: What actually went down on the night of October 14? Well, twenty-five years later I slotted a videotape of the play into my VCR and watched it over and over, listened to commentary by Joe Garagiola and Gary Carter, and tried my best to keep from seeing things through a disappointed Sox fan's eyes.

It was a job. I was astonished, delighted actually, that one single play could be so complex. Yet that is part of the allure of baseball, that it can be so simple and so complicated at the same time. After my repeated viewings, my conclusion was that there are five crucial questions about what transpired on the field during and after the "Armbrister moment."

First, was it interference? Second, should it have been called? Third, did Barnett in fact call it? Fourth, what is Fisk's responsibility in all this? And fifth, what happened down at third base? In order:

1. *Was it interference?* Unquestionably. Baseball rules were deliberately designed to favor the fielder over the runner on plays where they get tangled up. It cannot be otherwise, else there would be a whole bunch of purposeful collisions in every game. Thus, although the runner has a right to advance (Armbrister, in this instance, had the right to start toward first), the fielder has a superior right to an unobstructed opportunity to get to the ball (Fisk *must* be allowed to cleanly field the bunt).

   Some contend that Armbrister had no *intent* to interfere, and therefore the umpire shouldn't call it. Others, like Gary Carter, maintain that it's the catcher's job to clear the area around home plate. Because Fisk was able to do this—that is, to push Armbrister well out of his way *before* the throw—and to thereby gain a clear throwing line to second, it doesn't really qualify as interference. I'm unconvinced by either of these arguments.

   Armbrister was in Fisk's way when he went after the ball. No doubt about that. In fact, he halts and then seems to almost deliberately position himself in front of the onrushing catcher before getting shoved aside. But questions of intent and Fisk's ultimate field of vision are beside the point, as far as I'm concerned. The rule book is pretty unambiguous about this.

   Section 2.00 states: "Offensive interference is an act which interferes with, obstructs, impedes, hinders or confuses any fielder attempting to make a play." And if that's not clear enough, Section 7.09 reiterates: "It is interference if the batter fails to avoid a fielder who is attempting to field a batted ball or intentionally interferes with a thrown ball."

   Armbrister didn't interfere with the thrown ball, as Carter points out, but so what? He clearly obstructed, hindered, and impeded (and probably confused) the fielding play that preceded the throw, and there the question of intent does not apply. The batter is out, the runner is returned to first. Or if, in the opinion of the umpire, a double play could have been made, it may be awarded.

This is a basic principle that must be among the first things taught in umpire school. Yet it appears to have eluded Larry Barnett, and not for the first time. Recall that in Game 1, when he was at second base, he failed to call Yastrzemski out when Yaz flagrantly obstructed Joe Morgan's attempt to field a ground ball.

So it was a blown call, cut and dried. Or . . . was it?

2. *Should it have been called?* This question seems at first glance to be merely an extension of the first. Answer one, you answer the other. Sadly, though, they are two separate considerations.

Because . . . as it turns out, prior to the games, the umpires in this World Series had received a "supplemental instruction" from the front office of Major League Baseball. And that instruction read: "When a catcher and a batter-runner going to first have contact when the catcher is fielding the ball, there is generally no violation and nothing should be called." Presto! Barnett is absolved; the call is now seen as having been right and proper, end of all arguments. Except, of course, that the fan is left wondering why MLB felt obliged to tweak the rules in the first place and which god bestowed upon them the authority to do so.

(During my research, I asked just about everyone involved, including Darrell Johnson, whether they had heard this story. No one had. But my source—Roger Angell, who published the surprising directive in *The New Yorker*—has impeccable credentials, and when he says he has a copy of the document in question, I'm inclined to believe him.)

3. *Did Barnett in fact call it?* We are still left with the nagging suspicion that Barnett *did* in fact call Armbrister out but somehow changed his mind. Examine the tape. There is no question that his right fist flies up in the traditional *Out!* signal. Gary Carter contends that he could also have been signaling that the bunt was a fair ball. Maybe. Sure looks like he's calling the out, though.

4. *What is Fisk's responsibility in all this?* Despite the controversial nature of the noncall, shouldn't Fisk shoulder some of the blame? Yes, indeed. He has no way of knowing what the umpire is going to rule, so his job is to make some kind of play, to ensure that his team doesn't come up empty. The simplest thing is just to tag Armbrister. Or he could go to first for the easy out there. Or he could nail the speedy Geronimo. He fails to accomplish *any* of these. Bad news all the way around, Pudge.

5. *What happened down at third base?* The final question is one that is seldom asked, yet it might be the most important one of all. While Barnett's call can be reasonably debated—because it was wrong according to the rule book but correct in light of the "supplementary instruction"—what happened at third base looks indefensible.

Although nearly everyone is drawn to the commotion at home plate, things continue to happen in the field. Play is not dead until the umpire says that it is. So, after Fisk's throw sails into center, Geronimo lights out for third. Fred Lynn fields the errant ball and fires it to Petrocelli, who puts the tag on the sliding runner. And holds it there. Say again: *And holds it.* Now, Geronimo clearly beats the throw. Initially. However, his body is way out on the left-field side of the base, and during his slide his lead foot (the left one) comes off the bag, while his trailing right foot never makes contact with it. His whole body is skidding past the base a few inches away from it, and he doesn't touch it again until he grabs it with his left hand. Umpire Maloney makes the initial, and accurate, *safe* call, and then he apparently looks away, his attention perhaps diverted by the fierce debate that's developing at home. He misses Petrocelli making the putout.

When I interviewed Rico in 2002, I asked him if he realized what had happened, because on the tape you can see him look up and away after he gets the tag down. It's apparently the first time anyone has brought this up with him. He's surprised.

"No," he said. "I was looking to second, to see if I should throw down there. I heard the umpire call the runner safe, so I shifted my attention. I had no idea the runner came off the bag."

Not so Fred Lynn, who made the throw. He watched the whole thing. "Geronimo was out," he told me. "He was off the base and Rico still had the tag on him. That's the way I saw it."

It's the way it looks on the tape, too. So this, to me, may be the real Blown Call of the inning, and perhaps it is Maloney's name that should live in the Red Sox' Hall of Infamy as much as, if not more than, Barnett's. He didn't do a third-base umpire's job, which is to watch the play right there in front of him, until it's over.

In any event, the Red Sox don't wind up with a bases-empty, two-out situation, as they might have if Barnett had ruled that the interference cost Boston a 2-6-3 double play. They don't get one out, with Geronimo returned to first, the most logical call. They don't even get one out and Armbrister on second as, failing all else, they should *at least* have. What they're left with is no outs and runners on second and third. Ugh.

All that remains is to play out the string, without much hope that the Reds can be kept off the scoreboard after being gifted with this situation. The Sox try. Lefty Roger Moret comes in for Willoughby and gives Pete Rose an intentional walk, loading the bases and creating a force play all the way around. Then he battles pinch hitter Merv Rettunmund and eventually strikes him out on a low fastball that immobilizes him.

That brings up Morgan. Darrell Johnson frantically waves his outfielders in. Everything is staked on a double-play ball. Moret, though, is primarily a power pitcher. He doesn't generally force a lot of grounders, and he doesn't get one here. Morgan lofts a fly to center that'd be a routine out with normal positioning. With Lynn playing in, though, it's over his head. Cincinnati gets the win.

Fisk flings his mask at the backstop in disgust. It won't help. Nor will Bill Lee's angry assertion that fans "are going to start sending letters to [Commissioner] Bowie Kuhn, start calling his house. There's going to be such an outcry that they're going to have to play the game over tomorrow. You wait and see."

Anyone who heeded Lee's words is still waiting, of course. The Reds, with another gracious helping hand from the baseball gods, have taken the lead in games, 2–1. Nothing, but nothing, will alter that.

Get After Him Good

From a paper by the American Sports Medicine Institute on the bio-mechanics of pitching:

> "Extreme external rotation during throwing makes the shoulder prone to injury. As the shoulder externally rotates, the humeral head translates anteriorly. At maximum external rotation, the posterior rotator cuff may become impinged between the glenoid labrum and the humeral head. This 'over-rotation' injury can cause degeneration of both the superior labrum and the rotator cuff" [the rotator cuff being the cluster of muscles and tendons that allows the arm to pivot in several different directions at the shoulder].

Not only that, but, "Near the end of arm cocking, the shoulder is in extreme external rotation, the elbow is flexed approximately $90°$, and the forearm is in a valgus position. To resist valgus stress, a large varus torque is produced at the elbow. Tension in the ulnar collateral ligament (UCL) provides nearly half of this varus torque. This high tension is near the ultimate tensile strength of the UCL, leaving the UCL susceptible to injury" [the UCL being the ligament that, basically, holds the whole elbow together].

In lay terms, pitching is a hell of a physically stressful occupation, and the risk of blowing out either the shoulder or the elbow is ever-present.

And this covers only the major potential injuries. Left unmentioned is the fact that each and every time a pitcher goes out there, he suffers minor injuries in the form of microtears to the muscles and tendons of the arm and shoulder. Such tears require time to heal. If ample time for recovery is not allowed, they will get worse, until the player can no longer perform. So, how much rest is enough? Or, to put it another way, what constitutes the ideal pitching rotation?

The question has been debated endlessly. In the past, it was near universal for teams to use the four-man rotation, which meant that their starters would take a turn every fourth day. That allowed them to carry only nine pitchers—four starters and five relievers—and gave them a lot of flexibility with regard to the other eight positions.

Around the early '70s, however, there was a general change of philosophy that was embraced by just about everyone. Three days' rest was deemed insufficient—pitchers were getting tired and sore-armed too frequently—and the five-man rotation was adopted as the new standard. Now, clubs will typically carry five starters, two long-relief men, and four highly specialized short relievers, including a lefty, a righty, and a closer.

(It is entirely proper here to ask how, if three days' rest is truly inadequate, the old-timers did what they did without their arms falling off. Cy Young, for example, pitched more than 7,300 innings during his twenty-two-year career, or about 335 per season, and he averaged 34 complete games a year; Old Hoss Radbourn set the all-time standard with 73 complete games in a year in which he pitched the unthinkable total of 678 innings; and, while records from the Negro Leagues are spotty, it has been estimated that Satchel Paige pitched 2,500 games, winning 80 percent of them. Such feats should be impossible and, to the best of my knowledge, no one has yet come forth with a viable explanation.)

In any case, the Red Sox began 1975 with four starters: Lee, Tiant, Wise, and Cleveland. When the team struggled early on, Darrell Johnson made the decision to add Roger Moret to the rotation and give his other pitchers an extra day off. That, according to Bill Lee, was the key to the pennant-winning season. Moret was brilliant, the rest of the staff was better-rested, and "after that we started winning left and right," Lee says.

All thoughts of an ideal pitching rotation go out the window during the postseason, however. In a five- or seven-game series, you have to go with your best, no matter the condition of their arms. For the League Championship or World Series, the starting five is normally pared down to three or four, with the others relegated to long relief. Should the staff ace be far better than the number two man, he may be forced into action on a scant two days' rest, as the Red Sox' Jim Lonborg was in 1967. And if the manager has a particularly dominating starter, he may even ask that player to give him an inning or two on little or no rest at all, in a situation requiring that someone get a few key outs. Thus did Randy Johnson receive the call to close out Game 7 of the 2001 Series, despite having pitched seven innings the day before.

The short series is all about jockeying for position, allocating your resources as best you can. You don't want to bet your whole stake too early, but you also don't want to leave anything on the table for a deal that may never come. Which is the dilemma Darrell Johnson had to face in determining his Game 4 starter.

According to Bill Lee, Luis Tiant "used marijuana, but he never smoked it." Lee claims that the wily Cuban had his pitching arm rubbed down with a secret salve a couple of hours before each turn on the mound. The salve was purportedly made up of honey, liniment, and a mixture of herbs, including marijuana. One of the trainers, oblivious of its contents, would massage it in.

Lee goes on to note, with tongue probably firmly in cheek, that the trainer "was always very happy after working Luis over." It's well to remember that this is from the guy who claimed that he sprinkled pot over his morning flapjacks.

Whatever the case may be, I hope that Luis has used the marijuana mix or some other magic potion on his arm on October 15. He's sure going to need it before this night is over.

Tiant has had only three days' rest since pitching a complete game in Boston, yet Darrell Johnson feels it is imperative to start him. Behind two games to one, this is a must-win situation for the Red Sox. Johnson wants to save Bill Lee, who is much better suited to Fenway, for Game 6—provided the teams return there. Should the Sox lose tonight, then Johnson will have to start Lee tomorrow, hoping to salvage the final game in Cincinnati and extend the Series. But that would render his sinkerballer unavailable for the last two games. Bad.

Alternatively, the manager could still hold Lee in reserve, even following a loss. But if he did, the only option for Game 5 would be to go with one of his other two starters, the up-and-down Reggie Cleveland or the youthful, unpredictable Roger Moret. Johnson surely doesn't want to have to make that kind of choice if Boston is one game from elimination.

So the pressure is on to win tonight and ensure a return home either way, one game up or one down. Because Johnson wants to maximize the probability of getting the victory, he's forced to go with his ace. El Tiante.

(For his part, Tiant has said that he "didn't have my good fastball that I had against Oakland" when he pitched Game 1 against the Reds. He feels like he's going to need it. Well, uh, OK, Luis. Maybe if you got that heater, instead of a 5-hit shutout you'll pitch a 3-hitter.)

Despite needing to use his ace on short notice (and despite the potential absence of the fastball), the manager feels pretty good about his team's chances. First of all, even though Luis did go the distance in Game 1, he didn't throw all that many pitches. Second, Luis Tiant's record over his past six appearances (the final four games of the regular season, with the division title on the line, and one each in the American League Championship Series and World Series) is as follows:

W/L Record: 5–1
Innings Pitched: 49
Hits: 27
Runs: 6
Earned Runs: 5
Shutouts: 3
Earned Run Average: 0.92

These are truly astounding numbers. Tiant averaged more than eight innings per outing and essentially pitched a 4-hitter each and every time. Without question, it's a Hall of Fame–caliber performance under pressure.

For their part, the Sox will be facing Fred Norman.

Now, Norman's not exactly a slouch. Though he's been all over the place during his career, with a lifetime record hovering around .500, he never gives up a lot of hits and usually has a decent ERA. He had a great year in '75 and pitched well against Pittsburgh in the NLCS. Pitching coach Larry Shepard says before the game that Norman has the full complement: fastball, curve, change, and screwball. He induces a lot of ground balls. But his big weakness is that he has a tendency to nibble at the plate too much, and when he does he can lose it entirely.

The book says to get to him early. If you do, he'll try to compensate by pitching too carefully. Then you've got him. He's no Luis.

As it turns out, getting to the pitchers in the early innings will be the story of this game, which starts out very inauspiciously for Boston.

It's drizzling slightly at game time, but it isn't cold. There was rain earlier in the day. The field, however, is in as excellent a shape as plastic can be. Think Zamboni machine, which the Reds have one of. This squat, ugly contraption somewhat resembles the truck that washes your city streets and behaves like the offspring of a giant vacuum cleaner mated with a hair dryer. Normally used to condition ice rinks for hockey and figure skating, it also works wonders on artificial grass, and here it has turned a saturated surface into something very playable.

Johnson has tweaked his lineup for the left-handed Norman. He's starting right-hander Juan Beniquez in left and batting him leadoff. Yastrzemski returns to first base. And lefty Cecil Cooper, struggling at a ghastly 1 for 13 so far, goes to the bench; perhaps this breather will be what Cooper, a fine natural hitter, needs to get his stroke back. Other than this one substitution, the lineup is exactly the same as it was in Games 2 and 3.

It would appear to be a logical move, until you consider that Beniquez, twenty-five years old, has been no more than a utility player for the entirety of his brief career. Not that he hasn't been valuable. He can play both infield and outfield, and in '75, just his second full year of major league ball, he hit .291. On the other hand, he appeared in only 78 games and drove in a scant 17 runs in 254 at-bats. He isn't what you'd call seasoned, nor does he deliver very often in the clutch.

However, on a team that is painfully slow afoot, Beniquez has some speed, certainly more than any other starter. And so, after the national anthem is flawlessly rendered by fading heartthrob John Gary—a "popular entertainer and one of Cincinnati's favorites," according to the public-address announcer—Juan goes out there to take the first pitch of the game.

This will turn out to be Beniquez's only World Series, although he will go on to have a seventeen-year major league career, remarkable longevity for a nonregular. He'll appear in exactly 1,500 games, with 4,651 plate appearances. He will hit over .300 four times and .274 lifetime. He'll play every position except pitcher and catcher, including DH. And he'll be traded, on average, every other year.

I caught up with him near his home in Carolina, Puerto Rico, in 2002. Beniquez was quite fit, despite being a little thick through the middle. He had the massive arms and chest of a dedicated iron freak. Listed at 150 pounds when he first came up as a shortstop, he started putting on weight when he was moved to the outfield ("I had a strong arm, but wild," he admitted to me), and must tip the scales at more than 200 now. He had a stroke in 2001 and was in a coma for three days, but he recovered completely.

When I met him, I found him to be quite an affable fellow. He was sharply dressed in slacks and a sport shirt, had a heavy gold chain around his neck, and wore what looked like an expensive watch. He still had a full head of dark, curly hair, though it wasn't quite as long as the Afro he sported as a skinny youngster in '75.

I asked him why he got traded so much.

He shrugged. It's just baseball.

To tell the truth, I hadn't followed his career after he left Boston and never realized he lasted for so long. Which teams did he play for, then?

He ticked them off on his fingers. Boston, New York, Texas, Seattle, California, Baltimore, Kansas City, and Toronto.

Eight?

"I hold the record," he said with a grin. "Most different teams by one player, all in the same league. . . . Well, it was the record at the time. I don't know if it still is."

Me, neither. But if it isn't, it must be a close second. He was obviously proud of his place in the record book and of his overall accomplishments. As well he should be. Not many players log more than a decade and a half in the Show.

The last thing I asked him was whether he believed in the Curse.

"Oh, yeah," he said. "Definitely."

It'd be nice if Juan Beniquez, in his first at-bat as a World Series starter, helps begin the breaking of the Curse by hitting a mammoth home run, or even one that barely clears the fence. But he doesn't. He flies out to center, and Game 4 is under way. It'll offer up the longest two hours and fifty-two minutes that a fan can endure before it's over.

Doyle follows with a groundout to second, and, after Yastrzemski slaps a line single to right, Fisk waves pathetically at a screwball and strikes out. Easy inning for Norman.

But it's gonna be a much more soul-testing ride for Luis. Right from the get-go, he's in trouble. Leadoff hitter Pete Rose swings at a ball down around his ankles, not at all a bad pitch, and grounds a single up the middle. Ominously, Rose has worked an eight-pitch at-bat that consumes two and a half minutes. This is how it will go all night. Outs will be very difficult to come by.

Griffey then turns on a first-pitch fastball and creams one into the left-center-field gap. Tiant is down a run before getting anyone out. Fortunately, though, Ken tries to stretch his lazy double into a tough triple. Lynn makes a strong throw to Burleson, who pivots and rifles a perfect, chest-high one-hopper to Petrocelli. It's a textbook illustration of the importance of hitting the cutoff man, indicative of the kind of defense both teams are playing in this Series. Griffey is tagged out and, for once, aggressive baserunning has hurt Cincinnati instead of Boston.

Good thing, because Joe Morgan draws a base on balls. He walks on a pitch over the outside corner that plate umpire Dick Stello could've called either way. Little Joe gets the break, rather than Tiant. Luis shakes his head, and not for the last time. At this point, it's simply disappointment. *Oh well, I didn't get that one, I'll get the next.* That's a pitcher's reality, and you have to be philosophical about it.

As the game goes on, though, Tiant's displeasure will turn to disgust and a hard, cold anger. This will become one of those days when every marginal call goes against him, thereby not only adding extra runners but also inexorably ratcheting up his pitch count.

Now Morgan is at first, creeping across the dirt around the bag and putting one foot on the artificial surface for the biggest possible lead. So far, Joe has done this with his base-stealing opportunities: persuaded the pitcher to balk him to second (Tiant in Game 1) and been gunned down by Fisk (in Game 2). He's now on record as having boasted that "I'm not going to get thrown out again in this Series."

Tiant immediately makes a quick throw over and nearly picks him off. Then he goes over there again, and yet again. Each time it's close. Each time, Morgan brushes his uniform off and takes the same substantial lead. He's still ready to go, but he won't get the chance.

When Tiant finally comes to the plate, Tony Perez hits a slow roller to short. Burleson comes in hard and makes an off-balance throw to first that arrives on the bounce. Steady Yaz scoops it up, and he just nips Perez. Tony is probably the only man in the lineup too slow to have beaten that one out. The runner moves up.

Then Johnny Bench waits on a slow Tiant curve, and waits. By the time he finally swings, the ball is nearly past him, and he drills it to the opposite field. Both Lynn and Evans give chase, and both have a shot at it, but they seem to hesitate at the last moment, in order to avoid colliding. The ball falls into the gap and bounces up against the wall. Morgan scores easily, and Bench stops at second.

George Foster works Tiant to another 3–2 count before hitting a sharp one-hopper to Petrocelli at third for the last out. Luis, untouchable in Game 1, has been rocked here. Nearly everyone hit the ball hard, and he's lucky to be down only 2–0.

The Red Sox put another man on in the second. After Lynn chases a high curve and strikes out, Petrocelli continues his hot hitting, lining a single to left. But Evans forces him at second, and Burleson grounds out. For his part, Tiant settles down, retiring the side in order on a couple of grounders and a weak fly.

Norman runs into trouble in the third. He begins with the classic no-no: walking the opposing pitcher. It's the second base on balls Tiant has drawn in the Series. He takes a very short lead. But he's off and running when Beniquez makes contact. Uh-oh. It's a sharp ground ball, right at Luis. Somehow, Tiant gets his bulk up into the air and leaps over the ball like Edwin Moses clearing a hurdle. Or . . . maybe not quite like Moses. He does avoid getting hit, though. And, after El Tiante rounds second and bluffs a dash to third, the Sox have two on, nobody out.

Denny Doyle is up, with the heart of the order to follow. It's a clear bunt situation, yet there are two things working against it. First, the artificial surface makes sacrifice bunts difficult; the ball gets to the infielders more quickly, so the first and third basemen don't have to charge down the line as far, and the ball tends to come up in the air rather than hug the ground, increasing the likelihood that it'll be handled cleanly. Second, Darrell Johnson wants to do the unexpected.

So Doyle shortens up on the bat, showing bunt. The fielders at the corners advance toward the plate, then drop back a little. Doyle makes a half-swing, trying to slap the ball past Rose into left. He misses. On the second pitch, he doesn't even bluff. He takes a full cut and flies to center. One down.

Yastrzemski is up, the tying run at first. He hits a blistering two-hop ground ball, right at Joe Morgan. It's a 4-6-3 double play. Norman is out of the inning unscathed.

In the bottom of the third, Tiant is hit hard again. Rose smacks a line shot, but to straightaway center, and Lynn gathers it in. After Griffey bounces back to the mound, Morgan hits another line shot, this one hauled in by Beniquez in left-center. Though there's no damage, Luis clearly doesn't have his best stuff. If he's to make it any deeper into this game, it's apt to be a struggle. Which is just what it turns out to be.

Luckily, before Tiant can completely implode, the Sox give him some breathing room.

What does it take to produce a winning baseball team?

Some think that all it requires is gathering together the best talent available. And it's indisputably true that you can't win without highly skilled players, of which the Red Sox had an abundance in 1975. Why did they? Because of one man: Dick O'Connell.

O'Connell—an old-school, hard-drinking, cigar-smoking Irishman— was simply the finest general manager the Red Sox ever had, and one of the greatest in major league history. I tried to interview him for this book, to ask how he had put together the '75 team, but by the time I got him on the phone he was already seriously ill and could remember little. Sadly, he passed away in August of 2002. I will have to be content with the privilege of having spoken with him at all.

Dick saved the Red Sox. The once-proud franchise had had losing records every year from 1959 to 1965, when he was hired as GM. Attendance at the ballpark was pitiful, fan interest moribund. In '65, they lost one hundred games.

O'Connell started from scratch—drafting, promoting, trading. In the process, he put an end to the institutionalized racism that had defined the franchise (Jackie Robinson broke the color barrier in 1947; Boston fielded its first quality African-American player, Reggie Smith, twenty years later). Dick was interested in talent, period. Two years after he took control— following a season of ninety more losses and a next-to-last-place finish— the Impossible Dream Red Sox were in the World Series, and a tradition of at least contending was begun. It has continued ever since.

The 1975 Sox were perhaps O'Connell's finest achievement. Imagine having overseen a farm system that delivered to the majors, within a four-year span, the following players: Jim Rice, Fred Lynn, Carlton Fisk, Rick Burleson, Cecil Cooper, Dwight Evans, Bill Lee, and Roger Moret. *That* is the nucleus of a winner. Add in the savvy moves that brought to town Luis Tiant, Bernie Carbo, Rick Wise, Dick Drago, and Jim Willoughby, and you go to the World Series.

So Dick O'Connell assembled the talent without which no team can succeed. Yet something more is needed to win, and win consistently over a 162-game season. If that weren't true, the Sox would have reeled off several pennants in a row. They didn't. So, if the talent was still there, which it was, there must have been some missing ingredients. What did that '75 squad have that subsequent editions lacked?

Well, one thing that club *didn't* have was contract uncertainties. A year later, following the Messersmith decision (which began the free-agent era), every player in baseball was suddenly adrift on the brand-new, uncharted waters of free agency. Fisk, Lynn, and Burleson (unsigned at the start of the season, and therefore potentially eligible at its end) decided to stick their toes in those waters by holding out for new contracts.

The dissension this caused probably doomed the team, right there, and if it hadn't, the collapse of the pitching staff would have: though Tiant had another superb year, Bill Lee was injured in a brawl in New York and won only 5 games; Roger Moret (a 14-game winner and rising star) was traded for journeyman reliever Tom House because, apparently, no one in management could figure out how to relate to him; and closer Dick Drago was also traded, for reasons that remain unclear. And, too, everyone in the organization had to deal with the death of popular longtime owner Tom Yawkey.

OK, these were weights on the ball club, no question. But what about the other side of the coin? During my interviews for this book, I asked the players, coaches, and beat writers about the positives, too. What, outside of the talent, went into making the '75 edition such a great team? The answer: strong leadership, excellent work ethic, dedication to playing the game the right way, a no-nonsense attitude on the field, and, perhaps most important, a loose, jovial atmosphere in the clubhouse.

Same things as always, with any team, any sport. Clichés, even. Yet seemingly so difficult to bring together all at the same time. The Sox did it.

Carlton Fisk was a leader. He hated to lose and detested sloppy play. When he went to the mound for a conference, pitchers told me, it wasn't to say: "Maybe we should try a curveball on this guy." No, more likely the message he delivered was, "What kind of shit are you throwing up there today? Come *on!*" Rick Burleson was the same kind of player. He was hard-nosed and would get his whole 165 pounds right in your face if you slacked off. Nobody challenged the Rooster.

Carl Yastrzemski, by his own admission, was "not a rah-rah guy," but he led by example. He worked and worked. He brought everything he had to the park, every day, and left it on the field. He played hurt (for much of '75, he was trying to swing the bat with painfully pulled shoulder ligaments). And he showed how the little things bred success: throwing to the right base, hitting the cutoff man, decoying runners, knowing on whose arm you could score from second. At thirty-six he was the elder, an inspiration to the younger guys, continually proving that he could still bring the goods.

Bill Lee, though irreverent and often a distraction off the field, was all business between the lines. No one on the starting pitching staff was a fiercer competitor. And Dick Drago brought the same kind of fire out of the bullpen.

Then there was the superglue, the one person who held it all together: Luis Tiant. Everyone agrees that he was that glue.

According to Yastrzemski, the man who spanned the years between the '67 and '75 pennant-winning teams, everything changed when Luis arrived. Whatever tensions had existed in the clubhouse soon evaporated. A somber place was transformed into one of light and laughter. Losses were taken in stride instead of getting the players down.

Luis brought style. He arrived at the park every day dressed in his white linen suit and bright white sombrero, with a big and highly illegal Cuban cigar protruding from his mouth. He brought a commitment to winning, which he accomplished with greater regularity than anyone else; but he refused to give in to his bad outings, shrugging them off with something like, "No problem. I get them next time." He tormented the English language, and his accent was so thick that he was hard to understand even when he got the words right. Yet everyone knew what he was talking about when he would say, "Hey, cut out the *bool cheet*."

Suddenly, the Red Sox locker room became Prank City Central. The players, led by Tiant and Yastrzemski, began giving one another hotfoots;

pouring ice water on someone who was trying to nap or sitting on the toilet; short-sheeting hotel beds; putting itch powder in jockstraps; slicing in half a tie that a guy was wearing; cutting the trouser legs off of pants and the sleeves off of shirts, and slitting sport jackets up the middle of the back; and nailing pairs of shoes to the floor. Yaz wound up wearing his grungiest clothes to Fenway, so as to maximize his chances of having something to go home in.

Today, this seems like extremely childish behavior, wantonly destructive and personally hurtful. (Luis routinely called Yaz "Polack." When I asked him if anyone called Tiant "nigger" in return, he said, "No, never." There were limits.) How, for example, would the tailor who worked hard to make that suit feel if he knew it was being cut to ribbons by a "practical joker" with a razor blade? And what about the financial hardship on someone in the pre-big-bucks era who had to replace his clothes all the time?

It's easy to be disappointed, even shocked, that this sort of thing was condoned, although it helps to remember that a lot of ballplayers are still little more than kids when they make it to the Show. But there is another side to the story.

All the players I talked to believed that the clubhouse hijinks created a very positive atmosphere. They brought an added exuberance to winning and lightened the burden of defeat. The Red Sox were loose and happy. They had that great intangible: good "chemistry."

And they won. If that's your bottom line, then whatever helps get you there is probably worth it.

Fisk leads off the fourth by shooting a liner into the gap in left-center. Normally, this would be a double. But Gold Glover César Geronimo is on duty out there, and he plays the artificial turf perfectly, cutting the ball off before it can bounce past him. For once, the Sox choose not to be overly aggressive on the base paths, and the nonspeedy Pudge doesn't challenge Geronimo's arm. He pulls up at first with a single.

Fred Lynn works Norman to a 3–2 count, then foolishly hacks at ball four. Fortunately, he fouls it off. Doubly fortunately, he drills the next pitch to right. Fisk barely avoids being hit, and Boston has its first two batters on.

Petrocelli, who's been on a tear so far, pops to short. I groan. Another rally on the verge of slipping away.

Not. Because Dwight Evans, fresh off his game-tying ninth-inning homer the night before, is up. Evans swings at a low fastball and takes it to the opposite field with full power. Not even the fleet Geronimo will get this one. It's all the way to the wall. Fisk scores, Lynn scores, and Evans is waved around toward third. Concepcion takes the relay and makes his throw to third. It's in the dirt and skids past Pete Rose.

Fred Norman, who should be backing up the play, isn't. He seems confused and is just now making his way over there. Evans has a notion of trying for home. But the ball hits a section of fence in front of the dugout and bounces right back to Rose. Evans settles for having tied the game.

It doesn't stay that way for long. Rick Burleson is ready. The rally juice is flowing, and he absolutely cannot wait to swing the bat. He jumps on Norman's first pitch, a high fastball, and lines a clean single to left. Not only that, he doesn't even hesitate at first, just keeps on going toward second. The Sox are running on George Foster again. As well they should. Foster's throw is off line on the third-base side and has nothing on it. Burleson slides in safely.

The Sox lead, 3–2, and that's it for Norman. Pedro Borbon relieves.

Borbon does no better, even though the first batter he faces is Luis Tiant. Tiant, however, has discovered that his unsightly swing has some hits in it. He promptly lines a single to center. Burleson rounds third with a full head of steam, fully intending to score, but Don Zimmer forces him to put the brakes on, so hard that he jams his ankle. Foster they run on, Geronimo they don't, simple as that. Good thing. Geronimo's throw hits Johnny Bench right in the glove, on the fly. Burleson would've been meat.

Tiant, though, has a notion. With Perez near the mound playing cutoff, there's no one guarding first. Portly Luis makes a wide turn and bluffs toward second. Bench looks at him as if to say *you've got to be kidding*. He is. He retreats to the bag, chuckling to himself.

Runners at the corners, still only one out.

Beniquez is up. Borbon serves him a high, tight fastball that Juan tries to bail out on but can't. The ball strikes high on the bat and dribbles slowly toward first. Bench has no play. Perez, not a great fielder in the best of times, charges in and makes a game try at it, but he can't come up with the ball. Burleson scores, Tiant goes to second, and Beniquez is safe as Perez, perhaps a bit uncharitably, is charged with an error.

Doyle fouls to third, but Yaz, jammed with a fastball, hits a broken bat looper to right-center. Geronimo charges, then has to pull up when he realizes he isn't going to catch it. Still, it almost hops over his head. He jumps in the air and traps it at chest level. Tiant, running with two out, scores. Beniquez thinks about it, too, but Zim holds him as, yet again, they decline to test Geronimo.

When Fisk, who led off the inning, flies to left, the rally is finally over. As in Game 1, the Sox have bunched their runs into a single frame. Six there, five here. Now the question becomes: Can the struggling Tiant defend a three-run lead?

Early answer: it doesn't look like it. After a commercial break in which a pitchman with coiffed hair down over his ears tries to sell Sears Men's Store suits for sixty-nine dollars, Luis returns to the mound for the bottom of the fourth. He takes most of the breathing room his teammates gave him and gives it right back.

He looks strong at the outset, getting Perez on a strike three foul tip that Fisk holds onto ("That's luck," former catcher Garagiola says. "You can't practice that.") and Bench on a soft fly to left. Tiant has retired nine in a row, but the streak is about to end.

Oddly, the Reds rally with a string of soap bubbles rather than the hammer. First Foster hits a slow grounder to Denny Doyle's right that's just beyond the second baseman's comfortable fielding range. Doyle gloves it but is forced to pivot in the air and make an off-balance throw. It's up the right-field line from first, and it gets by Yastrzemski, sending Foster to second. George gets credit for an infield hit; Denny is charged with an error. OK, he probably should have held the ball. Yet the error came on the overthrow, and that could just as easily be laid on Yaz, who compounded the mistake by staying on the bag until it was too late to scoop up the errant toss.

It's only one base runner, though. Uh-huh. As if bad fortune never has a way of compounding itself.

Here's that guy again, Concepcion, who hit the Baltimore chop that tied the score in Game 2. Another day, another cheap hit. This time, the ball squibs off the end of his bat and flares out into short left-center. Lynn, Beniquez, and Burleson converge on the pop fly, and it falls in between them all. Foster scores; Concepcion winds up on second.

Jim Burton and Dick Pole begin warming up in the Boston bullpen.

Geronimo follows with another bloop hit, this one the opposite way, to left. Beniquez, unused to artificial grass, misplays it. At first he comes hard, thinking he has a chance to catch it. He runs out from under his hat, as he often does. Considering how much of his springy hair he's cramming up under there, it's surprising that he can keep it on at all.

By the time Juan realizes he doesn't have a prayer of making the play, he's overcommitted. The ball bounces high off the AstroTurf, goes over his head, and rolls all the way to the wall. Concepcion scores; Geronimo winds up on third. Because Beniquez never touched the ball, it's a straight triple, rather than a single and an error.

Terry Crowley comes up to pinch hit for the pitcher and Luis nails him, this time not taking any chances with his fielders. He strikes the hitter out on a nasty low fastball over the outside corner that Crowley waves at feebly as it goes by.

Tiant's pitching line for the home fourth will show that he yielded a single, a double, and a triple, and boy is that misleading. This is an inning that Luis could very easily have been out of without any damage at all. He must be muttering to himself. On a day in which he doesn't have his good stuff, neither is he getting one solitary break.

The Red Sox have a skinny one-run lead with five innings to go. Among all the world's certainties, this would appear to be one of the most certain: Luis Tiant will never be around at the end of this one. Well, we shall see.

Clay Carroll comes in to pitch the fifth for Cincinnati.

Fred Lynn, impatient at the plate, grounds out to second on the first pitch. Petrocelli also chases the first pitch, almost turning himself inside out in an attempt to go downtown. He swings and misses and later is called out on strikes.

Evans is up. With his scowl and clenched teeth, he looks like he wants to kill someone. And he nearly does. He hits a vicious line drive directly at Clay Carroll. Luckily, the impact point is six inches below Carroll's chin, because Clay doesn't even have time to get his glove in front of the ball. It ricochets off his chest and rebounds all the way into short right field.

Onto the field come the Reds' manager and trainer. But Carroll is having none of it. He stalks around the mound, avoiding them—playing tough guy, doing the never-let-the-opposition-know-you're-hurt thing. Finally he stands still long enough that the trainer can have a quick look at him. He's shaking his head at Anderson, though. As if to say, *no way, Sparky. It is the World Series, and you're gonna have to pry the ball from my cold, dead fingers before you get me out of* this *one.*

The manager leaves him in, and, after a couple of warm-up tosses, he induces Burleson to hit into a force play.

Looie's ordeal, protecting that 5–4 lead, now begins in earnest, and he starts off by doing the one thing he shouldn't. He walks leadoff hitter Rose.

Perhaps overcompensating, he then serves up a fat fastball to Ken Griffey. Griffey launches it toward the right-field fence. Evans retreats, stops at the warning track, drops his glove, half-turns, and looks up as if to watch it leave the park. It's going, going . . .

Just how good a fielder was Evans?

Good enough to win eight Gold Gloves, for one thing. That's a lot for an outfielder, considering that each year he's competing against all other outfielders, not just those who play the same position. Should there be a sudden glut of fine centerfielders, he could get squeezed out.

There is little doubt that he was the premier rightfielder of his day. He had one of the two or three most powerful throwing arms, and the most accurate. He played the different parks, including tough Fenway, to perfection. And he was smart, very smart.

Nobody, but nobody, ran on him.

I asked Evans's former manager, Don Zimmer, how he'd rate his old rightfielder. When I met him, Zim was getting ready to retire after a half-century in organized baseball. I wondered if he had the most World Series appearances by someone with more than one team. He went three times as a player with the Dodgers, in '75 as a coach with the Sox, and four times as a coach with the Joe Torre Yankees. Eight trips to the big dance with three different clubs (or four, if you differentiate between the Brooklyn and L.A. Dodgers). I didn't know if that was a record, and neither did he.

But Zim, who was rated by several of the players I interviewed as having one of the best minds in baseball, had a definite opinion about Dwight Evans.

"How good was he?" he said to me. "Let me ask *you* something. Do you know the difference between a ground-rule double and fan interference?"

I said that a ground-rule double was one that bounced into the stands and that it was interference if a fan touched the ball before it left the playing field.

"Right," he said. "So a guy gets two bases if the ball goes into the stands on its own. What's he get if the fan interferes?"

I wasn't sure. "A double?" I tried.

"Wrong," Zim said. "The home-plate umpire, with his best judgment, places the runners where he feels they oughtta be. So . . . when Boston was playing and there was fan interference on a ball hit down the right-field line, guess what?"

I shrugged, still not getting it.

Zim clapped his hands together. "The hitter would be awarded first. Period. Well, the other manager would always come storming out, screaming bloody murder. 'That's a double! Fan interference! Should be a double!' And the home-plate umpire would just smile and point to right field and say, 'Uh-uh. Not with that guy out there.' Meaning that unless you hit it over his head, Evans *always* held you to a single. If you tried to stretch it, he threw you out."

Finally I understood. It was one of those little games within the game that most fans never see. Even those who, like myself, have been watching for fifty years.

"So," I said, "when even the umpires were in your corner . . ."

Zimmer grinned. "You got it. *That* is how good he was," he said.

Soon, *everyone* who doesn't yet know will be made aware of just how fine a player this young man is. It will happen out there on the field, right before their eyes, so that there can be no doubt. But that moment still lies six days in the future.

Right now, it's a decoy. The youthful rightfielder, already showing a mature player's guile, is pretending that the ball is a home run—in the hope of selling the lie to Pete Rose, in the hope that Rose will start lazily toward second.

With a lesser luminary on first, he might succeed. Rose, however, is a pretty crafty guy himself, and he ain't having it. So, when Evans turns back toward the diamond at the last minute and puts the routine fly ball away, Pete has plenty of time to return to the bag before Dwight's throw arrives.

After Griffey, the last thing Luis wants is to go 3–0 on Joe Morgan. So he goes 3–0 on Morgan. That brings pitching coach Stan Williams to the mound. Tiant backs away from Williams, clearly upset, though it's impossible to tell if it's because the coach is suggesting he come out or because the ball/strike calls aren't going his way. Whatever the case, he stays in there and goes right after Morgan.

Little Joe, who probably always has the green light on 3-0, swings mightily and misses. Then he swings again, at a low pitch that might be ball four, and fouls it off. But then he walks. Two on, one out.

Fortunately, Tony Perez is up. Now normally, this is not good fortune; the future Hall of Famer isn't batting cleanup because he's a lousy RBI man. But it's a good deal here because (a) Tony is in a horrible slump, is in fact oh-for-the-Series, and (b) he's slow.

Sure enough, he hits another lazy grounder up the middle, and Doyle gets him at first. For the second time in the game, Perez has made a big out in the middle of a rally due to his lack of speed. The runners do move up, though.

That leaves first base open and, as announcer Joe Garagiola puts it, "I've got more chance of hitting in this spot than Johnny Bench." Meaning that the intentional walk is a given. Well, guess again. For reasons known only to the managerial mind, Darrell Johnson elects to let Luis fire away.

Tiant responds with a pitching clinic. His first offering is a fastball low and on the outside corner for a called strike. Then he goes high and away, followed by high and tight. Balls one and two. Next he challenges Bench with a fastball at the letters. Johnny takes a big cut and misses. Finally, Luis deals him a beautiful straight change. Bench is way out in front of it and flies out weakly to left.

Still 5-4.

Tiant is due to lead off the top of the sixth. Will Johnson hit for him? Nope. Luis bats for himself and is called out on an inside curveball that gets him hopping mad. You can almost hear him shouting at Dick Stello, *Hey, you don't give me that one when I'm pitching; why you calling it against me?*

Beniquez, first pitch swinging, grounds out to third. Doyle singles up the middle for Boston's eleventh hit of the game, but he's stranded when Yaz hacks at ball four on a 3-2 pitch and bounces out to the pitcher.

At the beginning of the home sixth, Rick Miller trots out to left field, replacing Beniquez. Juan, the converted shortstop, has already cost the Sox at least one run because of his inability to play the artificial surface correctly. Miller is an excellent defensive outfielder who doesn't hit much. So

Johnson is all but publicly announcing that, if the one-run lead is all he gets to work with, then he's going to try to win with it.

Back out goes Tiant, who is already at the hundred-pitch mark. He gets Foster and Concepcion on fly balls. Joe Garagiola announces that Simon and Garfunkel are going to be reunited Saturday night on NBC and muses, "Simon and Garfunkel. To me, they're Ruth and Gehrig." Tony Kubek wonders how much longer Tiant can go. Maybe not much. "But," he adds, "he certainly has the heart."

Just when Luis is thinking he might have an easy inning, he throws a sloooow hesitation curve to Geronimo with two strikes on the batter—a pretty cagey pitch. César waits and waits on it, though, and dumps a single into center.

Now, who to pinch hit for Clay Carroll? Sparky opts for Darrel Chaney, who batted .219 on the season, rather than Dan Driessen, a left-hander with some pop in his bat. Presumably, Anderson wants to save his power hitter for some more clutch situation, later in the game. Will Sparky sing *Je ne regrette rien* about the decision? Probably not, because Driessen will, in fact, never come up. This was his moment, and it goes by the boards.

Instead, the clearly overmatched Chaney takes his cuts against Tiant and strikes out on a tepid swing at a low, outside fastball. The portly one chugs back to the dugout with his lead intact.

For his pitching choice, Anderson doesn't hesitate to come right back with Rawley Eastwick, despite the reliever's poor performance in Game 3 (the ninth-inning homer Evans hit off him). Eastwick, his composure seemingly intact, retires the side in order on two grounders and a pop-up.

In the seventh, Tiant continues to feud with Stello, who fails to give him either of two low strikes against Rose. Luis is pissed. But he comes back to retire Rose on a liner to second and Griffey on a ground ball to the same spot.

Morgan is a problem, once again. You can't give Joe anything good to hit, especially clinging to such a slim lead. But the borderline pitches are all being called balls. And you certainly don't want to walk the guy; that's tantamount to giving up a double. Luis shakes his head as he falls behind 3–0 on what looks like a perfect strike at the knees. Now he's forced to come in with something hittable.

Joe, of course, is swinging away, and he gets a very big piece of this one. He hits a long fly to dead center. It's the hardest kind of ball on which to judge distance, the one right at you, and Fred Lynn initially takes a step in. But then he corrects and sprints back to the warning track, where he makes a pretty routine catch. Luis has his first one-two-three inning since the third and, as it turns out, his last.

The score is 5–4 after seven full.

Evans nearly plays hero again leading off the eighth, but Geronimo hauls in his long fly in deep center field, and Burleson grounds out. Had either of those two reached base, there's no way Tiant would have come to the plate. With two out and none on, though, Johnson sends his pitcher up there. He's going to pull as many innings out of the guy as he possibly can. Tiant, the accidental hitting star, grounds out, then trudges back to the mound.

It looks like he might actually, somehow, impossibly be getting stronger when he gets Perez on a fly ball to Miller and strikes out Johnny Bench on three pitches. But Foster rips a single up the middle. Darrell Johnson is poised on the dugout steps, and if a left-hander were coming up he'd probably go to the bullpen. But it's righty Concepcion. Johnson stays where he is, and Davy flies out to shallow right.

One inning to go.

It'd be nice if the Sox could tack on an insurance run or two, but it ain't gonna happen. Eastwick is cruising, pitching like the stopper he's been all year. He gets Miller and Doyle on easy ground balls to Morgan. Yaz works him a little, finally drawing a walk on the 3–2 pitch. But Fisk pops to Concepcion in short left field and now, improbably, we're heading for the bottom of the ninth with the score stuck at 5–4.

Who will pitch it? Johnson has plenty of choices. His closer, Drago, hasn't pitched since Game 2. He's ready. Or, with the left-handed Geronimo set to lead off, he could bring in one of his lefties, Burton or Moret, to face him, then make another change depending on both the outcome of that at-bat and who Anderson chooses to hit for the pitcher.

A modern manager would take one or the other of these options. Most would likely send their closer out to close. Let him start the inning with no one on and go flat out. Of course, nobody managing today would have stuck with Tiant this long in the first place. That kind of confidence disappeared from the scene years ago.

Darrell Johnson is managing in a different era, true enough. Even so, when he elects to have Luis Tiant try to finish the game, it's astonishing.

When I interviewed Johnson, he admitted that he "rassled with taking Luis out." Why didn't he? Because "Tiant had been super in the toughest part of the game, and that's where we were. I just thought, 'You know, the man's too good. I'm not gonna take him out.'"

And when I asked Don Zimmer if he might've questioned Johnson's judgment, Zim shook his head and said, "No way. I always said that if Luis got you to the ninth, you could sit your bullpen down. He knew how to finish a game."

I, of course, don't have the benefit of access to the coach's or manager's mind at the time. I have only the edge of my seat for company. But I try to think positive. Well, I consider, Luis *has* looked a little stronger the past two innings, so maybe the ninth will go easily for him?

Fuggedaboudit.

Geronimo comes up first, Geronimo who has owned Tiant on this night, Geronimo whom Luis has not gotten out since the second inning. And he doesn't get him here. César jumps on the first pitch and singles to right.

Now what?

For his part, Sparky decides to play the percentages, move the runner up, try to at least tie the game and send it into extra innings. And of course he nominates his designated bunter Ed Armbrister for the job. Armbrister. Already! Less than twenty-four hours removed from the raging controversy of Game 3's tenth inning. To bunt. *Again!*

I'm squirming in my seat, as is every sad inhabitant of Red Sox Nation. No good can possibly come of this.

Johnson's decision time. He stays with Tiant.

And the play unfolds uneventfully. Armbrister pushes a bunt toward first. Tiant fields it and takes the sure out, getting the batter. Ed doesn't even look like he's trying very hard to beat the throw. All very civilized.

The tension level drops a hair. But there's still that tying run perched at second. Geronimo, who has excellent speed. With the top of the order coming up and one out. Only Pete Rose, Ken Griffey, and Joe Morgan.

Tiant falls behind in the count on Rose. Maybe it's intentional, with first base open. Give Rose the base, pitch to Griffey. Apparently not, though, because Johnson chooses this moment to go talk to his pitcher. He seems to have decided, against the book, to pitch to Pete.

Tiant, Johnson, Burleson, and Fisk gather at the mound. Johnson is wearing a lapel mike, in order to record a sound track for the film the team is making of the game. So, years later, you can eavesdrop on the ensuing conversation. It turns out to be rather undramatic.

"What do you guys think?" Johnson says. "I got a left-hander down here, Luis. Can you get him?" "Him" presumably referring to Rose, not the reliever.

Tiant mutters something in either Spanish or English so heavily accented it's indecipherable. Johnson probably doesn't understand a word of it. The gist is plain, though. Luis is saying, *Yeah, I got gas left in the tank.* But how much of it could he possibly have? His arm must be howling in pain.

"OK," Johnson says, "OK. You get right after him. If that ball comes back to you, make sure of one out. Now get after him good. Come on."

Johnson walks away.

When I talked with him, I asked Darrell if Tiant's words, whatever they were, convinced him to leave his pitcher in.

"No," Johnson answered emphatically. "I *never* went to the mound without knowing what I was going to do beforehand. I learned that from my first manager, Rogers Hornsby. He never even left the dugout. He'd just whistle out to the bullpen for a pitching change." He laughed. "He didn't want the pitcher trying to talk him out of the decision.

"But I always had a purpose to going out there. So when I asked Luis if he could get the next guy and he said yeah, my purpose was to get him pumped up a little, to get the adrenaline flowing. That was my goal. It helps guys sometimes if they think they're part of the decision. I was never gonna take him out, though."

Perhaps Tiant now decides to pitch around Rose on his own, perhaps not. But walk him he does. If semi-intentional, it's not a bad move. It sets up the potential game-ending double play and takes the bat out of the hands of a very dangerous hitter. On the other hand, both Griffey and Morgan are very fast and, as lefties, start out closer to first. They don't hit into many double plays.

In any event, if he did it purposefully it's contrary to what his manager wanted. And if he didn't, his control may be slipping. It's clearly time for Luis to get the hook. He's struggled all night, and now there are two hard-hitting left-handers coming up. No-brainer. Put a fresh arm out there.

But, no. Incredibly, Johnson *still* sticks with his starter.

And Griffey immediately makes him look like a fool. Almost. Griffey smashes one to dead center field. It's off the wall, for sure. Two runs score,

Reds win. Except . . . that's not the way it happens. Fred Lynn, with a terrific jump, goes back, goes back, and, running flat out now, makes a gorgeous over-the-shoulder catch in the middle of the warning track. The flabbergasted runners, halfway to home, have to retreat to second and first with no chance to tag up and advance.

It's down to the one person you'd most want to have hitting in this situation (if you're a Reds fan): Joe Morgan.

"*That* was the biggest battle I had mentally in the whole thing," Darrell Johnson told me. "Joe Morgan up there with two out. But I decided to stay with my man."

Tiant works slowly, carefully to Morgan. After all, he'd probably rather face the next batter, right-handed oh-fer-the-Series Tony Perez, with just one out to get. Then, as Luis delivers his 163rd pitch of the evening, the Reds make a crucial mistake. Geronimo lights out for third!

Recall how Morgan said that he hates to have base runners take off when he's up, because it adversely affects his concentration. Consider, too, that Geronimo has very little to gain by stealing the base. True, if he succeeds he'll be set up to score the tying run on an error or an infield hit. But he's already in scoring position on just about any base hit that Morgan delivers, as long as it gets to the outfield. And the risks are that he could get thrown out, or he could mess with Little Joe's at-bat.

On balance, with two out in the ninth and the batter focusing as fiercely as he ever has in his life, this is not a wise move.

Now look at the pitch as it heads toward the plate, from Morgan's point of view. Right there, streaking across his field of vision as he attempts to pick up the rotation on the ball, is Geronimo. Joe has had no indication from the third-base coach that this is supposed to be happening. Did he miss a sign? Is he supposed to take the pitch? If not, does the runner distract the batter by taking action on his own?

"I always felt that Morgan was distracted," Darrell Johnson told me. "We knew he had a great knowledge of the strike zone, but there he went and chased a bad high fastball. Geronimo should never have done that."

Morgan swings, and his swing is the slightest bit off, just under the ball instead of squarely on it. The resultant pop-up soars high into the air and then falls back and settles gently into Carl Yastrzemski's glove.

It's over. Two hours, fifty-two minutes of burning, arm-deadening hell—163 pitches drawn from a seemingly bottomless well of skill and cunning and courage. Luis Tiant has another complete-game victory. Sox fans fall back into their seats, drained, savoring every second. Luis has salvaged a win in Cincinnati. Now, no matter what happens tomorrow, the Series will return to Fenway. We have the momentum. We can win.

Forget for a moment that Luis may have left everything he has out on the field tonight, that he may be unable to answer the bell for the seventh game, if there is one, just four days from now. Give some appreciation instead to his amazing performance. Tiant has given up two runs in the first inning, two more in the fourth. He's been touched for nine hits and has yielded four bases on balls. He's put men on base in each of the final five innings save the seventh and has stranded eight runners overall. He's had every borderline pitch called against him and hasn't received the support of a single double play.

And still, he's finished what he started.

It's a feat for the ages, one that will remain frozen in print and on videotape, never to be repeated. *Nobody* is allowed to throw 163 pitches anymore. *Nobody* struggles that deep into a game without yielding to a middle reliever. *No* team makes it to the World Series these days without having a stopper who automatically pitches the ninth if the score is even remotely close.

We don't know any of that yet. For now, mobbed by his running, leaping, bounding teammates, Tiant is a hero. And Darrell Johnson, who for the first and last time in the Series has thrown the book of baseball out the window and managed strictly from the gut, is a genius.

It remains to be seen how long the glow will last.

DAY FIVE

Interregnum

N othing exists in a historical vacuum. There is always context. Because 1975 marked the end of the war in Vietnam, the most divisive foreign entanglement in U.S. history, it seems appropriate to take a moment to examine the relationship of major league baseball to that conflict.

Reflect first upon the musings of David James Duncan, whose narrator speaks the following words in his wonderful (sort of a baseball) novel *The Brothers K*:

A pro contract is a kind of vow: a man agrees, in signing it, that he will perform as though his personal life, his family, his non-baseball hopes and needs do not exist. He is paid to aspire to purity. For the duration of every game he has not only to behave but really to feel that the ballpark is the entire world: his body is his instrument, so any lack of feeling will soon be reflected in his play. Everett [narrator's brother] has poked fun at the analogy, but the purity of commitment really isn't much different than that of the Hinayana monks whom Peter [another brother] so admired, they with their one robe, one bowl, one icon; ballplayers with their uniforms, their bats, their gloves.

But purity has a brutal side. Sometimes a strikeout means that the slugger's girlfriend just ran off with the UPS driver. Sometimes a muffed ground ball means that the shortstop's baby daughter has a pain in her head that won't go away. And handicapping is for amateur golfers, not ballplayers. Pitchers don't ease off on the cleanup hitter because of the lumps just discovered in his wife's breast. Baseball is not life. It is a fiction, a metaphor. And a ballplayer is a man who agrees to uphold that metaphor as though lives were at stake.

Perhaps they are. I cherish a theory I once heard propounded by G. Q. Durham [a fictional character who appears to be the voice of the author] that professional baseball is inherently antiwar. The most overlooked cause of war, his theory runs, is that it's so damned interesting. It takes hard effort, skill, love and a little luck to make times of peace consistently interesting. About all it takes to make war interesting is a life. The appeal of trying to kill others without being killed yourself . . . is that it brings suspense, terror, honor, disgrace, rage, tragedy, treachery and occasionally even heroism within range of guys who, in times of peace, might lead lives of unmitigated blandness. But baseball, he says, is one activity that is able to generate suspense and excitement on a national scale, just like war. And baseball can only be played in peace. Hence G. Q.'s thesis that pro ballplayers—little as some of them may want to hear it—are basically just a bunch of unusually well-coordinated guys working hard and artfully to prevent wars, by making peace more interesting.

A nice little irony in his theory: even warlike ballplayers fight for peace by making it more interesting . . . [Ty Cobb, e.g.] was a man who upheld the metaphor so long and ferociously that he never did reenter any sort of outside world: 'til the day he died. Cobb defined himself purely in terms of a baseball world—a world in which war never has and never shall exist.

Interesting thoughts, are they not?

Now consider this: in the course of researching this book, I began to wonder who among major league ballplayers of the era had served in Vietnam. So I looked into it. And I looked. And I enlisted the aid of some SABR (Society for American Baseball Research) members with vast databases devoted to the sport. And I asked every member of the '75 Red Sox team whom I interviewed.

This is what we all came up with: zero. To the very best of my knowledge—and if I'm mistaken, please write and correct me—not a single player was ever drafted out of the major leagues and sent to Southeast Asia. Nor did many minor leaguers go, especially if they were highly regarded prospects.

As writer and former Phillies pitcher Larry Colton put it in his book *Goat Brothers*, if you wanted out of the war, "organized baseball was the safest place in the country to be."

This is not to say that no Vietnam vets ever made it to the Show. I've been informed that Al Bumbry was one such (and a decorated one), as were Garry Maddox and Bobby Jones. Bill Campbell and Ed Figueroa have also been suggested. And there are undoubtedly others.

Some professional players also died over there. Minor leaguers Udell Chambers and Charles Chase were killed in action in 1968, Eddie Glinnen in 1970.

Others were inducted and for one reason or another not sent to fight. Boston's Doug Griffin is in this category. He told me that after being drafted he volunteered for submarine service, served eighteen months at Pearl Harbor, played some ball, and was discharged a short time before his unit shipped out for Asia.

This list, however, is not lengthy. And all of the men on it were drafted and served their tours of duty *before* the start of their major league careers. My assertion, that no *active* big leaguer became a veteran, stands.

So what happened to all this potential cannon fodder, all those physically gifted young men who came of draft age during the prime call-up years? The answer—despite David Duncan's argument that baseball is inherently antiwar, which means that the military should have a vested interest in sabotaging the game's stability—appears to be that there was a cozy little "understanding" between MLB and the Pentagon.

Baseball took care of its own, and the government cooperated. Larry Colton claims in his book that the front office of every major league team in those days had someone whose assignment was to make sure the talent in which the club had invested didn't get lost to war. I haven't been able to verify that allegation. But, while I'm not particularly inclined to doubt it, it hardly matters. Even if no one person was working under that specific job description, *somebody*—the general manager, one of his close associates, whoever—was busting his butt to make it happen.

Thus the players, without their having to lift a finger, were commonly shunted into either the reserves or the National Guard, options not generally open to members of the socioeconomic groups from which most soldiers were drawn. In fact, those alternatives were supposed to be closed to *anyone* who had received the dreaded letter that began, "Greetings." Before you were drafted, you could volunteer for the reserves or Guard; once you'd been ordered to your physical, you couldn't. (This is obvious, isn't it? If you could opt out afterward, nearly everyone would have done it, leaving no troops for the front lines.) So, if you passed the physical, in you went. Period. That was the rule.

The rules, of course, did not apply equally to everyone. The children of wealth and privilege enjoyed some advantages over the rest of the field. Former vice president Dan Quayle is perhaps the most notorious example of a well-connected fellow who managed to slip into the Guard even though his number had come up.

Many ballplayers, though they may not have shared the blue of blood, fared as well as the future politicians. Bernie Carbo, for example, was informed by the Reds that all he had to do was call them when he "got the paperwork," which he did. Thus, even though he had his induction notice in hand, he was told, "Come to Cincinnati and you'll be in the reserves." And presto, he was.

One of the nice things was that you didn't even have to enlist in a unit from your home state. Larry Colton served in Nevada, which he had never visited prior to his posting there. Boston's Bill Lee, from California, spent two weeks slogging through the Louisiana swamps each summer.

Other players, like their counterparts elsewhere, found their way into one or another type of deferment. Some got married and, when that ceased to work, had kids. Some, like Carl Yastrzemski (who was twenty-six when the buildup started in '65), were old enough that they never got called. Some got lucky. The Red Sox' Fred Lynn became eligible for the draft after the installation of the lottery; he had a high number. And, difficult as it may be to believe about those pursuing a career in athletics, there were even some who got excused because they failed their physicals. Jim Willoughby, one of the anchors of the '75 Sox bullpen, had a bum knee that didn't pass muster.

Whatever. The simple truth is that baseball was indeed the place to be if you wanted to live. Those with talent rarely went to war. Those who had already made it to the Show never did.

Today, the war in Vietnam is fast fading from our collective consciousness. We presently have a sitting president and vice president who both worked the system to avoid active duty, as did the president before them. Their records didn't prevent Bush or Cheney or Clinton from being elected to the highest offices in the land. Nor should it have; they only followed the same path as millions of their peers. And if these very prominent men have escaped being tarnished by their distinct lack of willingness to fight for their country, then it would hardly be fair to throw stones at the professional baseball players who used similar mechanisms to protect their own skins. I'm not about to cast aspersions on one group that behaved no differently from dozens of others. Guys do what they gotta do.

Nevertheless . . .

Tens of thousands of Americans did die. Very few of them were like Al Gore, well-off kids who felt honor bound to enlist despite their awareness of the kinds of avoidance procedures available to politicians' sons, doctors- and lawyers-to-be, and athletes with ninety-five-mile-an-hour fastballs. It's a harsh reality that begs us to be judgmental, yet to do so would be to open a jar of poison that's best left closed.

Better that, as we relive the joy of this great series of games, we also pause for a moment to remember one simple thing: other boys their age fought and died so that these boys, the boys of October, could play.

At this point, after the high tension of the previous four games, the fans need a break.

Baseball, of course, is not the only game in town. A Boston resident, should he or she be suffering emotional burnout or simply choose to ignore the struggle between the Reds and Red Sox, has plenty of alternative activities to select from.

There's shopping, for example. Duddy's Radial Tire Center is selling snow tires for the upcoming winter season, starting at $19.95. Filene's has wide flare jeans (which are still called *dungarees*) for $3.99, leather-look vinyl handbags for $2.99, and hand-embroidered all-cotton blouse tops for $4.99. If the larder is bare, you can hop on over to the Capitol Supermarket and cash in your ten-cents-off coupon on a box of new Freakies Cereal and, while there, stock up on butternut squash for eight cents a pound, cod fillets for $1.29 per pound, and quart jars of Vlasic pickle chips for fifty-nine cents.

If you just feel like driving around, National will rent you a Vega for $13.95 a day, unlimited mileage.

Driving stress you out? Try the recipe in the *Boston Globe* for a new drink called the Los Angeles, a "tall cool mixture of Crème de Banana,

Triple Sec, lemon juice, pineapple juice and that lovely, lovely whisky, Early Times."

You can also go down to Boston Garden and buy your tickets for the Celtics' home opener (introducing their "newest All-Star, Charlie Scott") against the Houston Rockets just eight days hence. If you want the really good seats (priced at $9 and $7.50), tough luck; they're all sold out. But tickets remain at $7, $6, $5, and, somewhere up under the rafters, $3.50.

And there's always the movies: Sidney Poitier, Bill Cosby, and Jimmie Walker star in *Let's Do It Again*, Al Pacino in *Dog Day Afternoon*. Cult classic *A Boy and His Dog* draws the young and hip; pointy-headed intellectuals can catch a return engagement of *The Lion in Winter*; and, down in the Combat Zone, the raincoat crowd is filing in to see a double bill featuring ultra-skinny Marilyn Chambers and behemoth-breasted Chesty Morgan ("Two Unique Examples of Womanhood!!").

Those who stick with baseball are treated to Game 5 of the World Series although, as is often the case in these days, if you want to spend your evening with both a movie *and* a ball game, there is nothing stopping you. And you don't even need TiVo. You can catch a film at six, leave for home ninety minutes later, grab a bite to eat, turn on the TV at eight-thirty, watch the entire game, and still be in bed by eleven.

Movies are shorter in 1975. Ball games are faster. If your entertainment goal is variety in manageable bursts, these are the glory days. But, because this book is not about Hollywood, I have no desire to ponder whether the transition from the hour-and-a-half film to the two-hour version has been a good thing. Rather, I want to concentrate on the other half of the equation, and the seemingly eternal question: is baseball too slow?

Well, at the opening of the twenty-first century, nine-inning baseball games are almost never completed in fewer than three hours and often stretch closer to four. Compare that to the lengths of the 1975 World Series games. Game 1—2 hours, 27 minutes. Game 2—2:38. Game 3—3:03. Game 4—2:52. And these weren't games in which runs were not scored. They were 6–0, 3–2, 6–5, and 5–4. Game 3 ran a little long because it went ten innings.

Game 5 is no exception. It is played in two hours, twenty-three minutes, just under the average for the Series. From the Red Sox point of view, it is the least interesting game between the two teams. It serves primarily

Old Stoneface, Sox manager Darrell Johnson, sports a rare smile as he greets Sparky
Anderson. (WIDEWORLD)

The Red Sox coaching staff (left to right): Don Bryant, John Pesky, Darrell Johnson,
Stan Williams, Eddie Popowski, and Don Zimmer (PHOTO FROM BOB MAYHALL AT
SPORTING NEWS)

Game 1: Dwight Evans, trying to score from second in the first inning on a ground ball off Joe Morgan's glove, is thrown out at home by Davy Concepcion.
(Bettman/Corbis)

The Sox Golden Boy: American League Rookie of the Year and MVP winner Fred Lynn
(Bettman/Corbis)

Pudge Fisk connects for a home run off Gary Nolan in the second inning of Game 3. (Bettman/Corbis)

Bill Lee, tabbed as flaky by the press for his unconventional off-field behavior, was all business between the lines. (BETTMAN/CORBIS)

Don Gullett, Sparky Anderson's surefire future Hall of Famer, brings some of his 95-mph heat. (BETTMAN/CORBIS)

Last chance for the captain: thirty-six-year-old Carl Yastrzemski singles home a run in the fourth inning of Game 4. (WIDEWORLD)

The Master of Deception: Peerless Luis Tiant goes for his third victory of the Series in Game 6. (BETTMAN/CORBIS)

Rico Petrocelli (number 6) congratulates Lynn, Fisk, and Yaz after Lynn's three-run homer in the first inning of Game 6. (BETTMAN/CORBIS)

Bernie Carbo jumps for joy after his pinch-hit, three-run homer tied the score in the eighth inning of Game 6. (BETTMAN/CORBIS)

The magic moment: Carlton Fisk wills his long fly ball to stay fair in the twelfth inning of incomparable Game 6. (WIDEWORLD)

It's a mob scene as Fisk jumps on home plate after hitting the dramatic, game-winning homer that ended Game 6 at thirty-five minutes past midnight. (WIDEWORLD)

Game 7: Yaz rips a single to right off Gullett in the third inning, driving in the first run of the finale. (BETTMAN/CORBIS)

Fisk shows the ball after leaning into the stands to catch Bench's foul pop, ending the top of the seventh inning of Game 7 with the bases loaded. (BETTMAN/CORBIS)

Pete Rose dives into third ahead of the tag in the ninth inning of Game 7, after Joe Morgan has driven in Ken Griffey with the go-ahead run. (WIDEWORLD)

The Cincinnati Reds celebrate their hard-earned victory. (WIDEWORLD)

to set the stage for the drama of Games 6 and 7, and so I shall recap it only briefly.

The primary difference between the Reds and Red Sox at this point is their respective pitching rotations. With the Reds up a game after three, playing at home, Darrell Johnson was looking at almost certain elimination if his team lost Game 4. So he was forced to pitch his ace, Luis Tiant, on only three days' rest. Luis responded with the gutty win, but he threw so many pitches that it might be a goodly while before he's ready again.

Sparky Anderson, by contrast, had the luxury of a game in hand and so could give his pitchers at least four days off between starts. Thus is well-rested ace Don Gullett primed and ready for Game 5, and itching to atone for his on-again, off-again performance in Game 1.

Darrell could come back with Bill Lee, who pitched magnificently in Game 2. But that would mean throwing another guy out there on three days' rest. Besides, Lee's style is far less suited to Riverfront Stadium than to Fenway. Lee gets a lot of ground balls. That's great on natural turf, not as good on the artificial surface, where grounders are apt to take high hops or scoot quickly through the infield. So Johnson has to toss a coin between Reggie Cleveland and Rogelio (Roger) Moret.

Though Reggie is only a year older than Roger, he's more the veteran, with five full seasons in the bigs vs. Moret's three. He's also faced the Reds in the past, during his years with the St. Louis Cardinals. And he's put up decent numbers in '75, with 13 wins against 9 losses, some of the victories big ones down the stretch. On the downside, his ERA is a marginal 4.43, he yields a hit an inning, and his walk/strikeout ratio is high.

Moret is a brilliant young talent. He's gone 14–3, with an ERA of 3.60. He has a live fastball that can be overpowering when it's on. After he moved into the starting rotation, the team went from good to great. He can be erratic, however, and his control is even worse than Reggie's; he gives up a walk for every strikeout.

Cleveland is a right-hander and Moret a southpaw, but that doesn't enter into the equation. Cincinnati has about as balanced a lineup as you can have: four righties, three lefties, and one switch hitter.

When I asked Darrell Johnson what went into his decision regarding his Game 5 starter, he couldn't remember who it was. Reggie Cleveland, I told him. That didn't help. "I don't know why I went with Cleveland," he said.

"I made all of my decisions based on what I thought was our best matchup. So that's what I must have thought."

When I interviewed Roger in 2002, I asked if he recalled being passed over. He sure did. "Yeah," he said, "they picked that fat guy instead of me." Then he laughed. He made the remark good-naturedly, in a teasing rather than an insulting way. He held nothing against Reggie Cleveland, who he hastened to add was a "good pitcher," yet he still believed that that was his game to pitch. He felt he'd earned it with his regular-season performance.

"I was ready," he said. "I could've beaten that team."

This is the only chance Roger Moret will have in his life to start a World Series game, and he won't get it. He's exiled to sulk in the bullpen while Cleveland goes out to oppose Gullett. Which, as it turns out, is a mighty thankless task. The night is cold, but Gullett is red hot.

As in three of the four games so far, the Red Sox score first, right in the opening inning. Denny Doyle triples with one down and scores on a Yastrzemski sacrifice fly; 1–0. And then Gullett slams the door with a big bang. The next fifteen Boston batters are retired in order. Fifteen in a row, before Juan Beniquez draws a harmless two-out walk in the sixth. Gullett then gets ten of the next eleven, yielding only an eighth-inning single to Dwight Evans. He has a 2-hitter with two down in the bottom of the ninth.

For his part, Reggie Cleveland doesn't do all that badly. He shuts the Reds out for the first three innings before giving up a solo home run in the fourth. Ominously, the homer is by Tony Perez, hitherto hitless in fifteen at-bats in the Series. He's the last person the Sox want to see heat up. But heat up he does.

Cleveland gives up another run in the fifth when the opposing pitcher singles and comes home on Pete Rose's double. Still, only two runs to the mighty Reds in five innings . . . not too shabby. Then in the sixth the roof falls in. Joe Morgan walks after three very close pitches, none of which goes Reggie's way. He's fuming at the home-plate umpire and now has to deal with Little Joe dancing off first. He throws over there perhaps seventeen times. His concentration presumably in tatters, he yields a single to Johnny Bench and then the clincher, a 3-run homer to Perez.

That's it for Cleveland and, for all practical purposes, for the Sox. Darrell Johnson seems to sense this, too. After getting two good innings out of reliever Jim Willoughby, he goes to the end of the bullpen bench and in the eighth calls Dick Pole and Diego Segui, both of them making their first and last appearance in the Series. Pole gives up a run on no hits; Segui gets all three batters he faces.

In the field, Boston continues its fine defensive play. Burleson, for example, makes a spectacular leaping catch of Joe Morgan's liner in the seventh, to start an inning-ending double play.

But it's wasted, even though Gullett suddenly falters with two out and nobody on in the top of the ninth. Yastrzemski, Fisk, and Lynn all reach him for base hits, with one run scoring. Sparky, though, is not wedded to the idea of Gullett getting the complete-game victory. Without hesitation, he goes to his bullpen stalwart, Rawley Eastwick, who immediately strikes out Petrocelli to end the game.

The Reds win and go up three games to two. With the Series now moving back to the Hub, the prospect of the Sox winning out at friendly Fenway would seem to be well within the range of possibility. Yet there's not room for a whole lot of optimism. Bill Lee is scheduled to pitch Game 6 on the 18th, and he's had plenty of rest. Well and good. But for Game 7 on the 19th? Can Tiant come back only four days after he threw 163 pitches and expect to be at all effective?

Idle speculation, as it turns out, because the weather gods intervene. The skies over Boston open up, and it rains for three days straight. Instead of being played on the 18th, Game 6 has been pushed forward to the 21st, giving the two managers time to set their pitching matchups for the big finale.

The Sox might have to face Gullett again, if the Series is extended to seven, a prospect that is very pleasing to Sparky Anderson. Boston has now seen the real Don Gullett, Anderson says, the guy who's a surefire Hall of Famer.

When Bill Lee hears that Sparky is once again beating the Cooperstown drum for his pitcher with the five-year major league career, he replies in his own fashion. "Yeah," he says, "Gullett's going to the Hall of Fame and I'm going to the Eliot Lounge [a Boston watering hole favored by athletes]."

Now, to return to the question I posed earlier about the changed pace of baseball.

Clearly, the game no longer has the grip on the public imagination that it once did. Yet it does endure and remains very popular despite the astonishing proliferation of competitive entertainment options we've witnessed in recent years. Which isn't to say that it might not need a bit of a face-lift.

There are obvious problems, most notably the escalating salaries that have rocketed the average major leaguer's annual pay from around $50,000 per year in 1975 to almost $2.4 million today. That's a forty-eight-fold increase, which is, um, a *tad* more than general inflation. Think about this: if the inflation rate for consumer goods had kept pace with that of player salaries, here's what you'd be paying for some of the items mentioned earlier in the chapter: one tire—$958; pair of jeans—$192; jar of pickles—$28; one-day car rental—$670. (And salaries *adjusted* for inflation? Nah, you don't want to know.)

The inevitable result has been to run up ball game ticket prices. Not as fast as salaries, OK. But still, a family evening at Fenway is now beyond the reach of most of the working people who used to constitute the bedrock of fan support.

This situation, however, will eventually be resolved by market dynamics. When the customers stop coming to the park, salaries (and ticket prices) will de-escalate. The market will also deal, albeit harshly, with perennially noncompetitive teams that no one wants to pay to see. They'll go out of business. Sorry.

Of course, a system of revenue sharing between the major and minor media centers and/or some form of salary cap would help with both issues, but whether either will happen remains to be seen.

Revising the length of the season should also receive some consideration. If ownership wants to preserve the current playoff setup because of the revenue generated, then so be it. Just shorten the season, guys. Even a return to the old 154-game standard would make a big difference. Baseball should not be played in November. End of story.

But in a sense these are all peripheral issues. Let's leave them to union/management negotiations and direct our attention to the play itself. Might we identify some things there that are worth fiddling with?

After meditating on the brisk, exciting pace of the first five games of the 1975 Series and how markedly it differs from the contemporary version, I picked up Bill James's *Historical Baseball Abstract*. In it, he tackles what's wrong with baseball as it's currently constituted, from a strictly mechanical viewpoint, and what could be done to fix it. (The Red Sox, let it be noted, had the good sense to hire James in late 2002 to perform statistical talent evaluations for them.)

I found that his take was quite similar to mine. One of the primary difficulties, we agree, is that a game that is so engrossing to us can be perceived as glacially slow by so many others. Why is this? The easy answer, as it's usually presented in the press, is that the games are too long. But, as James insightfully points out, that isn't really the problem. It's not the length of the games per se, it's that there's too much time when *nothing is happening*. And that's not built into the game itself.

Right on. Taking in a ball game is a lot like watching a movie. You can sit enrapt for three hours if what you see on the screen is continuously compelling, whereas a bad ninety-minute film will have you squirming, looking at your watch, and taking unnecessary rest room breaks.

James proceeds to compare baseball with college basketball, which both he and I also love. He points out that the sport has evolved over the years, with changes constantly being instituted as needed, in order to preserve the beauty and original intent of the game, as well as to maximize fan interest (which may amount to the same thing). Example: when Dean Smith's Four Corners "offense" caused excruciatingly boring games, it had to go. It wasn't necessary to outlaw Smith's strategy. All the NCAA had to do was add a shot clock. Then ball-possession rules were changed so that even milking the clock became more difficult. Simple as that, the game evolved, its flow was restored, and the Four Corners was blessedly buried forever.

Baseball's powers-that-be, however, have a more slavish devotion to the rules, as handed down through the generations. And when they do tinker, it's generally in large ways and to the detriment of the game: interleague play, the wild card, the designated hitter. These are hardly inspired innovations. Lowering the pitcher's mound and shrinking the strike zone also have not helped.

Today, we are too frequently offered contests that merely crawl along, with a lot of nothing sandwiched around a couple of home runs; .230 hitters swing for the fences (and all too frequently reach them), pitchers strive for high radar gun readings above all else, and defensive skills are relegated to the back burner. The results are predictable. Strikeouts are up, and homers are up. These may seem to be good things, or at least neutral, but they're not. Strikeouts mean that the other eight guys on the field are picking their noses. And home runs, which used to be exciting when they were relatively rare, are much less so when almost everyone is a threat to hit one and when the offense is pretty much based around them.

This represents a basic change in baseball attitude. Why bother to scratch and claw to manufacture a run—by, say, working hard to draw a walk, then executing a hit-and-run, and finally bringing the man home with a groundout to the right side—when the next seven guys in the lineup can achieve the same result with one swing of the bat? Why, indeed? Well, how about because it's from just such niceties that the maximum enjoyment of baseball derives.

So, perhaps the rule makers—and the lack of some strong, central governing body is definitely a major part of the problem here—are looking in all the wrong places. If the question is simply how to move the game along while returning to a more exciting form of play, then the answer may lie in a few subtle adjustments, swatting the fly with that floppy plastic thing instead of a lead pipe.

First, as I indicated previously, one of the nice things about reviewing the '75 Series was the discovery of how little time was wasted between innings. This was due to the network running only two or three thirty-second ads, to a finite number of replays, and, as is the case in college basketball, to the teams being ready to play as soon as the station break is over.

The latter two could be easily implemented by putting the umpire back in charge of controlling the pace, as he was back in the days when games *had* to be completed before nightfall. Once ads are finished, he could tell the teams to "play ball" and require that they be ready to do so.

(Reducing the sheer volume of advertising is not play-related, and it's a tougher nut to crack. But Bill James speculates that if the number of ads was curtailed a bit, thereby increasing their scarcity, advertisers would be willing to pay more for the resultant greater effectiveness. There might thus be no net loss of revenue. I don't know about this, but it seems worth a shot. Aren't the stations having trouble filling all their ad spots now? That would appear to be the case, based on how many ads are repeated over and over as the game goes on.)

Second, again as I pointed out before, in '75 at-bats were considerably shorter because the batter stepped out far less frequently than he does now, when it happens on nearly every pitch. This is a problem easily solved by making the umpire a timekeeper. James comes to the rescue here by reminding us that the batter cannot call time-out, only the umpire can. The batter can *ask* for time, but the umpire must *grant* it. Just stop granting it, except when obviously necessary—when the batter fouls a ball off his foot, for instance, or a spectator throws a beer can at his head. Otherwise, when the hitter enters the box, he stays there. Period.

Likewise with the pitcher. Construct some sort of "no-dawdling" rule, and give the umpires a means of enforcing it.

These are simple things, requiring little adjustment on the part of pitcher and batter. James would go further and limit the number of times the pitcher can throw to first to hold a runner on. His suggested rule change would grant the pitcher two free throws without something happening. On the third, he'd either have to pick the runner off or suffer a ball being called on the batter. This is a more radical change but well worth considering. True, it does strictly limit one of the pitcher's weapons. On the other hand, there would be more stolen-base attempts and pitch-outs. We might even see increased pickoffs, as well, because a base stealer would be more likely to get caught leaning the wrong way if the pitcher had already used up his freebies. All of the things gained add to the excitement of the game.

Third, and here I'm entirely indebted to Bill James, limit the number of pitching changes per inning. He points out that since the mid-'80s, the number of relievers used per game has increased by *50 percent*. Ball clubs keep specialists on their rosters who are brought in to face one batter in a specific situation and then are gone. This has made the managerial chess game more complex, but the truth is, it's a terrible drag on the action. James suggests one solution: that a manager be given one free midinning pitching change per game. After that, a pitcher can't come out before the inning's over, unless he gives up a run.

Does this, as some will undoubtedly argue, curtail a manager's strategy? It may seem to, but no. All it really does is limit his options. Strategy would then have to be thought out in a slightly different way. I like it.

Now, as for reducing homers and making a run more precious, James proposes two adjustments that are very minor but have far-reaching consequences. I can't help but see the wisdom of both of them.

To begin with, specify that a bat must have a minimum weight and circumference. The modern trend toward light bats with ultrathin handles and hollowed tops—with the goal of increasing bat speed through the strike zone—has been a major contributor to the phenomenon of marginal power hitters swinging for, and reaching, the fences. Phase those bats out over time and bring back the older, thicker style and you'd have far fewer splintered bats, for one thing; every time one breaks, it creates a pause in the action. Not to mention endangering the health of whoever's head the shattered half-bat is spinning toward.

More important, though, would be the long-term effect. Offenses, James writes, would be "based less around bat speed, and more around bat control; less around power, and more around contact. Baseball would still have power hitters . . . but we'd have fewer strikeouts, fewer walks, fewer homers, more hits, more doubles, and more contests between fielders and baserunners." A very worthy trade-off, in my opinion.

Finally, James advocates moving the batter's box away from home plate, incrementally (an inch a year), until it's four inches farther removed. This would decrease hit batsmen and probably eliminate the grotesque, unbase-ball-like spectacle of burly men striding to the plate encased in what amounts to armor, then leaning out over the plate and daring the pitcher to try throwing inside. It would also cut down on opposite-field home runs (the proliferation of which Greg Maddux calls the single biggest change he's seen during his career) and make homers hit off pitches down the middle a little more scarce. It would be yet another step toward reasserting bat con-trol's proper place in the game.

Baseball does need help, we all agree, and what I've listed are some deceptively simple ways in which to begin making it more fun again. Bill James understands this better than most, so I'll let him have the last word:

> We don't *need* to take dramatic, flashy actions to change baseball into something new and different. We need to take gauze-thin actions designed to tell the participants to *stop messing around and play base-ball* [italics mine]. This is understood by the men who run the NFL; it is understood by the men who run college basketball. It is not understood by the men who run baseball. If we'll just do that much, or that little, we can show younger fans how exciting baseball is sup-posed to be.

To which I say: amen.

And, just to prove that four consecutive hours of baseball can be *com-pletely* riveting, we now turn to Game 6 of the 1975 World Series.

The Serendipitous Rat

Baseball is not a matter of life and death, but the Red Sox are.
—MIKE BARNICLE, *BOSTON GLOBE*

Then come the rains.

For three days and nights, it rains and it rains and it rains. Each day, Baseball Commissioner Bowie Kuhn checks the forecast and goes out to inspect the field. Each day, he turns thumbs down. *No. No game today.*

A delay like this brings on the silly season. The ballplayers are restless, sitting around, itching for a resumption of action yet forced to wait for a moment that continues not to arrive. The last thing they want is to talk to the press. Talk they must, however. It comes with the territory, and now there are hundreds of journalists from around the country, trapped in boring Boston hotel rooms, desperate for some story to file.

On and on it goes. The players and coaches get interviewed beyond their ability to say anything cogent, and then reporters must range increasingly far afield in order to keep the words flowing. They go after the participants' parents, wives, girlfriends, childhood chums, parish priests, orthodontists, whatever. There is, seemingly, no tale left untold.

The most ironic statement, though, almost certainly issues from the mouth of the Sox' fabulous rookie, Fred Lynn.

"It's incredible how much of the edge is taken off this thing now," Lynn says. "It just doesn't seem the same as it did a few days ago. Now it's just like any regular season game. The atmosphere and excitement sure have changed."

Oh, Freddie. Young Freddie. How little you yet know of the game of baseball. Before the penultimate game of this Series is over, you'll find that you haven't lost either your fire or your audience, not at all. Your own name will rise from the throats of tens of thousands as they holler themselves hoarse . . . and for one terrible moment will be caught in those same throats like a chicken bone.

The contest to come, Game 6, has been called the greatest World Series game ever played. If it isn't, well, it's up there in the top few. It will be a tooth-and-nail struggle, with lots of scoring, an unprecedented parade of pitchers, managerial moves and countermoves, sudden and shocking reversals of fortune, fielding masterpieces, baserunning blunders, a near-tragedy, and, what most people remember in the end, a pair of dramatic home runs. It'll feature everything that makes baseball so enjoyable.

Let's watch . . .

The first thing to be decided is who the starting pitchers are going to be. This is now wide open, because Game 5 was five days ago. Gullett faced Cleveland in that one. So Sparky Anderson could bring Gullett back here, on four days' rest. Or he could go with someone, anyone, else and save his well-rested ace for the seventh game, if necessary.

Sparky opts for the latter course of action, giving the starting nod to Gary Nolan. However, he vows to bring a merciless hook with him. At the first sign of trouble, a pitcher is coming out. He won't be too bummed if it comes to a Game 7 and Gullett, but he'd rather win it all right here, and he won't hesitate to use every single one of his other nine pitchers if he has to. As it turns out, he very nearly will.

Anderson's counterpart, Darrell Johnson, has a real dilemma. Bill Lee was scheduled to pitch this game, with Rick Wise available for Game 7, if the Series got there. Lee pitched great in Fenway in Game 2, and the sinkerballer is a prime candidate to take his allotted turn, especially because the slow, soggy field favors a ground ball pitcher.

Luis Tiant, however, is the staff ace, and the weather has now given him five days' rest. He can go. Of course, his last outing was the 163-pitch marathon in Game 4 that followed the complete game in 1, and it would be most prudent to give him another day off. Then, if Lee can beat the Reds here, a marquee best-vs.-the-best pitching matchup, reprising the Series opener, would follow in Game 7.

On the other hand, this is a single-elimination situation. Lose Game 6 and the Series is over. Because they must win here in order to stay alive at all, Johnson believes that it makes a good deal of sense to go back to his ace. If Luis prevails, as he has twice already, the Boston manager can come back with Lee to face Gullett tomorrow. He has to like his chances there, considering that Bill has pitched splendidly in Fenway and Gullett not so well. So he goes with El Tiante.

When I met Bill Lee in 2000, I asked him how he felt about the decision.

"I should've pitched that game," he said. "I had to win one of them anyway, so why not Game 6? I was the most rested. Luis would've been in much better shape the next day."

He paused, then added, "Of course, there was no way he could have picked me. I understand that. If he had, and I'd lost, he would have been ridden out of Boston on a rail for not pitching Tiant. He really had no choice."

So we shall see how much gas Luis might have left in the tank.

It's a beautiful night for baseball in Boston: sixty-two degrees at the 8:30 start time. Especially in contrast to the days of chilly rain, it seems like a balmy spring evening. And the wind, which in Games 1 and 2 was blowing in from right, is now blowing the other way, out toward the fences. There should be some homers before this one is over.

The fans are pumped. Though their team is on the brink of elimination, there is a feeling in the air, that maybe, just maybe, Tiant and Lee can propel the Sox past the Reds here at home and the team can claim its first championship since . . . well, forever.

The Reds have different ideas. Prior to the game, several of them say that they haven't been impressed with Tiant's fastball, especially in Game 4, and that they feel he's beatable, particularly if they can get to him early.

Right off the bat, notice is served that this may be a memorable game. Pete Rose loops a fly ball to left. Yastrzemski, who slips slightly on the wet surface, comes in on a dead run and makes a superb, diving catch for the out. Yaz is off the plastic now, back in his element.

Though there's a different home-plate umpire than there was in Game 4, in this case Satch Davidson, it looks as though Tiant might have the same difficulty getting calls that he did then. But Davidson, resting his hand on the catcher, squats down and really sticks his face in close. He seems to be trying hard to make the calls as accurately as he possibly can. Two consecutive borderline pitches, one of which looks like a perfect outside strike, are called against Luis, and Ken Griffey is handed a free pass.

Griffey steps away from the bag. Prior to the game, as always, he went out to first with Davy Concepcion for Joe Morgan's baserunning clinic. Morgan marked a spot between thirteen and fourteen feet from the base. This is the maximum lead he feels they can safely take. Griffey stops at the spot.

Morgan probably also reiterated that he doesn't want anyone running while he's taking his cuts, because Griffey doesn't go. Joe hits a high foul pop-up that the wind plays all kinds of tricks with. Fisk weaves, skitters this way and that, and finally makes a very nice catch.

Bench strikes out swinging to end the inning. Tiant looks as tough as ever.

Gary Nolan, though, stumbles out of the gate. He gets the first two batters easily enough, Cecil Cooper on a fly to shallow center and Denny Doyle on a grounder to Tony Perez that Perez bobbles before underhanding the throw to Nolan in time. Then the roof falls in.

Yastrzemski starts the rally by ripping a single through the hole between first and second. When Fisk follows with a single to left, Sparky Anderson, true to his word, gets his bullpen going. Fred Norman and Jack Billingham (who's angry he didn't get the starting role here after his fine performance in Game 2) begin warming up.

Fred Lynn is up. The TV announcers note that Lynn, dissatisfied with the way he's been swinging the bat in the Series, has been working out during the rain delay, practicing in the batting cage under the center-field bleachers. Not for the last time tonight, the guys in the booth prove prophetic.

Lynn's extra cuts pay off. He lays into a Nolan fastball out over the plate and, aided by the wind, bombs a four-hundred-foot home run over the bullpen in right-center field. The crowd goes nuts. The Old Towne Team has jumped out to a 3–0 lead before the end of the opening frame, on the first World Series homer by a rookie since (portentously?) Reggie Smith did it for the Red Sox in their most recent appearance, 1967.

Petrocelli then lashes another fastball to deep, straightaway center. The fans come to their feet, ready to explode again, but Geronimo tracks this one down and catches it at the warning track. Another drive of almost four hundred feet. If the Reds get to the pitcher's spot in the second inning, Nolan is history, believe it.

Luis goes out and strikes out Tony Perez as Perez, completely fooled by one of Tiant's herky-jerkiest motions, seems to lose sight of the ball entirely and winds up flailing helplessly at a low, outside pitch.

The fans cheer lustily. Tiant, we'll learn later, is pitching with a chest cold, but he'll claim that he scarcely noticed it. "The fans," he says, "they make me do what I don't think I can do."

Foster fouls to first and, when Concepcion flies to center, Tiant has retired the side in order for the first time. It will also be the last.

Between half-innings, NBC flacks its upcoming special, *A Quarter-Century of Bob Hope on TV*. You could probably get good odds if you bet that Bob would still be going strong another quarter-century later.

Nolan settles down in the second. He catches Dwight Evans looking at a slow, outside curve that's called strike three—Evans of whom Sparky Anderson has said, "He's much better than we'd heard." Just how much better Sparky is yet to see.

Burleson grounds to first. Tiant (batting .333 in the Series) strikes out on another slow curve, and Nolan has a one-two-three inning of his own. For all the good it will do him.

Just before the station break—which will bring Xerox's opportunity to advertise its revolutionary bidirectional automatic typewriter—viewers are treated to a picture of the left-field wall, the Green Monster. There's a square hole in it, just above ground level. Behind that, we are told, is a camera that will be providing us, throughout the night, with shots from its own unique perspective. In hindsight, it's another prophetic moment. Because, Lord, what shots they will be. One in particular.

Sparky starts making moves in the third. With Geronimo up, he sends Terry Crowley to the on-deck circle. But after César fans on a patented Tiant hesitation curve, Crowley gets called back. Anderson has been saving his best pinch hitters for times when there are men on base to be driven in. He sends up Darrel Chaney.

Chaney lofts a routine fly to left. Well, not exactly routine, not with tonight's wind. The ball carries, and carries, until Yaz makes the catch up against the Wall. Rose follows by waiting on a slow curve and lining it for a single to center. But Ken Griffey grounds out to second, and Tiant's shutout is intact.

Fred Norman comes in to pitch and fails to get out of the inning, as the Sox threaten again. He gets Cooper (his sweet swing gone to wherever sweet swings go when they abandon you) on a pop to short. But Doyle doubles down the right-field line. Yaz, uncharacteristically, reaches for a ball out of the strike zone and pops to second.

Now what? The right-hander Fisk comes up to face the left-handed Norman. No hesitation. Anderson has him intentionally walked. He doesn't want Cincinnati down another run and would like the force-out at any base. Also, Norman will now face Fred Lynn. Despite that Fred's bat is probably still ringing from his first-inning homer, it's the matchup Sparky prefers: lefty vs. lefty.

Lynn walks, not at all intentionally. Bases loaded for Rico Petrocelli, who's had a hot bat.

That's it for Fred Norman. Anderson plays Captain Hook once again and brings in Jack Billingham to make it righty vs. righty. Petrocelli works the count to 2–2, but then Billingham serves him a nasty outside curveball. Rico tries to check his swing and thinks he has. Umpire Satch Davidson disagrees and calls him out on strikes. The rally dies.

The fourth should be an easy inning for Luis, and isn't.

Morgan leads off. He has, by his own admission, been overreaching for pitches the whole Series. Now he does it again. Of course, it also helps that Tiant is consistently working the outside corner, to everyone. Morgan grounds out to second.

Bench next. Once again, Luis hits the outside corner, this time with a curveball that freezes Johnny in his tracks. He's called out on strikes.

Perez, though, lines a single to right. Evans, always thinking out there, fakes a bobbling of the ball, trying to induce Tony to try for second. But Perez is too smart (not to mention too slow) to fall for that one. He stays at first.

Foster then hits an inning-ending grounder to short. Or so it would be in a normal game. Not here. Burleson fields it cleanly but then, going for the force at second, throws the ball too far to Doyle's right for Denny to get his glove on it. It skitters into center while Perez slogs on to third. Runners at the corners.

Tiant, perhaps a tad miffed, really bears down and escapes the inning unscathed when Concepcion fouls out to first.

The home fourth brings more of the *mondo bizarro*. Evans, visibly talking to himself at the plate, rips a ground-rule double into the stands along the right-field line. Billingham, pitching extra cautiously with Tiant due up next, walks Burleson on four pitches.

Now there are conferences all over the place. Boston can smell the big inning that breaks open the game; the Reds will do everything in their power to prevent it. Thus Luis confers with third-base coach Don Zimmer to nail down what Tiant should do here. Bunt, almost certainly, although you never know. For their part, Rose, Bench, Concepcion, and Billingham gather at the mound, each wanting to be sure of what the other is going to do should the Sox spring some kind of trick play. Eventually, everyone is satisfied.

When Luis does square around to bunt, the Reds go into their pre-arranged defense. Perez and Rose charge from the corners. Morgan covers first, Concepcion third. If Luis tries to bunt down the third-base line, either Rose or Bench will have a good shot at forcing Evans. He has to go toward first, which he does.

It's a terrible bunt, the ball shooting up into the air. If Perez hadn't been charging, he would have caught it and probably doubled up Burleson. But he was charging. The ball flies over his head, and he has to turn around and run it down. He bobbles it. Still, that's old Luis running, and Tony has time to get a grip on the ball and throw to Morgan in time. Tiant has done his job, after a fashion. Evans and Burleson move up, putting runners at second and third with only one out. The big inning awaits.

Unfortunately, it's Cecil Cooper's turn at bat, and Coop couldn't buy a hit with all the tea in Boston. Anderson pulls his infielders in. He won't concede a run unless it's hit past them. It isn't. Cooper, after getting ahead 2–0 in the count, takes a horrible, indefensible cut at a pitch down around his ankles. He tops it, sending a chopper right at Perez. Tony keeps the ball in front of him and a sharp eye on Evans at third. He makes the play unassisted, with Dwight holding.

Two down, and still Sparky won't give an inch. He has Rose creep in from third on Doyle, guarding against the squeeze bunt, a play the Red Sox *never* try. Denny grounds out to second, and another fine scoring opportunity is wasted. We wonder, How many of these can they squander and still win this game?

Well, maybe a lot of them, if Tiant continues to hold the Reds at bay. He has now pitched a mind-boggling forty consecutive innings at Fenway without allowing an earned run.

End of streak. He starts the fifth by getting Geronimo to fly out to right on another of those slow curves. Bases are empty again, and Terry Crowley, who'd been waiting to hit for the pitcher, is called back. In his place, Ed Armbrister comes up. Ed is roundly booed. Sox fans will not forget Game 3. Not now, not ever. Armbrister walks.

Ed is speedy but is not an accomplished base stealer. He won't be running here. He waits on Pete Rose, and Rose, who is quietly building up his Series hit total, obliges by golfing a single to center. Now, when Fred Lynn has trouble getting the ball out of his glove, Armbrister does turn on the speed and races to third. Runners at the corners, one out.

Then the unthinkable happens.

Tiant comes in with a high curve, and Ken Griffey crushes it as though he's been waiting all his life for just such a pitch. The ball takes off, a rising line drive to deep center field. Lynn, with a good jump, races back.

With Yaz, Lynn, and Evans, Boston has assembled one of the finest defensive outfields ever. Each has the perfect set of attributes peculiar to excellence at his position. Dwight has the extremely accurate gun of an arm you want in a rightfielder, so that he can cut down runners going from first to third. Captain Carl's arm isn't as strong, but the leftfielder has a shorter distance to throw; Yaz is pinpoint to home and second, and he has an extraordinary instinct for the right play. And Lynn has the raw speed necessary to cover the vast amount of ground out in center. His primary job is to react in an instant and get to wherever the batted ball will land as quickly as possible.

That's what Freddie does now. Faster, faster he runs. He reaches the warning track, going flat out. He raises his glove. He leaps . . .

Though not, strictly speaking, a contact sport, the game of baseball is nevertheless physically brutal. The threat of injury hangs over it like humidity, ever present yet visible only now and then.

There are the everyday, nagging little injuries that the long, long season inflicts upon just about everyone: pulled muscles, sprains, bruises. There are the less common but still relatively frequent traumas that send a player to the DL for varying lengths of time or that signal the end of a season and a date with the orthopedic surgeon: broken wrists and legs, damaged elbows, torn rotator cuffs. Beyond those, there are the spectacular mishaps that place life itself in jeopardy.

In all of major league history, there has been only one play-related fatality, and it happened more than eighty years ago. Cleveland shortstop Ray Chapman died in August of 1920, after being hit in the head by a pitch from the Yankees' Carl Mays. ("Chapman Suffers Skull Fracture" read the headline in the following day's *New York Times*, just above a subhead that noted "Yanks' Rally Falls Short" and text that called the incident a "severe blow to the Indians' pennant chances.")

This is remarkable, given that a rocklike sphere is being hurled at batters at up to one hundred miles an hour and that it can be hit right back at the pitcher even faster. And especially because the modern batting helmet didn't become standard gear until the 1970s. It can be difficult—considering the hard plastic shielding with which some batters now gird themselves before stepping to the plate—to remember that in the relatively recent past they went out there entirely unprotected.

There have, of course, been some close calls. Herb Score for one, his career ended when he was struck in the face by a line drive off the bat of Gil McDougald. The Red Sox' own Tony Conigliaro for another. Tony, the youngest player to reach 100 lifetime homers, never fully recovered after getting hit near the eye by Jack Hamilton.

Then there is the most frightening moment I have ever personally witnessed. I was watching in 1974 when Doug Griffin, a member of this '75 Red Sox team, tried to crowd the plate against Nolan Ryan. Nolan may have been the hardest thrower of all time, with a fastball once clocked at 101 miles per hour. He also didn't allow hitters to dig in on him. Ryan came inside on Griffin, to back him off, and hit him in the ear. Doug went down as if he'd been shot, twitched a little, and lay very still. Blood trickled from his ear. He looked near death.

That's what Nolan Ryan saw, as well. "He wasn't moving," Ryan said later. "His eyes were rolled back up in his head. I thought I'd killed him."

Me, too. How could anyone survive such a thing?

I have no idea. So I found Doug, now retired, and called him at his home in central California. What's it like to get clocked in the head by Nolan Ryan? seemed a pretty dorky question to ask, even though that's what I really wanted to know. Instead, I asked him how he lived to tell the tale. And the answer seems to be that, granting the misfortune of having been hit in the first place, Doug Griffin caught a break.

"This was before the protective earflaps, right?" I asked.

"No," he said. "They had them. But if you'd been around for a certain length of time, you didn't have to wear them. I didn't like them, so I didn't use one."

Did he remember being beaned?

"Oh, yeah," he said. "I don't remember much after that. But being hit, yeah, I remember that."

So . . . how come he's still with us today?

"Well," he said, "I was lucky. They told me if it'd been an inch higher, I'd be outta here."

What difference that skinny little inch makes, I'll never know, but Griffin surely did pull through. In fact, the first time he was scheduled to face Ryan after coming back from the injury, he refused to sit out the game. And, in what must rank as one of the all-time gutsy performances, he got two hits off Ryan.

I expressed my admiration for that, but he dismissed it.

"If you're afraid to hit, you won't last long at the major league level," he said. "I was never afraid of anything. You just go up there and do what you're supposed to do." Casual as you please.

Uh-huh. Against Nolan Ryan, who's almost killed you. I can only imagine, and not very well.

Though Doug came back, he was never the same. Batting .347 at the time of the beaning, he missed fifty-one games and tailed off to .266. He hit .240 the next season. That fell to .189 in 1976, and by the end of '77, Griffin was out of baseball at the age of thirty. (Remarkably, Nolan Ryan, who was born the same year that Doug was, would play until 1993.)

The Griffin injury was truly terrifying. What happened to Fred Lynn in 1975 wasn't; it was, however, pretty damn scary.

Lynn, who's been tracking the ball over his shoulder, tries to make a leaping catch off the warning track. As he launches himself into the air, though, his foot slips a little on the concrete, causing his body to turn ninety degrees. He hits the wall at full speed but backward, striking it with his spine and the back of his head. The wall is cement and, at this time, there is no padding. Fred Lynn crumples to the ground below the 379′ sign, his arms and legs at odd angles, and doesn't move.

The 36,205 people in the stands hold their collective breath. They're all on their feet. The entire park is dead silent. Darrell Johnson and trainer Charlie Moss rush out to center field and stand over their fallen star. Long minutes pass.

When I interviewed Lynn in 2002, I asked him what was going on out there. Had he been knocked out?

"No," he said. "Most people probably thought I was, but I never lost consciousness. What happened was that I couldn't feel anything in my lower extremities, from about my waist down. I didn't want to move, in case I'd broken my back. It was like when you hit your crazy bone. After a while I felt a tingly sensation, then I started to get some feeling back, and I thought, I guess I'm gonna be OK. I was conscious the whole time; I was just scared."

I asked him if that collision with the center-field concrete caused him afterward to play with something less than the reckless abandon he'd always exhibited. He told me it didn't.

"I'm a football player playing baseball, basically," he said. He'd gone to USC originally on a football scholarship and starred as a wideout and defensive back there. "As a wide receiver, I was used to going up and catching balls in traffic. When you do that, you're gonna get hit. But I was pretty good at it, and to me the wall was like a tackler. I'm gonna take a hit from it, so I might as well make a catch while I'm doing it. My aggressiveness did cost me some games [to injuries] down the road, but I never changed my style. I don't think I could. I had managers *ask* me to change and I couldn't."

On October 21, though, we don't know all this. The only thing we're sure of is that, for what seems forever, the young, handsome, and supremely talented Freddie Lynn lies immobile.

Finally, he stirs a little. Then, slowly, painfully, he gets to his feet. He walks around, twisting and stretching his body. He's going to stay in the game. The crowd cheers but with a very muted enthusiasm. It looks like a bullet has been dodged here, that their golden boy centerfielder will be out there for years to come, just as they've envisioned, but it's still too early to tell for sure.

Meanwhile, there's a game to be played. Two runs have scored, and Griffey's on third with Joe Morgan up.

The normally disciplined Morgan proves overeager at the plate once again. Fooled on a Tiant change-up, he lunges after it anyway, making a bad and foolhardy swing. He pops out to third.

Johnny Bench then jumps on a first-pitch fastball and lofts it to left. Yastrzemski, who's boasted that he can play Fenway's left field in his sleep, goes into one of his "dekes." This is his term for a decoy move, where he sets up as if he's going to catch a ball he knows is over his head, then turns at the last minute and plays it off the Wall. The hope is that this freezes a runner just long enough that he's prevented from taking a base. In this case, Yaz wants Griffey to believe that he's going to have to tag up before he can go home, giving the fielder a chance to cut him down at the plate.

No dice. Griffey isn't fooled, and he scores. But what happens next reveals the true defensive genius of Carl Yastrzemski. In one fluid motion, Carl picks the ball cleanly off the Wall on the fly, whirls around, sees that Griffey is a lost cause, and then, without the slightest hitch in his step, rifles a throw to second base. First option, nail the lead runner. Second option, keep the batter from advancing to scoring position. He wants to accomplish one of the two, and he does. Bench holds at first.

How can he do that, so effortlessly? Practice. That's it, pure and simple. He's had thousands of balls hit to him out there in practice, until he knows at the moment the ball leaves the bat how far it's going and whether or not he can catch it. If he can't, he knows where on the Wall it will hit and what the resultant carom is apt to be like. He treats every batter as if that batter is going to hit to left. Every possible situation that might develop has been analyzed beforehand in his mind, and he knows what he'll do in all of them. After he comes up with a Wallball, he knows exactly what options are open to him and which one he'll pursue depending upon what he sees in the first instant after he turns.

Only someone with the dogged persistence of a Yastrzemski could have logged the sweat equity necessary to accomplish this. But the results make it all seem worthwhile. In his first nine seasons as a regular leftfielder, Yaz averaged more than 15 assists a year. That's a lot, but even that doesn't reflect his true value to the team. Because for every runner he threw out, there were probably several more who simply didn't try to take the extra base on him. There's no telling how many runs he actually prevented.

None here, though. Perez strikes out to end the inning. Tiant is so certain he's got him that he begins to trot toward the dugout before Tony has completed his swing. The crowd is pleased but still restless. Considering Lynn's close call, it seems anticlimactic that the score is now tied, 3–3.

The game does go on, rather quietly. With Clay Carroll now pitching for Cincinnati, Yastrzemski leads off with a single to left. Fisk grounds to third, and Pete Rose, though he stumbles on the play, nevertheless gets it to second in time to force Yaz.

Fred Lynn up. The fans cheer, tentatively. Lynn, as he has so often, swings at the first pitch and hits a pop fly to left that is no trouble for Foster. Announcer Tony Kubek says that Lynn's swing looked "weak" to him. Has Freddie been injured more seriously than he's letting on? No one knows.

Again in the sixth, Tiant starts the inning strong, then runs into trouble. He retires Foster on a checked-swing grounder back to the mound and Concepcion on a fly to center. After Lynn makes the catch, the camera stays on him and reveals a slight limp as he walks back to his position.

Geronimo then lines one inside the third-base bag, just fair. Out there in Fenway, the stands jut abruptly toward the field, creating a sharp corner within a foot of the foul line. To hitters, that corner giveth—creating bounces that take the ball away from a fielder—and it taketh away—preventing hits such as Geronimo's from bounding down the line into deep left. Thus is Burleson able to field the carom quickly and hold César at first.

Terry Crowley, who's been called back twice by his manager, now finally gets his chance to hit for the pitcher with a man on. That man, Geronimo, is not the prime base-stealing threat on a team that includes Morgan, Griffey, and Concepcion. But he's fast and has an excellent success rate in his attempts. He might go here.

Consequently, Luis makes his best move to first, nearly picking him off. Though Geronimo slides back in safely this time, the idea has been planted in his head that he'd better be pretty careful with Tiant. By showing that move, Luis will keep the runner a little closer to the bag and prevent him from leaning too much toward second, thereby accomplishing not one but two things. Most obvious is that it reduces the chance of a stolen base. But it also makes it less likely that César will be able to go to third on a single to right or center and, given the strength of the arms out there, increases the potential for throwing him out if he tries it.

Crowley, though, hits another inning-ending grounder to short. And, once again, steady Rick Burleson misplays it. This time, though, it's a mental error. With two out, Denny Doyle was positioned well off second base, to guard the right-side hole against the left-handed hitter. In that situation, if the ball is grounded to short, the fielder's proper play is to first, because the second baseman may not have time to get to his base for the force-out. Burleson knows this as well as he knows his own name.

Yet he has an apparent brain lock. He comes up with the ground ball and turns to flip the throw to second. Nobody's there. By the time he realizes what he's done, it's too late. Geronimo's on second, and Crowley has an "infield hit."

What it really is, is Burleson's second error in three innings. What will that do to his fielding confidence? Well, perhaps fortunately, he gets the opportunity to find out right away. Pete Rose hits a hard grounder right at him. This time, Burleson fields the ball and makes the play himself, running to second and stepping on the bag to force Crowley for the third out. It's a good finish. Luis has wriggled out of another jam, and Burleson has gotten back astride the horse that threw him.

As Cincinnati reliever Pedro Borbon takes his warm-up tosses, the TV announcers again flack the upcoming Bob Hope special. Joe Garagiola emotes: "And you talk about having some guests! Frank Sinatra, Bing Crosby, Lucille Ball! Sounds like the Hall of Fame."

Evans grounds to Morgan to open the sixth, but then Burleson works a walk. Although his new pitcher has faced only two batters, out comes Sparky Anderson. A very superstitious man, Sparky hops over the chalked third-base line rather than stepping on it. With Tiant up, Anderson presumably wants to be sure Borbon knows what to do in the event of the anticipated bunt.

A bunt it is. Luis tries once and takes a strike. Luis tries twice and fouls the pitch off. Luis tries a third time and, when the ball rolls foul again, he's called out on strikes. Probably doesn't matter, because Tiant is followed by Cecil Cooper, now 1 for 16 in the Series. Coop grounds out to second.

It's the seventh, and Tiant has truly run out of gas. For quite a while, he's been throwing fastballs almost exclusively. It's a sign of mental fatigue and an open invitation to the free-swinging Reds, since Luis's velocity is well short of his best. That Cincinnati hasn't taken more advantage is due entirely to Tiant's ability to spot the ball where he wants it, primarily on the outside corner.

Here, however, Griffey jumps on the first pitch and lines a single past the diving Cooper into right field. Evans bobbles the ball, this time for real, but in a close game Griffey isn't going to try to stretch it into a double.

When Joe Morgan follows with a single to left, there are two on, no outs. Darrell Johnson comes to the mound.

If Sparky Anderson is Captain Hook, the archetypal modern manager who uses his relievers early and often, then Darrell is the anti-Hook, a throwback to baseball days gone by. He's not afraid to stick with a starter beyond all logical limits. Witness Game 4. His reasoning, as he told me in our interview, was always: "I know what my man in there can do. I may not know what my man in the bullpen can do. That is why sometimes I stay with my man instead of going to the pen."

Still, at this time he has a pen chock-full of fresh arms, and he has one very tired arm on the mound. It seems like the perfect moment to grant Luis the rest of the night off. The big guy has given his all in this Series— two complete-game wins, including the 163-pitch job, and seven more acceptable innings here. But Johnson leaves him to sink or swim and, tantalizingly, it looks for a while as if the gamble will pay off, as if Tiant will stay afloat.

First he makes Johnny Bench look bad. Bench reaches for another of those great outside-corner pitches and foolishly tries to pull it toward the Wall. By the time he finishes his swing, he's hitting one-handed. Even so, Bench is Bench, and he drives Yaz to the warning track. After the catch, Carl makes a quick throw to second, just in case Griffey's napping back there. He isn't. But Perez flies out to right, and though that gets Griffey over to third, there are two down now and no runs in. Luis may make it.

There's another round of conferences, as the managers plot their moves. Reds' third-base coach Alex Grammas goes into the dugout to talk to Sparky, then comes out and whispers something to Griffey. Meanwhile, Burleson, Fisk, and Tiant are palavering at the mound, presumably deciding what to do if the two speedy runners try to pull off a double steal.

The Sox wind up negating that possibility by playing the infield back and conceding second base to Joe Morgan. He doesn't matter as long as they record the third out and, with the relatively slow Foster up, Johnson wants to maximize his fielders' chances of getting the batter. Morgan obligingly takes off for second on the first pitch. Foster fouls it off.

Announcer Kubek selects this moment to recall that Foster has given Luis more trouble than anyone, with two hits in Game 1 and two more in Game 4. Thanks a lot, Tony. On the next pitch, Foster rips one off the top of the wall in center field. Two runs score. It's 5–3. Now Tiant really looks tired, and, when he trudges off after getting Concepcion on a ground ball to short, it seems certain that he's pitched his last.

Wrong. After Borbon sets the Sox down one-two-three in the home seventh, back out goes Luis. Johnson is going to squeeze the last possible fraction of an inning out of him. It's beyond reason and just seems cruel. The guy has nothing left, and the normally weak-hitting César Geronimo slams his first pitch of the inning down the right-field line, where it curves just inside the Pesky Pole for a home run. It's 6–3.

Only now, finally, mercifully, is Tiant pulled. The portly warrior has given up 6 runs on 11 hits and 2 walks. It's time.

Looie gets a well-deserved standing ovation, but there's probably not a soul in the crowd who doesn't think it's too late. Sparky still has his best young arms waiting to come in. The 3-run deficit might as well be 100. The Sox will lose the Series; Tiant, for all his prior heroics, will go down as the loser in the final game.

If there is to be any hope whatsoever, it has to start here. The bullpen must shut down the Machine and give the offense a chance to come back in the final two innings. They can't afford to yield any more runs.

Johnson chooses to bring in Roger Moret. Moret, with his 41–18 lifetime record, looks like Walter Johnson out there, snapping off unhittable fastballs. He retires the side in order. On the final out, a fly ball to center, Fred Lynn initially starts in the wrong direction, backward, but recovers and makes the catch running in. You have to wonder how well he's seeing the ball.

Tony Kubek says: "There's been an eerie feeling here since Lynn hit the wall," and he's right. The fans are quiet, as if all possible wind has been knocked out of them. And, now that the visitors have forged what looks like an insurmountable lead, butts seem welded to hands, eyes seem to be gazing at the far horizon that is *next year*. Kubek leaves the broadcast booth and heads for the Reds' dugout, to be in position to interview the winners.

Well, not so fast, Tone.

Lynn leads off the eighth and—will he *ever* take a pitch?—sends Borbon's first offering right back to the mound. The ball strikes Pedro on the ankle and trickles off toward the third-base line. Borbon gamely gives chase, fields the thing, and turns toward first. But Johnny Bench, a take-charge guy if ever there was one, is waving his arms and screaming at the pitcher. *No! You're too late! Don't!!* He does everything but wrap Pedro up in a bear hug to prevent a potentially errant throw to first. It's sound base-ball. Up three in the eighth, you don't risk putting a man in scoring posi-tion. Borbon holds the ball.

Borbon, his ankle perhaps more sore than he would care to admit, goes to 3–2 on Petrocelli, then loses him. Two on, none out, tying run coming to the plate. This is not the scenario Sparky Anderson had in mind, and he doesn't hesitate another second to perform the yank job. Borbon leaves, and Rawley Eastwick, the Reds' sixth pitcher of the game, comes in.

This is a little early for the Reds' stopper but, despite the game-tying homer he surrendered to Dwight Evans in Game 3, Rawley has been out-standing. Four appearances, $6\frac{2}{3}$ innings pitched, 1 run, 4 hits, 2 wins, 1 save. That's a pretty impressive line, and now Sparky wants him to do one last thing: close out the Series.

It looks as though he will do just that. He strikes out his nemesis, Evans, on a wicked outside fastball. Then he gets Burleson on a fly to short left. Now, to bat for Moret, Darrell Johnson once again turns to the player who is perhaps the best tenth man in baseball.

Both those who celebrate and those who deplore the countercultural exper-imentations of the '60s tend to overlook the context in which they hap-pened. I can well remember the mystified expression on so many faces of that era; they seemed to ask *What on earth are my children doing? And why?* It was as if this generation of kids was an alien race that had dropped into their parents' lives from God-knows-where.

It's a silly notion, of course, especially where it pertains to drug use/abuse. Patterns of behavior do not arise in a vacuum; they are very much a reflection of what has gone before. And the simple fact of the mat-ter is that America is, was, and probably always will be a highly drugged-out society.

The "'60s generation" began taking drugs because that's what the role models in their lives were doing. When I was growing up, more than half the adults in the country were addicted to nicotine, just about everyone was hooked on caffeine, and alcoholics were regarded as the life of the party rather than people with a disease. If the kids hadn't made the mistake of preferring illegal drugs to the legal ones—always an arbitrary and essentially meaningless distinction—no one would ever have noticed.

Then there is the matter of prescription medications. Though folks were primarily bingeing on liquor, cigarettes, and coffee, prescription uppers and downers were not far behind in popularity. These were "legal" in the sense that you could buy them at the pharmacy if you had written permission from a doctor. That was supposed to be the protection against abuse. Har har. Remember the phrase "mother's little helper"? It referred to my own mom, and millions like her. My mother got amphetamines to give her energy, barbiturates to help her nod off when she couldn't sleep because of the speed, and whatever the hell else she asked for. She was a kind, decent person who railed against the use of marijuana and LSD but was addicted to a slew of compounds whose names I can no longer remember. I don't believe there was a moment in her whole life when she saw the irony.

If it was a simple matter for my mom to get loaded, then there is no question about the availability of drugs to professional athletes. They were *very* available. There was casual drug use, and serious abuse, and we should hardly be shocked that there were some casualties. Because, for young guys working their way up to the Show in the '60s, the biggest drug pusher of them all was major league baseball.

Time and again as I interviewed the boys of October, I heard the same story told in different ways. A couple of examples will suffice.

Dick Drago said that when he first broke in, a common locker room pregame comment was, "Don't go out there alone." Meaning, *remember to take your pep pills.*

Bernie Carbo related how, in his day, the training room had big glass jars full of pills for whatever ailed you. Painkillers if you were hurting. "Performance enhancers" if you were tired—which, given a 162-game season, everyone is at some point. Players could help themselves to whatever they fancied they needed. "Vitamins," they were called in Bernie's clubhouse, and people on the trainer's staff would sometimes ask him, "Have you taken your vitamins today?"

Jim Willoughby recalled arriving in the dugout for his first major league game. In the corner, there were two big Igloo-type coolers, which he assumed were filled with water for thirsty players. Well, one was, at least.

When Jim tried to fill a cup from the wrong cooler, he was quickly corrected. "Not that one," he was told. "The other one. *That* one's red juice." The "red juice" was an amphetamine cocktail, and rookies weren't allowed to partake. It was for veterans—those tired old guys—only.

Everyone agreed that the practice of doping ballplayers ended in the early '70s, but only after the owners got nervous because of a drug-related lawsuit brought against the San Diego Chargers by one of the team's former players. It was a legal decision, driven by self-preservation, rather than a moral one. The organizations could see that they'd soon come under far closer scrutiny, and so they cleaned up their act.

This doesn't mean that there is no illegal drug use or abuse in the major leagues today. Of course there is, just as there is at all levels of society. Some players still relax by smoking pot; others bulk themselves up with illegal steroids. Some are hooked on Andro (the legal "dietary supplement" Androstenedione). The only thing that's changed since the bad old days is that the ball clubs are no longer openly in collusion with them.

Perhaps the most important lesson to be taken from all this is that as we listen to certain of these players tell the story of their lives, it would be wise not to pass judgment without fully understanding the circumstances in which those lives were lived. They belonged to a subculture suffused with drugs, from Jim Beam and chewing tobacco to Dexedrine and opiates. Some of them were bound to be drawn in further than they would have liked. And a few . . . well, the most surprising thing may be that only a relative few truly crashed and burned.

Which is by way of introduction to the man whose voyage home has been the most harrowing and perilous of any of these October boys, Bernie Carbo. Bernie invited me to his place in late 2001, and we talked for two hours there.

He lives in a one-story brick Florida home in a neighborhood of identical houses near Mobile, Alabama. Inside, every cranny is filled with things, mostly religious plaques and artifacts. But there are whole walls of baseball photos and memorabilia, statues of horses, and other knickknacks. His office is a baseball shrine.

On the day I met with him, the Christmas tree was up, and Bernie had his baby-sitting hat on. His two grandchildren, Tyler and Schuyler, were staying with him while their mother worked. He seemed a very good granddad.

Carbo, a stocky man, appeared reasonably fit, though there was a lot of wear to his face. He was dressed in a T-shirt and jeans; the T-shirt bore the logo of his organization, Diamond Ministry, and said "God is Love" on the back. His hair was still dark and thick, combed back and longish, though not like the halo of curls he sported back in the day. He was friendly, but not personable, and very intense. When he talked he gestured a lot and got right in my face. He had a strong, loud voice that seldom quit, making it hard to get a word in edgewise. I sensed a great deal of pent-up energy, and it was easy to believe he once had a terrible temper.

He began by telling me that he grew up in Detroit, surrounded by his extended Spanish-American family.

"Most people think I'm Italian," he told me at the deceptively quiet beginning of what would become an emotional, brutally honest interview. "That's because when I got to Boston, they told me, 'You're Italian.' I said 'No, I'm not.' And they said, 'This is Boston. Here you're Italian.' Actually, my grandfather immigrated to the States when the Spanish Civil War broke out. He didn't want anything to do with that. He went to work in a coal mine."

Later, the family moved to Michigan, where Carbo passed a seemingly ordinary childhood. He played ball, had lots of friends, and enjoyed the proximity of grandparents, aunts, uncles, and cousins, "all living on the same block. It was nice."

Well, not exactly. Though it may have looked that way from the outside, this was decidedly not Beaver Cleaver territory. Dad was an abusive alcoholic. Mom lived in fear and resentment of her husband's philandering, at one point throwing herself from a moving car in despair over her life.

"My father and I never talked," he said. "It was an old-fashioned household. The women and children were together while the men hung out upstairs. Then there was TV, which was the worst thing to come into my house. After we got a TV, when it was on you weren't allowed to talk at all. So there was no communication between anyone."

Bernie's relationship with his father was further strained because the old man saw his boy as a competitor. He never showed love for his children, and he belittled them mercilessly. A sometime ballplayer himself, who'd never risen above the minor leagues, he nevertheless constantly crowed that he was better than his son.

"It didn't matter if I hit three home runs in a game. It didn't matter that I went on to play for the Cincinnati Reds," Carbo said. "I could never please him. He'd just sneer and say, 'I'm still better than you.'"

Worst of all, Bernie was sexually molested by a relative when he was nine years old. "I completely repressed the memory," he said. "And it didn't surface until I went into therapy thirty-five years later. Even now, I don't know whether it happened once or many times. But it affected the rest of my life."

Under the circumstances, it's a wonder that Carbo stayed straight as long as he did. A couple of years back, when he had a reunion with a dozen childhood chums, he found out that they were astonished at the turns his life had taken. "You never drank or did drugs back then," they told him. "We can't believe this is the same person."

An old, old friend's memory tends to be short. Or perhaps it's just that booze was such an ingrained part of social life in those days that no one noticed. But Bernie himself remembers things differently. He was an alcoholic by the time he was sixteen.

"Basically, I'd become my mother's husband," he said. "She would do anything for me, so I tried to protect her from the consequences of my father's adultery. I'd take phone calls from women who started talking to me, thinking I was him. I was on the receiving end of his anger. But none of this was ever talked about. I drank a lot."

Then he graduated to major league baseball, which, as we have seen, wasn't exactly the best environment for a kid who had substance abuse problems coming in. Soon he was living on a diverse psychochemical cocktail, cheating on his wife, being awakened by the maid in a hotel corridor with the room key still in his hand. And the thing about it was, his lifestyle was so common that he didn't think it a bit unusual.

"You have to look at what baseball really was," he said. "Baseball *was* drinking, it *was* pills, it *was* women, it *was* living hard. You get accustomed to living in the darkness, and you don't realize anything is wrong."

Things went from bad to worse. He started smoking pot to complement the alcohol. By the age of twenty-three he was popping pills: codeine, Dexedrine, and just about anything else that ended in *-ine*, all courtesy of his employers. By twenty-five, he was a full-blown coke freak.

Yet he continued on as a professional ballplayer. Like many gifted athletes he was able, for a time, to shrug off the ravages of his drug-fueled life.

Age and addiction would eventually catch up with him, as they will. But not until he had forged a career that created a decent market for his services. He could play both left and right field, took pitchers the opposite way, slugged home runs, had a rifle arm, and was a premier pinch hitter. A lot of teams would have liked to have him. Boston really wanted him, and they traded for him in 1974. He was perfect for Fenway Park, his stroke made for popping line drives off the Wall, and he did everything the Red Sox asked of him.

Which included the request to deliver a fairly key hit in the '75 World Series.

If you look at the tapes of Game 6 with the benefit of hindsight and TV camera close-ups, it's easy to conclude that Bernie Carbo sure looks wired on *something*. But that's not what we see at the time. All that interests us in the moment is that here is what may be our last, best chance to get a run or two across, and we have the right man up there to do it.

Especially considering the right-hander out there on the mound. That Carbo would be batting against Eastwick at all is a major surprise. Lefty McEnaney is ready and waiting. And surely Anderson remembers the last time he left a righty in to face this guy. Carbo took him downtown.

Bernie himself recalled: "I was completely unprepared. I went to the on-deck circle thinking there was no way I was getting into that game. Darrell Johnson would announce me and then Sparky would pull Eastwick and bring in the lefty, McEnaney. That's what Sparky *did*. Always. Which meant that I'd then be pulled for a right-handed hitter. It wasn't until I looked over at the Reds' dugout and saw Sparky standing there, not coming out, that I realized I really was going to hit. I had to pull myself together mentally in a hurry."

Ready or not, Carbo steps in, and we couldn't ask for a better matchup. He already has that earlier pinch-hit home run, the solo shot that started the Sox on their comeback from a 5–2 deficit in Game 3. He stroked that homer, off Clay Carroll, the opposite way, to left field. That's where Bernie's power is. He seldom, if ever, pulls the ball. In order to negate his power, what you do is, you pitch him inside.

So of course Eastwick throws him a waist-high fastball smack over the heart of the plate that the stunned Carbo takes for a called strike one. After that, Rawley reverts to the book and comes inside twice, both pitches called balls. Then he grooves one, at the letters, right down the middle.

Carbo swings and misses. Of that swing, Rico Petrocelli will later say, "Terrible. A truly terrible swing. He looked like he was riding a pig out there." Rico will add that he doesn't know personally what riding a pig might be like; what he wanted to convey was the sense of a body jangling around disjointedly, of a swing that was impossibly out of sync.

One more strike and the Reds are out of the inning. Eastwick tries to get it with a fastball over the outside corner; Carbo chops a foul off to the left. Then he comes in with his strikeout pitch, and it's a beauty—a sinking fastball that might or might not just catch the inside corner. Bernie can't take a chance; he has to swing. He does. It's more like a half-hack at a ball that's past him, that he nearly plucks right out of Johnny Bench's mitt. (In fact, he recalled to me, he believes the umpire had already called ball three.) He gets just enough of his bat on it to foul it there at the plate.

Petrocelli will call this Carbo's second terrible swing of the at-bat, and coach Don Zimmer will pronounce it one of "the worst swings I've ever seen a big-league hitter take." Sportswriter Roger Angell will colorfully describe what he saw as akin to someone "fighting off a wasp with a croquet mallet."

Well, OK, guys. Time-out while I register a respectful second opinion. Awkward as he might appear, to me it looks like Bernie fights off one hellacious pitch, and there's simply no way to look pretty doing it. Joe Garagiola, calling the play-by-play for NBC at the time, concurs. "That's the kind of pitch," he says, "you get a piece of it you're happy. You did your job." However . . . none of this alters the perception that Carbo looks overmatched. There's probably not a soul watching who expects that he'll be able to handle whatever comes next. The man is burnt toast, and he looks it.

Eastwick certainly believes that. Perhaps frustrated that he didn't get the strikeout with his best pitch, he tries to throw one right past the batter. It's a fastball, and with utter disdain for his opponent he lays it out over the plate, about thigh-high, essentially daring Carbo to hit it. Which Bernie does, and how. Eschewing the opposite field, he puts all his muscle into one massive power stroke aimed at straightaway center. It isn't even close. The ball leaves the park and buries itself ten rows up in the bleachers, well over four hundred feet from home plate.

Was he stoned during the Series? I asked.

"Probably," he said. "But you have to remember that it wasn't like being stoned is to most people. I smoked a couple of joints and drank a few beers for breakfast every day. Add in some pills, and that was my pregame routine. That consciousness was my reality. I'd gotten myself to where I could function pretty well in that state. Or at least I believed I was functioning well. Actually, I was in a lot of pain, and that was my way of dealing with it.

"You know, every generation passes its problems on to the one coming up. What my dad did affected me, and the consequences of my behavior affected my wife, my children, everyone around me. They fell right into it. My ex-wife became as much of an addict as I was. My daughters grew up watching me roll joints, and they've had to deal with drug addiction and sex addiction and alcohol.

"All the time, I was bipolar, which I didn't realize until I got in therapy years later and they put me on lithium. Basically, I just created crisis wherever I went. I even confronted my dad once when I was drunk and stoned"—he slapped the table with the palm of his hand—"and said, 'Do you love me *now*? Do you love me like *this*?' I begged him to tell me he loved me, just once."

And did he?

"No, never. He couldn't. He didn't know how."

We paused and, after taking a minute to collect my thoughts, I steered him back to the subject of his career.

"That team in 1975 was the best one I ever played for," he said. "It was better than Cincinnati. I loved the Red Sox."

Bernie, at one time a member in good standing of Animal House, has become a very serious person. In the two hours I spent with him, he almost never cracked a smile. But at that point he did.

"I'll tell you a story," he said. "The first time I entered the Red Sox clubhouse, I saw some old guy there shining shoes, so I gave him ten bucks and told him to go get me a cheeseburger and some fries. He didn't bat an eye. Later somebody said to me, 'You know who you gave that ten bucks to? That was Mr. Yawkey.' The owner of the team, and I'd thought he was a go-fer. We became very close after that. He was another man who became a father to me, who liked me and took care of me. He kept giving me raises, bringing my salary up to what I was worth.

"Then, the year after that World Series, Tom Yawkey died, and I felt like my life was over. I loved him. Next thing I knew, they traded me to Milwaukee. I was devastated. My heart was with the Red Sox, and I wanted to end my career there. I'd been on top of the mountain, and now I had to start climbing up that mountain all over again. I almost refused to report to the Brewers.

"But I did, and while I was with Milwaukee Don Zimmer came to see me. Zim was another guy I used as a substitute father. And he told me—he'd replaced Darrell Johnson as the Red Sox manager at that point—'don't worry, I'm going to get you back.' Which he did. They traded for me that winter, giving up Cecil Cooper to get me and George Scott. So in '77 I was back in Boston."

Where, once again, he didn't last. I asked him if it was because he was one of the Buffalo Heads, a clique within the ball club that he hung around with: Bill Lee, Ferguson Jenkins, Rick Wise, Jim Willoughby, Carbo. Guys who made fun of Don Zimmer, who in turn reportedly hated the Buffalo Heads.

"No," Bernie said. "That wasn't it. What Zim didn't like was pitchers. But he liked me. He wanted me on the team. What got me released was my behavior. People were finally beginning to realize how screwed up I was and the new ownership put a private detective on me. When they called me in they had a book this thick on me"—his thumb and forefinger two inches apart—"and they showed it to me. I had a problem, and they knew it. But rather than trying to get me help, they just sold me to the Indians. Which I can't really blame them for. If I'd compiled a book like that on me, I'd have traded myself."

After being sold to Cleveland, the end was near for Bernie. He went back to the National League in '79 and got into 52 games with the Cardinals, for whom he somehow managed to hit .281. They released him the following year, after 14 games. He put in a 7-game stint with the Pirates, and then he was out of baseball.

Bernie Carbo was on the street, with no profession and an insatiable thirst for drugs and alcohol.

"It was bad," he said. "I went from making $125,000 a year to making $7,000. I headed back to Michigan and took a job bartending while I put myself through cosmetology school. Eventually, I opened up a hair salon that I had for eight years. But all the while I was still an addict. The only way I could support my habit was by selling drugs, so that's what I started doing."

He shook his head sadly. "You know," he said, "I can go to any city in this country, a complete stranger, and within a couple of weeks I can find

a supplier. Not just friends sharing joints, or some street dealer, you understand. A guy who'll deal in quantity that's only limited by how much
money I have. Now are you gonna tell me that the cops, who *live* there,
don't know where these guys are?"

I shook my head, too. I didn't have an answer for that.

"Anyway, after I sold the hair salon, I was pretty much living on the
streets. No job, no place to stay. Everything I did revolved around drugs,
selling them and using them. All my friends were the same. I was the only
one who didn't die or go to prison. I remember waking up in Chicago one
morning, in the rain, in the gutter. I'd fallen asleep there, and during the
night somebody had parked their car a couple of inches from my head. I
don't think he had any idea there was a person sleeping down there. I probably should have died that night. I should have died over and over again.
But God had a different plan for me, and He spared my life."

It was a horrible story, but one that obviously had something like a
happy ending. Because here he was, whole and healthy. I asked him how
he finally got straight, though I would have known the answer even without the reference to God's plans. Bernie proclaims his faith on his cloth-
ing and the walls of his home.

"I hit bottom in '93," he said. "My mother had committed suicide in
1989, and my dad died three months later. Then I was divorced in '92 after
twenty-two years of marriage. I was forty-five years old, broke, homeless,
still not knowing what I was doing, only that I just wanted to kill myself.
I called Bill Lee and he got in touch with Fergie Jenkins, and they put me
together with BAT, which got me into rehab."

BAT is the Baseball Assistance Team, an organization that helps former
ballplayers in need, no questions asked. Carbo was clearly a man in need.

"I was in the hospital for a couple of days, and after I'd dried out I was
still thinking, 'Why am I here? I don't need to be here.' Do you believe
that? I just wanted to get out and get high. But they put me in a bed next
to an old guy, and at one point he turned to me and said, 'Have you given
yourself to Jesus?' Given myself to *Jesus*? 'Nah,' I said. I hadn't been inside
a church in thirty years.

"That night, though, I had a dream. I saw a man dying and a hand
reaching out to save him. When I woke up, I knew that I was that man
and that the hand was God's. And I was reborn."

Simple as that?

"Well, nothing's simple," he said. "I have to face down the same temptations, drugs, sex, alcohol. I pray every day to keep the darkness out of my heart. But now I have the strength to do it."

It's worked. Bernie has been clean and sober for eight years, since he bottomed out in that hospital. He moved away from his old circle of friends, remarried to a woman who shares his beliefs, adopted her son, and founded the Diamond Ministry, which provides baseball instruction while it promotes clean living to kids. He's traveled to most of the fifty states and a number of foreign countries, including Saudi Arabia, telling his story and helping others succeed at the game that he still loves so much. When not on the road, he is a substitute teacher in the local high school. He's also shepherding his children through some of the same problems he faced, and he minds the grandkids. He fights the fight, one day at a time.

It's a grueling schedule, but Bernie Carbo would have it no other way. He considers himself a lucky man. And, though we sparred a bit when he took a stab at proselytizing me, I do, too. Like Bernie, I knew people who went down that particular rabbit hole and never came out. I have a lot of respect for those who made it, however they did.

"After all my addictions," Bernie said, "there's only one left. I choose to be addicted to Jesus now." For the second time in an hour he smiled. "You know, Christians used to be in the closet in baseball. When I played, no one would admit their faith. But that's all changed in the past ten years, hasn't it? They've come out of the closet. The way I look at it is that in the '60s in baseball you had alcohol, in the '70s pot and pills, in the '80s cocaine, and in the '90s Jesus."

I laughed. Maybe so. If the boys of October that I interviewed were any indication, there were a lot of deeply religious athletes out there.

As Bernie prepared to lay his closing statement on me, I realized that in all the time we'd spent together he hadn't once called me by my name. I wondered if he saw a person or simply a potential convert.

"And your last word is?" I said.

"The truth," he said, "will set you free."

Fair enough.

This particular moment's truth is that Bernie Carbo has just hit one of the most improbable home runs in World Series history. He trots around the bases as if he too is shocked by what he's done. His arms are thrust into the air, and his fists are pumping. As he rounds third, he yells at former teammate Pete Rose, "Don't you wish you were this strong? Don't you?" His second pinch homer has tied the World Series record. More important, it's tied the game. Perhaps now his dad will see him as someone of worth. Sure.

The fans are back in full voice, shouting themselves hoarse, and when Cooper strikes out swinging to end the eighth, it doesn't dampen their enthusiasm at all. It's a brand-new ball game. It's anybody's. No, it's ours.

Pete Rose is unruffled by Carbo's taunting. "Isn't this amazing?" he says to the third-base umpire as he leaves the field. "This is the greatest game I've ever played in." Already. And so much is yet to come.

Facing the revamped Red Sox defense—Carbo in left, Yaz at first, Dick Drago on the mound—the Reds do nothing in the ninth. Joe Morgan, with the fans cheering every strike the hard-throwing Drago gets, pops out. Bench grounds to third, where Rico makes a nice play, going to his left, to nail him. Perez fouls to first.

In the bottom of the ninth, the Sox put themselves in position to win it easily. Of course, we oughtta know by now that nothing will come easy on this remarkable night.

Right away, it seems as if Eastwick is still shaken by what happened to him the inning before. He walks light-hitting Denny Doyle. Now what? It's clearly a bunt situation—because all Boston needs is one run to win the game—but the batter is Yastrzemski. The announcers go scurrying for their record book and a moment later inform us that, sure enough, Yaz hasn't bunted all year. Not once. In fact, he's bunted so seldom in his whole superstar career that we have to ask ourselves, *Does he even know how?*

The question goes unanswered. On the first pitch, Yaz does indeed attempt to bunt, and he looks as foolish as some guy trying to thread a needle after his sixth beer. He fouls it off. Change of strategy. On the next pitch, he squares around again, then pulls back at the last moment and tries to slap the ball past the charging Pete Rose. It bounces foul to the left. OK, enough of this nonsense. Finally, Yaz simply does what Yaz does best. He takes an Eastwick pitch up around his neck and hammers it into right for a single. Doyle goes to third. The winning run is ninety feet away with no outs. The fans, those in Fenway and those of us watching on TV, are delirious.

Anderson has seen enough. He goes to the mound and calls for Will McEnaney. While he's making the pitching change, third-base coach Don Zimmer confers with Darrell Johnson in the dugout and with Johnny Pesky at first. Who knows what the Sox might have brewing?

Whatever it is, it'll have to wait. McEnaney, a left-hander, is ordered to walk right-handed Pudge Fisk, even though first base isn't open. Sparky is filling them up to create a double play at any base, and to have his reliever pitch to lefty Fred Lynn. He brings both his outfield and his infield in. It's a desperation move, because now almost anything will get the run home.

Anything, that is, except what actually happens. Up comes Lynn. Now Fred is a great hitter, but it's wise to remember that he's still a rookie. What's called for here—and what a veteran will do automatically—is for the hitter to work the pitcher deep into the count. You do that, you give an already stressed-out guy the chance to walk in the winning run. No extra effort needed. Lacking that, you want him to have to throw you something easy to hit, a nice fastball in the heart of the strike zone, which he will be forced to do rather than yield a base on balls. Then all you have to do is make decent contact and the run scores. Simple. Add in that Freddie has had very little success in this Series first-pitch hitting, and his course of action is written in stone.

Incredibly then, explicable only by his lack of experience, Lynn *again* swings at the first pitch. No surprise, he doesn't get much of it. He lifts a soft fly about halfway down the left-field line. It's drifting toward the seats, may be out of play, may give Lynn a precious second chance. Uh-uh. Foster goes over and, his shoulder brushing the stands, makes the catch. The ball isn't hit very deep, but George Foster is an adventure in fielding in the best of times. His throwing arm is suspect, and he's in an awkward position, and the fans are right there in his face, and this is unfamiliar Fenway, and he'll have to make a near-perfect throw to the plate, and . . . The air is filled with *ifs* and *ands*, but the Red Sox have been the riverboat gamblers through the first five games, and nothing's gonna stop 'em now.

Yet what transpires at third in that time-suspended moment between stillness and action has been the subject of some controversy. What does coach Don Zimmer say to his base runner? Is it: "Go, go, *go!*"? That's what Denny Doyle hears over the din of the crowd, and run he does.

Had Zimmer actually sent the runner, chancing a rally-killer with the game on the line? "No way," said Zim when I interviewed him. "Much too risky. It was only the first out. What I said was, 'No, no, *no!*' "

A couple of days earlier, I had asked Doyle the same question, and Denny was impeccably diplomatic. "Well," he said, "all I can tell you is that *go* is what I believed I heard. But Zim has the final word. He's the coach. If he says he said *no*, then he probably did."

Perhaps. But look at the tape. As Doyle streaks down the line toward home, there's Zim, standing with his hands at his sides, intently following the outcome of the play. Now, if he had actually shouted *no*, doesn't it make sense that he would have supported his command with some gesticulating, at least thrown his arms up with the palms out, in the sign that always means *stop* in the physical language of baseball? If it'd been me, and I didn't want my man going, I'd have done everything short of grabbing him.

Nope, said Darrell Johnson when we discussed the same play. Once a coach starts the runner in that kind of situation, he can't stop him. All he can do is hope for the best.

Zimmer backed his version of events by saying that he was right next to Doyle as the ball was descending and that he said directly to him, "You can't go anywhere." He also quoted third baseman Rose as telling the newspapers, "How many times do you think Zim told him not to go?"

I don't know. I guess it's advantage Zimmer here, but not by much.

In any event, there's no blame. Both coach and player believe they have properly communicated. Even if there has been a clear-cut decision to run, it isn't a horrible one. Nobody expects Foster to make a perfect throw, and he doesn't. On the other hand, he doesn't have to heave it very far. It arrives to Bench's right, to the fair side of the third-base line. Doyle goes the other way, trying to elude Bench to the catcher's left. Forget it. The greatest defensive catcher of all time fields the throw on one hop, lunges back over home, and makes a perfect swipe tag. Doyle is out.

Ironically, he probably should have been safe. With the luxury of replay we can see that, though the throw is there in time, it's up high. Had Doyle started his slide earlier, he would have been down in the dirt when Bench turned to tag him with the ball still at chest level. Johnny would have had to dive down there with him and most likely wouldn't have had time to apply the tag before Denny touched the plate. But he's just a fraction of a second late and can no longer slip under the tag.

"Yeah," Denny told me, "I felt really bad at the time. But . . ." He grinned. "If it weren't for me, Dewey and Pudge never would have had the chance to be heroes later on. That's the way I look at it."

OK. Me, too. But in the moment, as Johnny Bench yells down at his old pal Zimmer, "You're a kamikaze pilot," the out at home is a major downer. The fans, anticipating victory, now have to wait and deal with their first creeping doubts that Boston, even after the miracle rally, can pull this off.

It isn't going to happen in the ninth, of that we're sure, no matter that there is still one out to go. And we're right. Petrocelli hits a routine grounder to third. But wait. Pete Rose, going to his left, fields the ball cleanly, then . . . hesitates, almost as if he doesn't want the inning to end quite yet. Or maybe his nerves are as shot as everyone else's. Because when he finally does go to second for the force, he kind of pushes the ball toward the base with a puny little lob. In my youth, in the days before political correctness and the proliferation of fine female athletes, we would've said he threw it like a girl. Luckily for him, it's the unfleet Carlton Fisk chugging toward the bag, and he gets him.

On to extra innings.

After all the excitement, the tenth is blessedly anticlimactic. For the Reds, Foster bounces out to short. Concepcion gives Cincinnati fans a brief ray of hope when he grounds a single up the middle and then, after Drago nearly picks him off, steals second. Fisk would have had him, but the catcher, who isn't throwing well in this Series, is high again, and Davy slides under the tag.

There's no damage, though. Geronimo strikes out swinging on a pitch down around his ankles, and pinch hitter Dan Driessen pops a fly to short left, near the stands. Carbo, Petrocelli, and Burleson converge on the ball and almost lose it when a fan reaches out with his glove. But at the last minute, the fan withdraws his hand and Bernie, who has overrun the ball, leans back with his glove in the air.

"I was *really* scared I wouldn't make the catch," he told me. "The wind was blowing the ball back, and people were waving their arms, and the other guys were trying to get there, too. I just stuck my glove up there and hoped for the best. I never saw what happened."

What happens is that the ball plops into his outstretched mitt.

Pat Darcy comes in to pitch for the Reds. He's the eighth hurler used by Cincinnati, which ties the World Series record for pitchers used by one team, and the eleventh overall, also tying a record. With this pitcher, Sparky Anderson is essentially out of bullpen options but, fortunately for the manager, Darcy looks like a world beater. He retires Evans on a grounder back to the box, gets Burleson on a pop to short, and fans Carbo.

In the top of the eleventh, Pete Rose leads off. As he digs in at the plate, he turns to Fisk and says, "Isn't this something? This is what it's all about."

Drago comes inside, spins Pete around, and . . . hits him. Well, maybe. That's what Satch Davidson signals, anyway. The replay, however, shows that the ball's trajectory isn't altered in the slightest. If it does hit Rose, it just brushes his shirt, at best. Darrell Johnson comes out, and he and Fisk argue vehemently. To no avail, as always.

Griffey bunts toward third, but not far enough. Fisk barehands the ball and, a bit off-balance, guns a throw to second. Maybe he's better when he hasn't fully set himself, because the throw is perfect. Rose is forced.

Now comes All-Star Joe Morgan. First thing Morgan does is confer with third-base coach Alex Grammas, probably telling him that he doesn't want Griffey running with fewer than two strikes. With that straightened out, he settles in, watches the count go to 1–1, and then turns on a Drago fastball and smokes it.

I don't remember where, but I once read a comment that baseball is an "aerial" game.

Whoever made the remark was clearly a sage. For above all—and unlike any other team sport—that's what it is. Michael Jordan may have defined the parameters of individual, mechanically unassisted human flight, but baseball, in its very essence, *soars*.

Nowhere else is the flight path of the ball (puck, whatever) of such primary interest. Nowhere else (with the possible exception of golf) is there such a bewildering array of heights, spins, trajectories, and consequences of atmospheric disturbance. Nowhere else (golf again excepted) does the fan in the stands ever look up rather than down.

Face it, though there are interesting minor variations, if you've seen one jump shot you've pretty much seen them all. Same with the forward pass; if the quarterback expects to connect with his receiver, the parabola defined by the pass is completely predictable. Soccer yields some short passes and long, with little hooks and slices added for punctuation, but that's about it.

Football, rugby, and lacrosse are played mostly down in the dirt. Hockey is fast but totally flat. Basketball is about bodies banging each other on the hardwood. Soccer escapes terra firma at times, and is intriguing because it's the only game in which the head is used as something other than a mental weapon, but most of what happens is determined by who controls the relationship between the ball and the ground at any given moment.

Baseball's focus object, on the other hand, is nearly always in flight. Glorious, maddening, often unpredictable flight.

The pitcher initiates every play by putting the ball into the air, and never the same way twice. The pitch will be (relatively) fast or slow. If it's a fastball, it may be arrow straight, rise or sink, drift left or right. A forkball will fall suddenly, as if through a virtual trapdoor. A slider will move quickly down and away. A curve thrown at the batter's head will, at the last minute, sweep in a beautiful arc back over the plate. And a knuckler will head in directions unknown even to its author, dancing on the very molecules of atmosphere it's passing through.

And all of that happens before the batter even enters the equation.

Once he swings his stick, everything changes. If he makes contact, the ball takes off on an entirely different flight path. It may go backward (to the screen), left or right, fair or foul, high or low. Even if it is hit down into the ground, the play's denouement depends on how the ball comes back up when it reaches the fielder and how truly that fielder, having captured it, is then able to propel it toward the appropriate base.

Trajectory is crucial.

The pitcher's intent, other than getting the batter to whiff, is to have him hit it either straight down or high into the air (but not too far).

From the batter's perspective, the most successful outcome is for him to hit it hard, on a line, and with at least enough rise to it that it eludes a jumping infielder's outstretched glove. Or, better yet, to propel it at a slightly steeper angle, with enough velocity that it will travel the three hundred plus feet necessary to transcend the limits of the playing field.

In any event, the spectator will be treated to an aerial show. There are little bloopers that are either caught or just drop in for hits. There are vicious line drives that threaten to decapitate anyone in their way. There are long flies that may be tracked down, or fall to earth between fielders, or fly over the wall. And then there is the towering pop-up, hit so high it's nearly lost to sight, blown here and there by the prevailing winds, with the infielder skittering this way and that in an attempt to stay directly beneath it. (It is a measure of the big-league ballplayer's skills that most of the time he makes such an extraordinarily difficult catch seem routine.)

The variation in distances involved is mind-boggling. No rifle-armed quarterback can throw a football the length of the field, nor can the most powerful leg kick a soccer ball from goal to goal. A sixty-foot jump shot is out of the question.

Talented outfielders, however, can throw a baseball a hundred yards on the fly. (And hit a spot the size of a dinner plate.)

With batted balls, even one poorly struck might travel a couple of hundred feet. Home runs start about half again farther. A slugger will routinely break four hundred feet, and occasionally even exceed five.

In the vertical plane, we're also talking some substantial altitude. Assume that the batter strikes the ball at a thirty-five-degree angle with enough force to drive it away from him at 120 miles per hour (both of these are about optimal). The result will be a 450-foot homer that at the peak of its parabola is about 120 feet in the air. If he undercuts it and hits one of those sky-high major league pop flies, it will of course go much higher.

The persistent, ever-changing aerial ballet delights the fan and can't help but create a sense of awe at what is transpiring back down on the field. That our infielder can remain camped under a tiny white sphere being blown around a couple of hundred feet up is rather a miracle. (Just try it sometime.) Perhaps even more of one is that an outfielder can, virtually at the point that ball meets bat, launch himself into a full-speed run that will intersect the flight path of the ball at precisely that point where he can most comfortably catch it, approximately five or six feet above the field.

These guys are *good*.

How good?

Well, I'm reminded of the wonderful baseball movie *A League of Their Own*. In it, a crusty old manager, played by Tom Hanks, is confronting a member of his women's baseball team who wants to quit because, "I guess it just got too hard."

Hanks stares at her in amazement and then sputters, "*Hard?* Of *course* it's hard. It's *supposed* to be hard. If it wasn't hard, *everybody* would do it!"

Yes, we would.

The reason we don't is not that we lack the desire. It's that it is so god-damned difficult to play the game with skill and consistency. And if we require verification of this, we need only consider how difficult it is to make that outfield catch.

First, there is the "crack of the bat" phenomenon. No one, of course, can predict at that moment precisely where the ball is going. Some fraction of a second is needed for even the intuitive mind to process the information it has just received.

Nevertheless, within that split second the supreme fielder will note the angle at which the ball leaves the bat and know at least in which direction to begin running. He will also "know" how hard it has been hit, based on whether the pitch was a fastball or breaking ball, how full the swing was, and whether the sound of contact was explosive or dull.

Once in motion, he will turn his head to confirm that he's headed in the right direction at the right speed, and will repeat this—modifying his stride as necessary—until he arrives at the point where he has projected the ball will come down. At the last moment, he'll extend his arm and, he hopes, the ball will fall into his glove.

It's an extraordinarily complex sequence of decisions and adjustments; the available time in which to do it varies—for example, the path of a ball angling away from a fielder can be physically perceived in about half a second, while one hit directly at him requires a full second to pick up—but it is always small; and there is a hell of a lot of real estate to cover.

Take a ball hit straight toward an outfielder who is playing some 65 feet from a fence that's 350 feet from home plate and say that, if unimpeded, this ball will strike the wall at a height of 9½ feet.

For the first full second, the fielder can't truly know whether to run in or out (hence the occasional "misjudged" fly, where he breaks the wrong way). But assume he makes the correct guess, turns, and starts to run back, losing only half of that second in the process. Assume also that, half a second later, he's able to adjust his path as he perceives that the ball is actually tailing away from him. And let's concede that he's a very fast runner.

The amount of time it will take the ball to reach the fence is affected by the wind, of course, but on average will be slightly less than five seconds.

Our fielder, starting from a standstill and adjusting his direction to match the flight of the ball, has to cover perhaps seventy-five feet in the same amount of time. Once at the wall, he must then put on the brakes, set himself, jump as high as he can, extend his glove to just the right spot, and snag the ball.

It's physically possible to do all that in the time allotted (or baseball wouldn't exist), but just barely. There is no margin for error. Yet it occurs repeatedly, successfully, and sometimes in even more spectacular fashion.

Which introduces what happened next in this extraordinary Game 6.

Evans is off with the crack of the bat.

Later, when I interviewed Jim Burton, Jim would tell me: "I was in the bullpen, so I had one of the best seats in the house. And the most amazing thing to me was Dwight's reaction. He turned and started running the *instant* that ball was hit. I couldn't believe it."

It's a certain home run, or off the top of the waist-high right-field wall at the very least. Griffey scores, Morgan either trots home or winds up on second or third. Reds lead.

Back goes Evans. Back, back, running full tilt. He reaches the warning track, leaps into the air, and over his shoulder, somehow, improbably, makes an unbelievable catch just before the ball falls into the first row of seats. He comes down and bangs into the wall. He's made the Catch, the play of the game and of the Series, but he knows his job isn't done yet. Immediately, he pushes himself off the wall, whirls, and pegs the ball back to the infield. The throw is ten feet off line, toward the dugout. It doesn't matter. Yastrzemski is there, and Burleson has come all the way across the infield to cover the bag. With Griffey basically in denial—he was halfway to third—Yaz flips the ball to Rick to complete the double play. The crowd comes alive.

As Evans lopes back to the dugout, Fisk walks over to him and says, sarcastically, "Nice *throw*, Dwight."

When I interviewed him, Evans recalled the catch. "I did get a good jump," he said. "But I'd been going over in my mind exactly what I'd do if Morgan hit the ball. I was watching carefully, for the kind of pitch and how it came off the bat. I was ready. Still I made a mistake. If you look at the tape, you can see it. I was slanting toward the foul line, because usually when a left-hander pulls the ball he puts a left-to-right slice on it. Only this time, Morgan hit it straight. So if you look carefully, you can see that when I jump I have to reach back to compensate. I actually catch the ball a little behind my head."

Well, not so's you'd notice. I told him I couldn't see it. He shrugged. He should know. I asked him if it was the greatest catch he ever made.

"I don't know if it was the *greatest*," he said. He paused, then smiled. "It was a hell of a catch though, wasn't it?"

Sparky Anderson is a bit more effusive. Given the circumstances, he will say the following day, it's the greatest catch *he's* ever seen. Period.

The crowd is wild again. After that, the Sox will surely win the game in their half of the inning. *Not.* Darcy still looks unhittable as he retires Rick Miller, hitting for Drago, on a fly to left and both Doyle and Yaz on grounders to short.

Rick Wise is in, the Sox' fourth pitcher. Combined with Cincinnati's eight, the two teams have set a World Series standard for most pitchers used.

The twelfth inning begins a little ominously. Johnny Bench hits a foul pop-up back behind home plate. Fisk goes to the stands, misjudges it, has to backpedal furiously, and ends up falling on his backside. But he makes the catch.

Perez, however, grounds a single past Burleson into left, and Foster loops a single to left off the handle of the bat on a fastball that had him good and jammed. Two scratch hits that count the same as hard line drives. Wise is in trouble.

He bears down and gets Concepcion on a fly ball to right. With Evans out there, along with the mystique that now hangs over him, the runners don't tag. They go halfway, then return to their bases when Dwight makes the catch. Darrell Johnson goes to the mound, though he has no one warming up.

Sparky, though, has action in his bullpen. Should Geronimo walk, or otherwise reach base without scoring anyone, Anderson will undoubtedly pinch hit for his pitcher. So Clay Kirby, who has yet to appear in the post-season, is warming up. And Merv Rettenmund, just about the only hitter

Sparky has left, is swinging a bat. If Rettenmund does come up, and the game happens to go on for another ten innings, that's how long Kirby will have to stay out there. Other than tomorrow's potential starter, Don Gullett, there simply isn't anyone else left.

We're spared that scenario, though, for at least one more inning. Geronimo stares at strike three, an inside fastball at the waist. The Reds strand two.

As the bottom of the inning comes up, announcer Dick Stockton reminds viewers that the wind is blowing out, which is one reason there have been so many home runs. As if to say the game will probably end on one, too.

Carlton Fisk is the batter. Pudge is the all-time Golden Homeboy, a native of Bellows Falls, Vermont, and Charlestown, New Hampshire, who grew up dreaming of playing for Boston and who, when he finally made it, became an immediate and huge fan favorite. Which he will remain until he defects to Chicago five years later. Ultimately, he will appear in more games for the White Sox than the Red, but he will be forever rooted in New England and, when he's inducted into the Hall of Fame in 2000, he'll be wearing his Beantown cap.

Fisk takes ball one. Then he goes down and swipes at a fastball on the inside part of the plate at the knees. He launches a long, high fly to left. If it stays fair . . .

When my eldest son, born in 1986, was twelve years old, I decided it was important to acquaint him with some music from the golden age of rock 'n' roll. So I went rummaging around in my vintage vinyl collection and put on some Creedence Clearwater Revival.

After side one had finished, I asked him what he thought. His first comment was, "Gee, Dad, that was pretty short."

"That's all you have to say?"

"Um, well, it's not bad. I could listen to some more."

"Done," I said. "Don't worry, that's as long as they could make a record in those days. But we can flip it over and listen to side two."

He looked at me in amazement. "You can play the other side?" he said.

So it goes. Derek has never known a world without compact discs or VCRs, personal computers or microwaves, cable television networks or Toyota Camrys. None of those existed in 1975, either.

It was very much a *you-can-play-the-other-side?* kind of world, and one of the many things TV directors didn't have back then was a battery of cameras feeding a multitude of video recorders, so that they could archive every play of every baseball game, from every possible angle, to be instantly accessed and endlessly replayed should something controversial or spectacular happen. Videotape was of the one-inch variety, and the machines that recorded on it were big, clunky, and expensive. Filming for posterity on sixteen-millimeter acetate was more common.

Thus it is only by the merest chance that the magical early morning moment of Game 6 has been preserved.

There were multiple cameras in operation, of course. But in those days only the broadcast feed and perhaps one other were recorded. The director in the booth would look back and forth among the monitors, making instantaneous decisions as to which camera's point of view deserved air time.

When Carlton Fisk connected off Pat Darcy and sent that long, looping fly ball right at the left-field foul pole, one of the cameras providing coverage was in the room behind the Wall, shooting through the little opening in the scoreboard that the announcers had referred to hours earlier.

That camera was on-line after Fisk hit the ball, although the center-field camera was the one that caught the swing. A third camera tracked the flight of the ball from the first-base side. The director called for a cut, asking that the feed from the left-field camera be killed and taping of its signal halted.

But at that instant—and this is according to the Red Sox' official history of Fenway Park—the baseball gods themselves intervened.

The left-field cameraman was supposed to switch his camera off. He didn't. So the image he was relaying continued to be recorded. And why did this happen? Because a rat ran across his foot and he jumped back.

An apocryphal story, perhaps. But I've been in that room behind the Wall. It's a hot, narrow, claustrophobic hellhole, walls covered in largely illegible graffiti, stinking of generations of sweat and tobacco juice and hot dogs and God knows what else. That there might be many such rodents residing therein is surprise-free.

Whatever the truth, the tape ran past the recording heads as that camera remained trained on Fisk. If it hadn't, if the director had had his way, our only record of the moment would be the lifeless arc of the home-run shot, rather than the Series' most defining image: Carlton waving his hands, jumping up and down like a little kid, trying his damnedest to persuade that tiny sphere to stay fair.

It does, of course, although just barely. Pudge wills it. But it's as close as you can get. It hits the left-field foul pole and bounces back onto the playing field. Home run.

Fisk thrusts his arms into the air, claps his hands together, and skips joyfully around the bases as fans stream past the police and onto the field. Fisk is jostled rounding third, and for a moment he looks fearful for his safety. He runs faster and finally touches home plate. The game is officially over. It is, imagine this, at just over four hours, the second longest in Series history to that point, and our final trivia question to which Rick Wise is the answer may now be posed: Who was the winning pitcher in glorious Game 6 of the 1975 World Series?

After order is restored and he's done the obligatory TV interview (in which he claims to have "known" something good was about to happen), Pudge comes back out onto the field. One last time, he trots around the infield, this time with nothing at stake but his personal memories. Hardly anyone has yet left the park. Here is the local hero, and they can't get enough of him. In Bellows Falls, it is said, at a quarter to one in the morning, the church bells are sounding. If there were any justice in the world, the moment would never end.

But it does, and a long, sleepless night begins for Sparky Anderson. Despite all of his maneuverings, his team has lost. Its momentum is gone. And there remains one game left to decide the title, on Boston's home field, with both team and spectators euphoric. As Sparky lies there, with dawn creeping up, he thinks there is no way his guys can win. Nope, no way. Not now. Not after this.

The game, though, must still be played.

Candles in the Wind

It is foolish and childish, on the face of it, to affiliate ourselves with anything so insignificant and patently contrived and commercially exploitative as a professional sports team, and the amused superiority and icy scorn that the non-fan directs at the sports nut (I know this look—I know it by heart) is understandable and almost unanswerable. Almost. What is left out of this calculation, it seems to me, is the business of caring—caring deeply and passionately, really caring—which is a capacity or an emotion that has almost gone out of our lives. And so it seems possible that we have come to a time when it no longer matters so much what the caring is about, how frail or foolish is the object of that concern, as long as the feeling itself can be saved. Naiveté—the infantile and ignoble joy that sends a grown man or woman to dancing and shouting with joy in the middle of the night over the haphazardous flight of a distant ball—seems a small price to pay for such a gift.

—ROGER ANGELL, "AGINCOURT AND AFTER"

When I was a kid, Uncle Oscar used to take my brother and me down to the Cape Cod candle factory where he worked, on hot summer nights when the boss had gone home and the evening shift was on.

That factory was a strange and wondrous place, a ramshackle wooden building, dank and humid in the August heat, permeated with the smell of wax and sweat and sweet crushed bayberries. My brother and I would

run up and down the creaking aisles, half expecting our feet to go crash-
ing through the ancient floorboards at any moment. Then we'd stop at one
of the candle-making stations. There were a bunch of them, and they
were all the same.

At each the candlemaker stood, patiently dipping wire racks of would-
be candles into vats of wax, building them up layer by layer. The wax was
hot, but not scalding. We found we could stick our fingers into it without
risk of first-degree burns. Which of course we did, over and over, until a
nice thick faux finger had formed. Plunge it into cold water, wiggle a little, and off it would come. Over time, we collected wax fingers in all the
colors of the candles: spring green and dusty rose, burnt orange and lilac.
Our bedroom became littered with them.

The candlemakers somehow tolerated these two pesty kids careening
around their work space, stealing their wax on tiny child fingers.

I remember them all as one composite person. He's male, of course; the
women wrapped and boxed, even did hand painting, but they never
dipped. He's gaunt, with close-cropped salt-and-pepper hair and a couple
days' growth of grizzled beard on his face. His skin is sallow, because he
sleeps during the day. He puffs on his cigarettes, being relatively careful not
to drop any ashes into the vats of wax. There are deep sweat stains on the
back of his khaki work shirt. He gazes at something only he can see, as he
lifts and dips, lifts and dips.

And next to his workstation is a radio. It's an old maroon Bakelite with
an arrow that you guide around a lighted dial in order to find your favorite
station, or else a tinny transistor portable hung from a nail driven into one
of the beams that hold up the roof. It's set to AM, naturally, the only band
available.

The radio is on. There's a lot of static, but not enough to drown out the
play-by-play. For the radio, on all of those long, hot summer nights that
featured a game—which is every one, when you're a child—is tuned to the
Red Sox.

"The real activity," in Bart Giamatti's words, "was done with the
radio—not the all-seeing, all-falsifying television—as was the playing of
the game in the only place it will last, the enclosed green field of the mind.
There, in that warm, bright place, what the old poet called Mutability does
not so quickly come."

I don't know to what extent these men's minds are warm, bright, mutable, or any longer green. I do know that it was only with the stream of commentary issuing from the radio that the stoic demeanor of the chain-smoking candlemaker cracked, joy replacing despair replacing joy, as dictated by the ups and downs of his team.

With the Red Sox, there was nearly always hope and anticipation, and then, as the grinding summer wore on, the inevitability of disillusion. Before we knew it, we were already talking about "next year."

But not this time, not at the beginning of the ultimate game of the 1975 World Series. This time, the future is now.

I'm watching the game at Uncle Oscar's, the only place to be. He's as New England stoic as ever. Between us, like a dusty pile of old baseball cards, lie the jumbled events of all those years together: making wax fingers at the candle company; watching the slow deterioration of Cape Cod as it grew and grew; acknowledging my own failures as a player; surviving the '60s; pigging out on fried clams and 'Gansett beer; listening to the crackling AM radios of the night dippers; and rooting, endlessly rooting, for a team that always, always, always falters in the end. We have shared so much, and we never speak about it. We will share this one last thing, then I will move away from the Cape for good.

We talk about the Series and I wonder if Oscar, with his fatalism, is thinking that this may be his final opportunity to see the Sox win for the first time since he was about the same age I was when I started dipping my finger in hot wax: seven years old.

I push away the thought. I'm just happy that it's another great evening for baseball: dry, with the temperature in the fifties. The Sox enter the game on a roll, still high from Fisk's twelfth-inning homer sixteen hours earlier. They have everything going for them. They have momentum. They have home-field advantage. They have a very well-rested starter, Bill Lee, who baffled the Reds here in Game 2; and they have a much less heavily worked bullpen. They'll be hitting against a guy, Don Gullett, who struggled in Game 1 at Fenway. They're loose, facing a stunned team that is surely a bit tight after losing a game (and possibly a Series) that they appeared to have locked up.

And tonight the wind has shifted, now blowing from right to left, as it did in Games 1 and 2. That, coupled with Lee's sinkers and screwballs, should negate the Reds' advantage in terms of the long ball. A home run like Fisk's will not decide this one; a scratch hit, more likely.

One hopes for no further umpiring miscues. Larry Barnett—who has been assigned bodyguards in the wake of death threats he received after Game 3—is lurking out there at second base, but at least he's not calling balls and strikes. How could he possibly be objective if he were? Instead, the steadier hand of Art Frantz will be controlling the flow of the game.

Lee is ready. He's pumped. No more complaining about being passed over for the previous night's start. He's been waiting all his life to pitch a game this big, and he's eager to show what he can do.

He goes out there and immediately serves notice that he is *on*. He retires Rose on a fly to short right, then fans Joe Morgan swinging. It's Joe's first strikeout of the Series. When Bench goes down on a grounder to short, it looks as though we might be seeing the Bill Lee of Game 2, which is good news indeed.

First up for the Sox in the bottom of the first is Bernie Carbo. Bernie has been lobbying hard for the chance to start in left field, with Yaz moved to first and the slump-stricken Cecil Cooper sent to the bench. Now he's gotten his wish. It's not a tough decision for Darrell Johnson, considering that Cooper is 1 for 18 and Carbo has two home runs in four at-bats. The only surprising thing is that Bernie is batting leadoff, because that pits the left-hander against lefty pitcher Don Gullett.

Bernie strolls to the plate after having searched in vain for the bat with which he hit the dramatic homer in Game 6. It's been stolen.

Carbo facing Gullett is the sort of against-the-book matchup Johnson normally shies away from. But in this instance he probably reasons that Carbo, the natural opposite-field hitter, is ideally suited to take a fastballer like Gullett to the Wall. Which, as if he wants to waste no time in making his manager look good, is exactly what he does. He launches a long, high fly to left. Home run, everyone thinks. First blood drawn with the very first batter. But . . . no. The wind serves *its* notice that it is going to be a factor tonight. It holds the ball up and pushes it back. So, instead of being into the screen, Carbo's hit strikes high up on the Green Monster and Bernie has to settle for a double. Not as good as a homer, but a nice start nevertheless. Perhaps Gullett will get rattled early and the Sox can knock him out of there.

Not this inning. Doyle flies to right. Yaz, who has two game-winning RBI in the Series, grounds to second. And Fisk strikes out swinging on a letter-high fastball. That's the one they have to lay off of, announcer Tony Kubek informs us. When Gullett is going good, his high heater is about unhittable. You have to wait him out, force him to bring the fastball down in the strike zone, where it's less lively.

Tony Perez leads off for Cincinnati, and the second offering he sees is the "Leephus" pitch, a big, slow lollipop curveball that tends to freeze batters in surprise. Perez watches it roll past him. Watches carefully: *Where is the pitch thrown? What does it do?* Storing away information for possible use later in the game. For now, though, he grounds a sinker to Petrocelli, and Rico, who has played outstanding defense at third throughout the Series, makes a nice pickup going to his left and throws Tony out.

Foster follows by getting under one of Lee's pitches and lining it off the left-field wall. But then he tries to stretch it into a double. No, George. Not in Fenway. Not against a fielder with as powerful an arm as Bernie Carbo's. Bernie throws him out at second.

Concepcion grounds to short, and Burleson, who's had a couple of shaky moments in the field, almost makes another error when his throw pulls Yaz off the bag. But the old pro bails him out. Yaz makes a swipe tag to get the runner.

There's a moment of excitement in the Boston second. After Fred Lynn opens the inning with a walk, Petrocelli hits a long drive to deep left. It has home-run distance but curves just foul. Rico then strikes out, Evans fouls to third, and Burleson flies to right. Gullett isn't as sharp as he was in Game 5, but he looks like he has enough to go deep into this one. A pitcher's duel to decide the Series is shaping up.

Lee has a little trouble in the third. Griffey leads off with a single to right center and is erased on a 4-6-3 double play. Good thing, because Gullett follows with a single to right. But Pete Rose bounces one back to the box, and Lee forces Gullett at second. Despite the three hits in three innings, this is very much a Bill Lee type of game. No one has scored, and six outs have been recorded on ground balls.

The third starts harmlessly enough, as Lee tries a surprise bunt with two strikes on him and pops one foul for strike three. Then the roof falls in on Gullett, and it's his own inconsistency that kicks out the supports.

Bernie Carbo works the count to 3–2 and draws a walk. With Denny Doyle at the plate and the count 1–0, the not-very-fleet Sox are off and running. Carbo (two stolen bases all year) lights out for second. It's a hit-and-run, and Doyle fouls the pitch off. Perhaps that's fortunate, because on the next pitch he lines a single to right, making him the only player on either team to hit safely in all seven games.

Griffey throws right past the cutoff man in a vain attempt to nail Carbo at third. He doesn't get him. Equally important, savvy veteran Carl Yastrzemski is watching intently from the on-deck circle. He notes Griffey's mistake, which doesn't cost the Reds . . . this time.

With Perez holding Doyle on, Yaz grounds one through the hole between first and second to deliver yet another timely hit. Carbo scores and Doyle goes to third. Yaz, the previous play fresh in his mind, watches Griffey as he rounds first. Sure enough, Ken winds up and overthrows the cutoff man again. So Yaz never stops. Doyle is safe at third, and Yaz pulls into second standing up. Pete Rose fakes a quick throw to second and swipes a tag back at Doyle, but Denny isn't having any. He's camped on the bag.

Now Yaz's superb baserunning pays off. Had Carl held at first, Gullett would have pitched to the slow-footed Pudge Fisk and the Reds would have had a shot at a double play to get out of the inning. With first base open, however, Fisk has to be intentionally walked. This is the only way to create the double play opportunity, plus it takes the dangerous Fisk out of an RBI situation, and it sets lefty against lefty. On the downside, the lefty hitter is fleet Freddie Lynn, a much more difficult runner to double up than Fisk.

Gullett is clearly struggling and yet, incredibly, Lynn is once again overanxious. Perhaps envisioning the game-breaking grand slam, he goes after the first pitch. Even worse, it's the one Gullett pitch the Sox should all be laying off, the high heater. And worst of all, it's out of the strike zone. Lynn swings and misses at a ball up around his shoulders.

He swings at the second pitch, too, but at least this one is letter-high. He fouls it off. Then he finally lets the pitcher start digging a hole for himself. He takes balls one and two. Then, on 2–2, Gullett comes in with a very nice, tight fastball at the knees. There's nothing Lynn can do except look and hope for the best. The call could go either way. Had he not taken a foolish cut at that first pitch, it wouldn't matter; he'd either get ball four or run the count to 3–2. Unfortunately, he did swing at it, and now Art Frantz calls him out on strikes. Lynn argues, to no avail.

Gullett is almost out of the inning. But Petrocelli is up, with his powerful, compact swing. Gullett probably starts obsessing with the Wall again, remembering the foul home run Rico hit over it in the second. He's high and wide on every pitch and falls behind 3–0. Gamely, he struggles back, with Rico taking, and gets to 3–2. Then he loses it. Petrocelli walks, forcing in Doyle.

Gullet comes unglued. He completely loses the strike zone, walks Dwight Evans on four pitches—the fourth base on balls he's issued in the inning. Yaz scores. Gullett's on the ropes, but Anderson leaves him out there. Says Tony Kubek: "Sparky's managing with his heart now." He doesn't want to pull his ace at such a low point.

Three runs in. If ever there was a moment to let a pitcher finish hanging himself, this is it. Gullett can't find the plate with a searchlight. Yet here comes another guy with visions of that grand slam dancing in his head. Burleson—oh no, oh *no!*—swings at the first pitch, a fastball wide that's probably out of the strike zone. He fouls it off. He takes a ball low. Then he swings *again*, fouling off a low, outside pitch that would have been a borderline strike, at best. God. A fastball down the pipe, OK, maybe you take the big cut, try to put four runs on the board all at once. But this is pure junk Rick is hacking at.

The next offering is even worse, in the dirt, with Bench making a nice pickup to prevent the wild pitch. So, had Burleson merely stood there, with the bat on his shoulder, there's an excellent chance that he would have walked on four pitches. Just like the batter before him. Umpires rarely give marginal strikes to pitchers as wild as Gullett is right now. With a little self-control, Burleson would have driven in the fourth run of the inning, and the Red Sox would really be in the driver's seat.

Instead of trotting down to first, though, Burleson is staring at a 2–2 count. Thus, when Gullett serves up yet another borderline pitch, this one on the outside corner, Burleson is unable to chance taking it. Forced to swing, he strikes out and the inning is over.

Coulda shoulda. But a three-run advantage, hey, we'll take it. Or at least I will. Oscar is less sanguine. "Would of been nice to really blow it open," he mutters. Like any true Red Sox fan, he regards a modest lead as something to be frittered away.

But it holds up easily in the fourth. After Joe Morgan bunts his way on and steals second, Bench flies out to right-center, Perez flies to right, and Foster fouls to the catcher.

In the home fourth, Gullett goes back out there and is immediately in trouble again. Lee, the opposing pitcher, chops a single past Perez into right field, then lopes on down to second on a wild pitch. Bad start. "Knock him out," I urge my team. "Knock him out *now*." Sparky hangs with his starter, though, and miraculously Don rights the ship. He gets Carbo on a ground-out to second that allows Lee to advance. Man on third, one out. A key hit, even a fly ball, and the lead is padded.

It's not to be. Doyle grounds to third and is thrown out as Lee is forced to hold, and Yaz fouls to first to end it. Gullett survives. But he knows that if the Reds reach his spot in the order, he's gone. Though he can lose this one, he can't get his second Series victory today.

Lee has a tense fifth, through no fault of his own. First Davy Concepcion lays a perfect bunt down the first-base line and beats it out. Then Griffey's ground ball gets past Denny Doyle for an error, putting runners at the corners with nobody out. The Boston left-hander bears down. He catches Geronimo looking at strike three for the big first out. Then Merv Rettenmund, batting for Gullett, swings at a sinkerball and raps a perfect two-hopper to Burleson. It's a classic 6-4-3 double play, second of the night for the Sox, and they're out of the inning with no damage. Twelve outs to go for the championship.

Gullett's Series is over. He pitched well enough to win one game and poorly enough to lose two others. If he's to escape the loss in this one, the relievers will have to hold off the Sox until the Reds can put some runs on the board. Sparky's first man out of the pen—and it's one of life's few certainties that it won't be his last—is starter Jack Billingham. This makes sense, considering Jack's fine performance in Fenway in Game 2.

Looks like a bad choice. Billingham strikes out Fisk swinging, but then the road gets very bumpy. He walks Fred Lynn on five pitches, one of which hits the dirt and bounces right past Bench. It's Boston's sixth free pass of the game. Then steady Rico Petrocelli grounds a single between short and third. Lynn stops at second.

Evans unloads, driving the ball to the deepest part of center field. Of course, there just happens to be a Gold Glover out there, and if it's catchable Geronimo is going to get it. Which he does, at the warning track. Lynn tags and goes to third.

Burleson is up. His previous at-bat, he probably should have been patient, waited Gullett out, worked him for the walk that would have produced a run. Now, with Bill Lee to follow and runners at the corners with two out, he should probably swing away and try to drive the run in. He doesn't. On the other hand, Billingham doesn't give him much good to hit, anyway. Rick walks on a 3–1 pitch.

Bases loaded. The bad news is, the pitcher is up. The good news is that the pitcher is Bill Lee, and Bill—who receives a standing ovation—is a pretty good hitter. Consider that three years from now, after a decade with Boston, Lee's archenemy, manager Don Zimmer, will finally persuade management to trade him. The Red Sox will ship him to Montreal (a club in the DH-less National League, where he will be forced to bat) in exchange for a young but unpromising utility infielder named Stan Papi.

It is only one among many, many bad trades that litter the Red Sox' historical landscape like so many burned-out Studebakers—Jeff Bagwell for Larry Andersen, Sparky Lyle for Danny Cater, Brady Anderson and Curt Schilling for Mike Boddicker, and so on. But it's my personal favorite because, in this instance, not only will Lee go on to notch 16 victories for the Expos in '79; he will also, embarrassingly, *outhit* Stan Papi, .216 to .188. Forget the wins; if Boston had merely kept Lee around for his bat, they would have fared better.

But that's the future. In the present, the Red Sox just want Bill to make contact, to not strike out. Despite the pressure of the situation, it ain't likely that the veteran Billingham will cave in and walk him. He must put the ball in play. If he can, there's the chance of a hit or an error, which will allow the Sox to lengthen their lead.

It's Lee's opportunity to really help his own cause, and Lord, does he try. After fouling off the first pitch and taking a ball, he laces into a fastball and drives it deep to straightaway center. Gold Glover that he is, César Geronimo, who was playing shallow, reacts instantaneously. He turns and takes off. This one will clear the bases if it drops, and post a six-run lead for Cincinnati to chase. Should Sparky Anderson open his mouth at this moment, his heart will likely dribble off his tongue.

Back goes Geronimo, desperately, a full-speed no-tomorrow sprint, back, back, and right at the warning track he hauls it in. Without that damnable wind, it's . . . But no. Lee has given it his very best shot, the Sox have staged a rally that could effectively put the game out of reach, and all they have to show for it is three men left on base. It doesn't matter that the team is still out in front. Boston fans everywhere are squirming nervously in their seats.

"That hurts," I say to Uncle Oscar.

He sits there calmly, with his hands folded over his paunch, tapping his thumbs together. He just nods. He's been there and seen that.

And now, as if in direct response to our gnawing sense of unease, as if to justify the nagging suspicion that the Red Sox will always find a way to snatch defeat from the jaws of victory, the game takes the most bizarre of turns. Only in Boston, we'll be saying to ourselves for years to come. Only in Boston . . .

In the sixth, Pete Rose threads a single through the right side of the infield and, for the third inning in a row, the Reds' leadoff man has reached safely. Lee, though, is unfazed by base runners; in fact, he almost seems more comfortable with them on. So far, he's pitched his way out of every jam, and here it looks as if he'll do so again.

He gets Joe Morgan on a fly to right, as Rose holds. Then Bench hits a two-hopper to Burleson for the inning-ending double play. *Whew.*

Only problem is—oh no, oh God no—it doesn't happen. Burleson flips to Doyle, who steps on second, then turns and . . . sees Rose, Pete's face a twisted malice mask, barreling as fast as he can down the base path, fully intent on breaking the fielder's legs. Denny leaps out of the way and his relay throw flies over Yastrzemski's head, over the dugout, everything. It lands in the seats. Bench is awarded second, and the inning is suddenly not over, not at all. Not with a Hall of Fame–caliber player due up.

Over the years, there have been several theories advanced about Doyle's error. One has it that he was terrified by the sight of the maniac Rose coming at him. Another holds that Bench hit the ball so hard he tore the cover, and that Denny couldn't get a proper grip.

When I met Doyle, I put the question to him. What happened?

He just shook his head. "No," he said, "the cover wasn't damaged. I don't know how a rumor like that gets started. But it isn't true. And Rose didn't scare me. When you're in the air like that, you're not focused on the runner. You don't see his face. You want to get out of his way, of course, but you don't even think about who he is or what he looks like.

"Turning a double play is all about timing, and on that one our timing was just off. Mine and Rick's. I got the ball a little late to make a clean pivot. Which threw my throwing motion off. Which caused the ball to sail on me." He shrugged. "I just made an error. It was bad, but . . ."

"It didn't decide the game," I offered.

"No."

And he's right. The inning shoulda been over, OK. Yet the Red Sox still have the three-run lead, and there are two outs and a lone runner on. There is plenty of time to regroup.

Lee, though, is upset, very upset. He thought he'd pulled his escape act again, and now he has to pitch to Perez. When I met him, he told me he wished Darrell Johnson or pitching coach Stan Williams had realized his distress and come to the mound, just to talk for a couple of minutes, to calm him down. Well, maybe. Hindsight is 20/20. And when no one emerges from the dugout, there's nothing preventing Lee from calling his catcher out for a chat, using Fisk to help him regain his own composure. Or he could even walk around for a bit, until he felt ready to go on.

None of this happens. When Bill returns to the rubber, he's still agitated. Perhaps, in light of what now transpires, he's not thinking clearly. He misses with his first pitch, then makes a decision so poor that it becomes instant Sox history. Bad history. Miserable, heart-wrenching, weep-in-your-beer history. Because Space, guided by whatever intergalactic logic, decides to come back with the Leephus.

Most pitchers are fastball pitchers. The pitch is less complicated to deliver, gentler on the arm, and easier to control. It's the first thing kids throw, what they grow up with. You don't start by trying to put some tricky spin on that old rock. And later, when you finally reach the major leagues, the temptation is always strongest to get strikes by heaving the ball so hard the batter can't catch up with it.

Thus, most big-league hitters are fastball hitters. They attempt to get into a rhythm, to time the pitcher's fastball, guess when it's coming, and be prepared to hit it. If they're good at it, they're known as good fastball hitters. Whole teams—like the '75 Reds—can be known as good fastball hitters, or "free swingers," meaning they guess fastball a lot, are right more often than they are wrong, and hit a ton of home runs. But you have to be able to hit the breaking ball at least occasionally, by skill or by guessing, or your career is apt to be a short one. Pitchers soon learn if someone is a "dead fastball hitter," which means that's *all* he can hit.

Hitting a professionally thrown curve demands a more complex set of talents.

First, you must be able to see it. Different pitches put different rotations on the ball, visible to the keen, well-trained eye. You must be able to pick that up, to distinguish the heater from the breaking stuff, preferably just after the pitcher releases the ball. And you must have absolute faith in your ability to make the distinction.

Next, your timing must be impeccable. Breaking balls arrive at the plate pretty quickly in an absolute sense, but more slowly than fastballs. If you can't adjust, you'll find yourself way out in front of the one and swinging late on the other.

Then, too, you must be an excellent guesser.

And finally, you must be able to conquer your fear. Imagine that *you* are the batter. The pitcher winds up and then throws one right at your head. In a fraction of a second, you have to try to pick up the rotation, to determine whether you're about to get your brains scrambled or not. Is the pitcher a headhunter, or did his fastball just get away from him, or is this actually a breaking ball that will dive back over the plate and make you look the fool? You flinch, automatically, you can't help it. But do you also pull away? If you do, and it was in fact an errant fastball, you did the right thing; if it was a curve, you not only got beat, you handed the pitcher a big psychological edge the next time he comes inside on you. You can't do that.

These are the basic requirements for someone who wants to be a *good* breaking-ball hitter. To be a *great* breaking-ball hitter, you need to add one further ingredient. You must be able to guess fastball and still make contact when you *don't* get it. This necessitates abilities far beyond the ordinary. Players who can do it have to have the visual acuity to recognize their mistake; the skill to adjust their swing accordingly, in less time than it would take to think the thought; and the reflexes to bring it off. Not many have that complete package.

Tony Perez does. He's a great breaking-ball hitter.

And, in this instance, he just might have a helping hand. Johnny Bench, a catcher, is perched out at second, the perfect man to steal a sign.

Whether or not Perez has been tipped that the Leephus pitch is coming doesn't matter. Nor does whether or not he was waiting for something off-speed, or adjusted when he saw the rotation on the curve. All that is material is that Tony has seen this pitch earlier in the game, knows what it does, and is ready for it. He crushes it. In left, Carbo doesn't even move. This one won't be held up by the wind; it isn't going to ricochet off the Wall. In fact, it soars over both the Wall and the net and falls into the hands of some lucky pedestrian on Lansdowne Street.

The crowd, which had been cheering every pitch, goes silent and remains so even as Foster flies out to right to end the inning. Though the Red Sox still cling to the lead, in one irretrievable moment the whole ball of yarn has begun to unravel, and everyone in Fenway knows it.

Bill Lee nailed it down when he wrote that Boston fans, while the most wonderfully supportive people in the world, live "in a state of constant denial. Even when the team's going good, they . . . keep waiting for the other shoe to drop, knowing that it usually lands on their heads. New York fans let it all hang out, never worrying about tomorrow because they know tomorrow may never come. In direct contrast, Boston fans figure no, let's worry about tomorrow because the odds are it will probably get here, and when it does, it's going to rain. They realize death is lurking in the background of every celebration. It can't be avoided. Their city is filled with famous old cemeteries. Every corner you turn, there's John Adams or John Hancock. And they're all dead."

Well, OK, Lee is given to hyperbole.

But the Red Sox do go quietly in the sixth—how could they not? They're not immune to the malaise that's creeping through the stadium. And Billingham, on the verge of being driven shamefaced from the mound an inning earlier, seems rejuvenated by the turn of events. He sets the Sox down one-two-three.

To open the seventh, Darrell Johnson takes a calculated risk and sends Rick Miller out to play left field. He's making a statement. By sacrificing

Carbo's very hot bat for Miller's more accomplished glove, he's saying that he believes his team can hang on and win this game even if it doesn't score any more runs.

Concepcion starts the inning by grounding out to short, but then Griffey walks on four pitches. Lee is consistently missing low. Johnson immediately goes to the mound and finds that Bill has developed a blister on his pitching hand. This is no small matter; it's why pitchers normally work hard to keep calluses on their fingertips.

Did Darrell know about that blister ahead of time? I asked him during our interview. "No," he said. "I'm sure that I didn't. And I know that because, if it had been there before, Bill would have told the trainer and he would have come to me. That's the way it works and that didn't happen. But a blister can come on very quickly, and once it does it can throw your whole delivery off. The reason I went out there is that I knew something was wrong. A manager knows his pitchers. There's always a giveaway when something's wrong. If it turns out to be a blister, then you don't fool around. You want the guy to come out right away."

Watching the tape today, you can see Johnson look down at the hand, then without a moment's hesitation signal for his left-hander in the bullpen, to come in and face the left-handed Geronimo.

You can see the frustration in Lee's face, but he doesn't protest. When I asked him about it, he said, "Hell, no, I didn't want to come out. Are you *joking*? The seventh game of the freakin' *World Series*? I wanted to finish it. But my finger was bleeding." He paused, then went on. "You know, a couple of years later I found out up in Montreal there's some stuff they could've put on it, to cauterize the wound on the spot. And they didn't. Where the hell was [Sox trainer] Buddy Leroux when I really needed him?"

Well, nowhere near the mound, that's for sure. But even if he had been, Johnson assured me, Leroux wouldn't have done anything. "You don't fool around with a blister," he said, "not during the game. You have to open it and drain it and give it time to heal. It's a two- to three-day operation in the training room. You can't just treat it and expect someone to continue to pitch."

Lee departs, and the crowd gives him another standing ovation. He's done good. Among all the starting pitchers on either side of this Series, he has posted the lowest earned run average and has departed both of his games with his team ahead. Now he can only watch and wait. If the bullpen holds the lead, he will have his World Series victory. But if the Reds score another, both he and Gullett will get a no-decision.

In from the pen, making his third and final Series appearance, comes Roger Moret.

Dealing with the enigma that is Rogelio Moret has been one of my most difficult tasks in writing this book.

The basic story is simple:

Roger, from Guayama, Puerto Rico, was signed by the Red Sox out of high school, for the princely sum of eight thousand dollars. It was 1968, he was eighteen years old, and he had a world of stuff—fastball, curve, change-up—all potentially of major league quality. Moret moved quickly through the minors. He spent time at Waterloo, Iowa—a place he remembers now as simply "cold"—with Pudge Fisk and Bill Lee, moved up to Pawtucket, a Double-A team at that time, and was promoted from there to the parent club in 1970.

He remembers his first appearance in the bigs. "It was 1–1 when I came in," he recalled for me. "I pitched six innings and got the win."

And that was pretty much it for that year. He pitched two more innings before being sent down to Triple-A Louisville for seasoning. In '71, he split time between Boston and Louisville. For the Red Sox he pitched 71 innings and went 4–3 with an excellent 2.92 ERA. He was a rising star. But he backslid in '72, adding only 5 innings to his major league résumé.

"My arm was tired," he told me. "I pitched 60 games and five hundred innings the year before." *Five hundred?* "Yeah, between America and Puerto Rico. I was pitching for Santurce in the winter league. It was too much."

In '73, though, he came storming back. He pitched 156 innings for the Red Sox and went 13–2 with an ERA of 3.17. The next year, 1974, featured a disappointing won/loss record, 9–10, but his ERA was a respectable 3.75 and his hits/innings and walks/strikeouts ratios remained strong.

In both of these years, he was used primarily in long relief and as a spot starter. In 1975, after the season was under way, he was moved into the starting rotation, a promotion that was looking permanent after he won 14 and lost 3 and posted an ERA of 3.60.

Moret was traded to Atlanta following the '75 season, and after that his career went nowhere but down. He was exiled to the bullpen by the Braves, and his innings pitched fell to 77 while his ERA ballooned to 5.03. The Braves traded him to Texas, where he played in '77 and '78. His innings declined to 72, then to 15 and then, in 1979, he was out of baseball.

Well, out of the big leagues, anyway. He returned home to Puerto Rico, where he pitched for Santurce until 1994 or, in other words, until he was forty-five years old.

"You have to be forty-five to collect your major league pension," he told me with a smile. "That's when I quit."

Obviously, then, there was nothing wrong with his arm. And everyone agrees he had a world of talent. So what was the story behind these facts? Why the precipitous descent? How could someone with so much promise drop from sight before his thirtieth birthday? I didn't know. No one I asked knew. The only thing to do was seek out Roger himself and see what I could discover.

That's what I did, and it wasn't easy. But with the dedicated help of some new friends at the Puerto Rican Baseball Federation, I tracked him down. Roger lives at the end of the road to anywhere, in the town he originally came from, Guayama, a few miles from the southern coast of Puerto Rico. He doesn't have a car or a telephone. His baseball earnings sufficed to buy him a home, and he pays his day-to-day expenses out of his pension, which he told me is five hundred dollars a month.

To get to Guayama, you drive south from the heavily populated and touristed San Juan metropolitan area, to the opposite end of the island, where visitors seldom venture. You pass through any number of climatic zones. At first, there is the lush green of the rain-watered windward side of the island. The crumpled hills have small pastel-colored stucco houses tumbling down their sides like strewn matchboxes. Setting off the green are flamboyant trees with their brilliant orange flowers.

But the land gets drier and drier as the central mountains trap the moisture to the north. The population thins out. The hills turn brown and green, then to dry brown grass. Finally, there is nothing left but naked dirt and bare rock. A desert.

As I made my way to my meeting with the man, I pondered what I'd heard about Roger Moret. If no one could tell me exactly why he'd flamed out, there was general agreement that some of his behavior was "problematic" to management and that that was the kiss of death back then. The incidents that got him into trouble were well known and have been written up in the press.

In '75, he'd tried to drive to New York and back one night, during the season. He didn't make it. Sometime before dawn, he'd fallen asleep at the wheel and plowed into a truck, totaling his car and nearly decapitating himself. He went to the hospital, where they sewed up his head and released him the following day. He pitched the day after that in Chicago. But the brass was not pleased.

This is the incident, as Bill Lee recorded it in his book: "Roger was a good pitcher, but he was uncomfortable in the Boston organization. He felt misunderstood and mistreated. The players called him Wrong Way. He was usually headed the right way, but he did have a habit of falling asleep while going there. He did that once while driving his car. He was doing eighty when he nodded out. The car slipped under a rock, tearing off part of his roof and almost killing Roger in the process. Only the fact that he was so completely relaxed saved his life. He did miss that evening's game, spending most of the night in a local hospital. The next day, the front office read the riot act to him. I'll never forget how that stunned him. He sat in front of his locker, shaking his head, saying, 'They keep talking about fining me, or suspending me, or trading me to another club. But nobody has asked me how I am or what the X-rays showed.' That really blew him away."

And it probably helped get him traded.

Later, in Texas, things went from bad to worse. In 1978—in what was probably the most publicized event of his career—he experienced a total freak-out that left him catatonic in the Rangers dressing room.

This is the way Bill Lee told it to me: "Roger had girlfriend problems, everyone was hitting on him, everyone needed money, he was broke. He was promised a loan for a new car if he won this ballgame. He didn't quite win it and went to the GM anyway, who said, no, it was only if he won the game. So Roger goes out in the outfield, starts digging up the turf and burying all the batting practice balls, then running around. They tell him to get off the field. He goes in the clubhouse. Now he's lost baseball, he's lost his money, he's lost his family, he's lost everything, and he's standing there naked with a shower shoe in his hand and yeah, a lot of people woulda gone catatonic in that situation."

Ferguson Jenkins, who roomed with Moret in Texas, talked to me in a telephone interview. He also remembered that Roger "didn't get the car, the one thing he wanted. He had no wheels, and that bothered him."

Jenkins added that Moret, standing there in the dressing room, was unable even to recognize his roomie. Then general manager "Eddie Robinson slapped him," but it didn't do any good. So clubhouse medical personnel were called in; "they gave him a shot and took him to the hospital, the psychiatric ward at the hospital in Arlington."

Whatever happened to Roger, and whyever, it spelled the end of his sojourn in the big leagues. In those days, there was no psychotherapy, no Prozac, no counseling, nothing. If you got tagged a "head case," you were simply traded away, until nobody was willing to take a chance on you anymore. Then you got cut for good, as Roger was after '78. I couldn't help but wonder what kind of career Moret would have had in the modern era, when every team has a sports psychologist on staff, and when the use of antidepressants is commonplace.

Jenkins believes Roger would have flourished if only there'd been someone around with a measure of savvy about the problems of nonnative English speakers. In Moret's day, Latin players were still more of a curiosity than not, and those who struggled with the language had a particularly difficult time of it.

Roger "couldn't translate what he wanted very well," Jenkins said. "He didn't understand what people were asking of him. Because of that, he would sometimes agree to things that he didn't really comprehend."

Lee believes Moret was just a confused, sensitive, uneducated kid who needed to be hugged now and then. Fergie believes he should have had a translator. Beat journalists tend to see him as suffering from some unspecified variety of mental illness. Another teammate, himself a recovered alcoholic, thinks he saw in Roger the classic signs of substance abuse.

Enrique Sued, the gracious Puerto Rican baseball club owner who set up the Moret interview for me, was clear about one thing: I needed to talk to Roger in the morning, because in the afternoon, "the drugs . . ." When I pressed him on what he meant, he only shrugged. Was Moret doing illegal drugs, or was he on some prescription medication that kicked in during the afternoon? And what behavioral changes did I risk seeing if I waited until later in the day? I never got an answer to any of these questions.

I was going to have to take Rogelio Moret at whatever face value was presented to me. I drove. When I reached the end of the highway, I turned east. There was a sign advertising a new Chi Chi Rodriguez golf course but no evidence that construction on the course was under way. I was told later that the project was an attempt to bring more tourists to the south coast region.

The area could use them, if Guayama is any indication. It's a parched, paint-peeling town set in a bowl surrounded by ugly brown hills. It seems very poor. It's several miles from both the ocean and Chi Chi's proposed links. There's no reason to think that it will attract the mainland travelers' dollars anytime soon.

Somehow, using my phrase-book Spanish, I found my way through the town to our rendezvous point; a few minutes later, Roger came loping down the street. At fifty-two, he was still rail-thin and spindly legged. I could tell that he had once been quite tall—he claimed to be six five, which seems an exaggeration. In his playing days he was listed at six four, but the passing years had bowed him considerably, so that he didn't seem much over six feet anymore. He had a gray bush of hair on top and a gray mustache.

He might have been difficult to recognize from a photo, but in person you couldn't mistake the trademark grin. I recalled that during the introduction of the players prior to Game 1 of the '75 Series, he was the only member of the Red Sox who laughed into the camera. He was still laughing a lot, and when he did he was that twenty-five-year-old kid again.

Roger was accompanied by a young woman who stayed with us the whole time. I was never introduced to her, and she didn't speak. She was either his daughter or his niece, I think the latter. Both of them live with or near him. It certainly felt as if she was his chaperone.

Sr. Sued gave us the use of a storeroom at the rear of the pharmacy that he owns, and that's where I interviewed Roger. We talked for about an hour. And at the end of that time I knew little more than when I started.

Some things about him were evident from observation. He was a very cheerful man, whether or not he had chemical assistance in that regard, and never had an unkind word for anybody. He had an infectious laugh. He was easily distracted, playing with this or that in front of him on the table, but I couldn't say that it was pathological. And his mood underwent a sharp change in tone when we dealt with topics that made him uncomfortable. At those times he became very quiet and withdrawn, and he would remain that way until I changed the subject.

It happened when we talked about Luis Tiant. He liked Luis a lot, but his opinion of his fellow pitcher differed markedly from that of every other member of the team that I talked to. The others saw Tiant as the merry prankster, the guy who kept everybody loose; many called him the funniest man they'd ever known. Not Roger. Moret believed that the Sox made fun of Luis because of his fractured English and heavy Latin accent and that Tiant demeaned himself by playing the clown for them. He didn't like it.

I couldn't help but wonder how much Roger was actually talking about himself.

Another moment of silence came when I tried to steer him into talking about what happened in Texas. All he would say was that he hurt his shoulder down there and had to have an operation. When he came back, they wouldn't let him be a starter, which was what he wanted. Eventually, they sent him down to the minors.

That, he said, was when he did a sober evaluation of what remained of his career. He knew what the minors were like. He'd tasted life in the big leagues. Could he go back? "I asked myself if I wanted to drive fifteen hours on a bus through the dust to games again," he said, and the answer was, "No. I decided to go home."

That was it. No mention of any freak-out or time spent on the psychiatric ward. When I made one last attempt by saying I'd heard he got into a dispute with management over a car, he said he had no recollection of any such thing.

Roger did not strike me as a dissembler. His lack of memory of the car incident appeared genuine. Yet it is at variance with the stories told by his teammates. Fergie Jenkins, Moret's roomie, is particularly credible in this regard. I could only conclude that, at the conscious level anyway, he dealt with the past in the way that was least painful to him.

The same seemed to be true concerning his stay in Boston. He remembered the accident, but he shrugged it off. "I got seven stitches in my head and pitched the next day," he told me. He swore that he didn't miss his turn in the pitching rotation, although his teammates say that he did and that that caused the irritated response from the front office.

I prodded him. Wasn't his relationship with Red Sox management a little rocky? I asked him.

"No, no," he said. "I'm happy in Boston. I'm a good boy, Orlando Cepeda was my teacher. I didn't like that they traded him. They traded all their good players. But I'm happy anywhere, money is money. Boston treated me super."

I didn't doubt the part about him being happy anywhere.

The conversation turned to 1975, and there I found that Moret's memory for the World Series was unimpaired. He recalled in detail all of his appearances, especially taking the mound for the first time in Riverfront Stadium. That was thrilling. "Seventy-five thousand fans," he said (actually fifty-five thousand). "It was different. Not like that little park in Boston."

He pretended still to be seething about being passed over for the start in Game 5, though I believed it unlikely that Roger seethed about anything for too long. He laughed as he said it. Then he re-created how he struck out Merv Rettenmund in Game 3, noting every pitch he threw. He said he believed that after getting that out he was going to escape the inning unscathed and prolong the game. He remembered being elated at the weak fly ball Morgan hit next, until he realized that Fred Lynn was playing way in, to prevent a run scoring on a bloop single, and that this one was going to be over Freddie's head. That bummed him out. Having allowed the winning run to score, despite not being charged with it, was obviously embarrassing to him.

I told him he was a great player.

"Yah," he agreed. He grinned. "But I'm broke now." He got up abruptly. "I gotta go eat," he announced. "We done?"

Sure, I said, and, after he posed delightedly for a few pictures, he walked away down the dusty, potholed street.

As I drove back to San Juan, I thought about Roger. I'd found him to be very personable, eager to please, childlike in a positive way, with an infectious good humor. Being around him had lifted my spirits.

Something had derailed his career, yes. But I didn't know what it was, and I never would. Getting to the truth would be difficult and time-consuming, and I wasn't up to it. Moreover, I realized that I didn't care. Roger Moret was who he was. In the end, he was in some measure just like us all, a person whose past was a mystery to everyone but himself. I was happy simply to have met him.

Moret is throwing bullets, but it's anyone's guess as to where they're going. He falls behind Geronimo 2–0, then catches a break. César squares around as if to bunt but takes a half-swing and tries to chop it past the onrushing fielders. Instead, he pops it up. Burleson puts it away, and there's only one more out to get.

Here comes *that guy* one last time. Ed Armbrister, hitting for Billingham. Not much danger of a bunt here, of course, not with two out. Although you never know with Sparky. Petrocelli plays close to the line at third; they'll concede a bunt, if that's what Anderson springs on them, and guard against the double down the line that might score the fleet Griffey.

The count runs to 2–1 and, with the hit-and-run on, Armbrister swings and misses. Griffey's fast, but he's dead in the water when the batter fails to make contact. A decent throw and the runner is out. Yet once again, maddeningly, Fisk fails to make the play. Since he gunned down Joe Morgan in Game 2, Pudge has come up empty. The Reds have been successful on nine consecutive stolen-base attempts.

This one really costs.

Moret loses Armbrister, making two pitches out of the strike zone for the walk. Up comes Pete Rose. He gets a fastball, just low. Ball one. Moret knows he's got to throw some strikes, so he brings his next pitch up a little. A fastball, thigh-high. Pete is sitting on it, and he lines it into center for his Series-leading 10th hit. Lynn fields the ball cleanly but stutter-steps on his throw. It would almost certainly have been late anyway, but the slight hesitation cinches it. Griffey scores and the game is tied. Bill Lee, having for the second time pitched his very large heart out, will not (now or ever) win in the World Series.

The Red Sox, who have mostly played sound defensive baseball throughout, make a fundamental mistake here. There is no one in position to cut off Lynn's throw when it becomes evident that they won't get Griffey. So the ball bounces to the plate, allowing the runners to move up a base. Armbrister goes to third, Rose to second.

And the National League's Most Valuable Player is up. The percentage move is probably to walk Morgan intentionally, or at least pitch around him, then bring in a right-hander to face Bench. Oddly, Moret goes after

Little Joe, running the count full before coming in with what he undoubtedly hopes is a strikeout pitch, a fastball at the knees. It's maybe a little low, maybe not, but is in any case one of those borderline pitches, again, that will not be called a strike against Mr. Morgan. He takes the base on balls.

They could have spared us the unnecessary suspense of wondering whether Morgan was going to deposit one of Roger's fastballs in the bleacher seats and just walked him on purpose. Because now righty Jim Willoughby does indeed come in to pitch. Willoughby is a sidearming sinkerballer with a motion like a spastic rattlesnake. When he finally throws, the ball seems to explode out of a tangled mess of arms and legs, and it's very difficult to pick up.

Willow makes quick work of Johnny B., who tries to lift one of those sinkers, gets too far under it, and fouls it straight back. Fisk makes a nice catch leaning into the stands as the fans give way.

It's 3–3. We should be relieved, because it coulda been so much worse. We're not.

"We're gonna lose," I say to Oscar.

"I think so," he says.

That's what the heart says. The mind, though, says that the Sox have three more at-bats to mount a rally against a Cincinnati bullpen that has proven to be merely mortal. And now unpredictable Clay Carroll is out there, making his fourteenth World Series appearance. There is cause for hope.

Well, not yet. Carlton Fisk tries, of all things, to bunt. He fouls the pitch off. Pete Rose refuses to move in at third. If Pudge actually thinks he can bunt his way on, so be it. Rose is more concerned about guarding the line. Fisk strikes out on a slow curve after falling behind 1–2.

Lynn grounds to first, and Perez just gets the ball to Carroll covering in time to nip him. And Rico grounds out to short on a checked swing.

In the eighth, the fans get back into the game as Willoughby's sinker looks unhittable. He gets Perez on a pop to third, Foster on a grounder to short that Burleson makes a nice play on, and Concepcion on a grounder to third.

When Evans walks to open the home eighth, the noise level rises. Burleson squares to bunt. The pitch is high; he lays off. But no. Art Frantz calls it a strike. Burleson glares at him. You don't want to lose a precious strike when your purpose is to move the runner over. On his next attempt,

Rick gets his bat on the ball but bunts it foul. The bunt is off. Burleson takes balls one and two. Then he swings. And grounds it right at Pete Rose, who starts an easy around-the-horn double play.

And now it comes down to this. These two teams have gone at one another with everything they have for about twenty-one hours, spread over twelve days, and they're still dead even. It looks as though the winner will be the one who finds and exploits the skinniest little edge. Which means major, gut-check decision time for my man Darrell.

Everyone's a coach, and everyone's a critic.

Hard-core sports fans tend to be a highly opinionated lot, fanatically dedicated to their teams. They're apt to feel personally insulted when said teams do poorly. They'll gather over beers in the evening and endlessly gnash their teeth over their team's failure, consigning its manager to the lowest circle of hell for his latest transgression against the dictates of simple common sense. If, further, they happen to get paid to voice their opinions, then things can get downright ugly, right out in the open for all to see.

Big-league baseball managers, because of the complex strategies involved in playing the game, are particularly subject to the fans' ire. They know this going in. They also know there is a near 100 percent chance that they will never be liked, admired, or even sufficiently appreciated for what they do. All but one must fail at his job, every year, and fans do not take kindly to losing.

This goes at least double in Boston. Imagine managing there, and struggling not only against your team's opponents and the vagaries of the game but against the dreaded Curse that has held the city at arm's length from a Series championship for generations (if it holds, the drought will reach a full century's duration in just sixteen years). Everything a Red Sox manager does—every smallest move!—is fodder for the press and the team's rabid fans. Each misstep will be analyzed and reanalyzed, not just at the time but for months and years later. Just as I, in fact, am doing more than two and a half decades after October of 1975.

It made me wonder why anyone would want to subject himself to such continual abuse, and I put the question to three former Red Sox managers: Don Zimmer, Darrell Johnson, and Johnny Pesky, a lifelong Red Sox man who was born in that same autumn in 1919 when Babe Ruth was shipped down the muddy river to New York and who has served the ball club in every conceivable capacity over the years.

Neither Johnson nor Pesky answered me. It didn't seem as if they didn't want to. It was more like the question didn't register. Everyone wants to manage a big-league team, don't they? And once you're there, you shed criticism like duck feathers do water. You do your job for as long as they let you, and you're happy for the chance.

Zim didn't directly address the question, either, but he did have this to say: "Sure, I got booed all the time in Boston. And I loved it. *Loved* it. You know why? Because I knew that come September we'd be fighting for the championship, every year."

Regardless of how they felt about it, though, all of these men, at one point in their careers, lived their lives being continually second-guessed. It's an accepted, unquestioned part of the game. Yet, if you give the matter any thought, all of it is hogwash. Call it the fixing-the-blame fallacy, if you want. The truth is that there are, in baseball, no brilliant managerial moves and no boneheaded ones. Period. It's that simple. To believe differently is to ignore the basic realities of the game.

To begin with, brilliance and boneheadedness are revealed only in the rearview mirror. A manager makes a choice, based on his best reading of the situation, and it either succeeds or it doesn't. It can always go either way. If it works, you did good, and if not, you screwed up. But none of that exists except in hindsight. That's all.

In addition, although there are always crucial events—again in hindsight—no one of them can be said truly to determine the eventual outcome of a game, no matter how close it is, much less of a series. Games are an accretion of meaningful moments, and of managerial moves and countermoves, and all are subject to the weight of circumstance. An error is inarguably "costly" if it allows the winning run to score, but it is apt to be meaningless if the team committing it has a 10-run lead. Not to mention that the "costly" game-deciding run must necessarily have been preceded by some equally costly hits, walks, or whatever.

And, finally, there is the bottom line. Managers may look like players. They, unlike their counterparts in other sports, wear the team uniform (picture Mike Krzyzewski pacing the sidelines in Blue Devil shorts, or Bill Parcells in helmet and shoulder pads . . . well, maybe Parcells), complete with cap and nonfunctional cleats. But they do not play. They don't throw ninety-five-mile-an-hour fastballs at hitters; they don't slug five-hundred-foot homers; they don't make spectacular diving catches. Only the players do those things, and only the players, by their actions, determine who will win and who will lose.

By way of illustrating the fixing-the-blame fallacy, we have to look no further than the Red Sox of 1986, who were involved in what is widely regarded as the worst managerial blunder in World Series history. In the sixth game of that Series, as every fan of the game knows, manager John McNamara failed to insert a defensive replacement for gimpy-kneed Bill Buckner at first base in the tenth inning, with the Sox leading by two runs and needing only three more outs to celebrate a victory in the Fall Classic for the first time since . . . well, since the Curse was laid on.

The rest, as they say, is history. Excruciatingly painful history for a Boston fan. Buckner, unable to coax a routine play out of his aching body, allowed Mookie Wilson's two-out ground ball to trickle between his legs. The winning run scored, and the Mets went on to win the Series.

It's a moment frozen in time and disbelief, the single dismal moment for which McNamara, a highly successful major league manager, and Buckner, an outstanding major league hitter for more than twenty years, will be primarily remembered. That is harsh, and cruel, and worst of all unfair.

In retrospect, the manager committed a terrible mistake in not making the defensive substitution for Buckner (something he'd already done in seven consecutive postseason games). Or did he? McNamara has always defended himself, maintaining that he wanted to honor Buckner—whose 102 RBI in '86 had been indispensable in helping the Sox reach the Series in the first place—by having the man on the field for the final out of the final game. Who can say that that wasn't a valid decision? After all, the Red Sox were up two, the champagne had been broken out, and the TV crew had already set up in the Boston dressing room, preparing for the post-Series interviews and the awarding of the MVP to Sox pitcher Bruce Hurst. Probably the only person in creation (outside of cynical long-term Red Sox fans) who didn't believe it was over was Gary Carter, who stroked the two-out single that began the debacle.

And before any further abuse is heaped upon Johnny Mac and Billy Bucks, it should be remembered that Buckner's error hardly determined the outcome of the Series. It ended the sixth game, yes, but all that did was pull the Mets even in games at 3–3. The Red Sox still had the seventh game in which to prevail. They didn't, despite jumping out to an early three-run lead (sound familiar?).

Furthermore, by itself the error didn't even decide the game in which it was committed. Boston pitchers did that, when they blew numerous chances to make that one final outstanding pitch, to get the one out they needed when they most needed it. Buckner didn't allow the tying run to score. That happened on a Bob Stanley sinker that Rich Gedman couldn't handle. Wild pitch or passed ball, take your pick. The first baseman had nothing to do with it.

And did the "fatal" error even matter at *all*? The person who should know best has always said, "No way." Mookie Wilson maintains that it would've made no difference if Buckner had handled the chance cleanly. He couldn't have outraced Wilson to the bag himself, and Steamer Stanley, never swift afoot, was too far from the base to have covered it either. Mookie had it beat out no matter what, he claims.

Nevertheless, McNamara was vilified and hounded out of Boston for doing what managers are called upon to do. He made a choice. Because it didn't "work out," he must act the scapegoat and be held responsible by the fans for losing the Series. He didn't, but it is in the nature of things that it must seem as if he did.

It's in this context that we must consider Darrell Johnson's final managerial decisions of the 1975 World Series. If they succeed, he will be lionized. If they fail . . .

So what do you do? It's the deciding game of the World Series, eighth inning, tie score. You're playing at home. There are two out, nobody on. Your reliever of the moment has the opposition talking to themselves, plus he's not a bad hitter himself.

Do you let him come up to bat, in the belief that it's better to stick with an effective pitcher in the late innings and utilize the home team's final at-bat advantage and if the guy delivers a hit, so much the better? Or do you send up someone who can start a two-out rally, and possibly put your team ahead with one swing, then count on whoever's left in the bullpen to close it out?

It's not an easy choice, but Johnson has been thinking about it at least since Willow mowed the Reds down last inning. At that point he knew both how well Willow was pitching and that Jim's spot in the batting order would roll up right about now. He's decided in advance what he will do if there are one or two runners on, depending on where they are, and what he'll do if, as turns out to be the case, the bases are empty.

He's going to hit for Willoughby. But with whom? With right-hander Clay Carroll still on the mound, you want a lefty. Carbo, the main home-run threat, is already out of the game. Miller is in the lineup. That leaves two possibilities: reserve catcher Tim Blackwell, a switch hitter, and Cecil Cooper of the 1-for-18 slump.

No contest. Cooper hit .311 on the season, with 14 homers; Blackwell hit .197 with none. Sure, this pressure cooker is hardly the ideal situation into which to drop a second-year player with the bat-swinging willies and expect him to break out. But slump or no, it's got to be Coop.

Cecil walks to the plate, and the fans let out a collective groan, at least those who can see his face. "No," I say to the TV more than to Oscar, as if in some mystical way Johnson can hear me. "No. Let Willow hit." Cooper looks as though his confidence level is at zero, which it probably is. He looks as though he can't wait to get this at-bat over with, which is what he does as quickly as he can. On Carroll's first pitch, he lifts a weak foul pop to third that Rose puts away for the final out.

Now Johnson must face the consequences of his decision. He has to bring in a new reliever. He consults the lineup card. Griffey, a left-hander, will lead off for the Reds in the ninth. Geronimo, another lefty, follows. And then the pitcher's spot and a probable pinch hitter who could bat from either side. Then switch hitter Rose and lefty Morgan.

The percentages favor a left-hander, at least to face the first two batters. Then, if Sparky sends up a righty, Johnson can change pitchers again. Here's the problem, though: there are only three lefties on the staff and two of them—Lee and Moret—have already pitched in this game. That leaves Jim Burton, a rookie who is very short on seasoning. He was used only sparingly during the stretch run for the pennant, failed to appear in the ALCS, and has pitched to exactly two batters in the World Series (he gave up a walk and a sac fly back in Game 3). The rest of the pen is heavy with veterans—Rick Wise, Reggie Cleveland, Dick Drago, Diego Segui; hell,

if you absolutely *had* to go to him, the exhausted Luis Tiant could probably get you a couple of outs—but they all throw from the right side. So
what'll it be, the percentages or the experience?

Johnson places the call to the pen. Send in Burton.

Perhaps if he'd had the luxury of my 2002 interviews with Jim and
Drago, he would've done it differently. Who knows? But neither of those
two was happy with the decision.

"Should it have been you?" I asked Drago.

"Absolutely," Dick told me. "That was my spot. I was ready, I was on
my game. I should've gone in."

I reminded him that he'd pitched three innings during the marathon the
night before. Three superb innings, yes, but nevertheless, that's a lot for a
reliever.

"Oh, come on," he said. "I was a starter before '75. I pitched over two
hundred innings a year. And this was the World Series, for Christ's sake. You
don't leave anything on the table. I was the closer and I wanted the ball."

Not so Burton.

"I wasn't ready," he admitted to me. "I'd hardly pitched at all the previous month. I was rusty. When I was warming up, I couldn't get loose. I
could tell I didn't have anything."

"Did you want to go in anyway?" I asked.

He paused, then answered honestly. "No," he said. "Not really."

Hindsight is beautiful, but Darrell Johnson doesn't have the slightest bit
of it at his disposal, not on October 22, 1975. His gut tells him to throw
the rookie out there, and that's what he does.

Burton, who will later tell me that, quite frankly, he was terrified, needs
a full at-bat in order to settle down. That batter is Griffey, and he walks.
With the lead man on, Anderson wastes no time. Geronimo immediately
lays down a bunt in the direction of third. Petrocelli, charging, fields the
ball but slips on a patch of wet grass and falls. His only option is to go to
first. That's where he throws and somehow, against all odds, he makes a
spectacular play, nailing the speedy Geronimo while sitting on his butt.
Could be a crucial out.

Now who's going to pinch hit? Two of Sparky's right-handers, Armbrister and Rettenmund, have already appeared in the game. That leaves
light-hitting Darrel Chaney. Or he could go with one of the lefties, Terry

Crowley or Dan Driessen. He picks Driessen. Wrong choice. With a shaky rookie on the mound, you want to force him to go deep in the count if you can. But you can't do that if you jump on the first pitch, which is what Driessen does. He grounds to Doyle as Griffey holds. Only one out to get.

Johnson makes a trip to the mound. He isn't asking Burton if he wants to come out. No, they discuss whether or not to go ahead and intentionally walk Pete Rose. They decide not to do that but to pitch around him.

Burton follows orders. With the exception of one fastball for a strike at 3–1, Rose sees nothing but breaking stuff at the edges of the plate. If the Series' leading batter intends to swing no matter what, he's going to have to hit a curve. He lays off and takes ball four on a high pitch that Fisk just does snag.

Now comes Joe Morgan. You're the manager; what the hell do you do with Joe Morgan? With Morgan, who has boasted that there's not a left-hander in baseball who's too quick for him to pull with power? With Morgan, who can slice and dice someone with a mediocre fastball, like Jim Burton? With Morgan, only 7 for 26 so far, yet still one of the best clutch hitters in the game?

Well. You could put him on, deliberately loading the bases, and bring in your best right-hander to face Tony Perez, who's batting .185 in the Series. That'd be very gutsy, but it has some appeal. Or you could pitch around Morgan like you did Rose, hoping for him to swing at a pitch on the fringe of the strike zone, and not worry overmuch if he walks; of course, this presupposes that your rookie has that kind of control. Or you could just order Burton to go after him, lefty vs. lefty, and let the chips fall where they may.

Decisions, decisions. Whatever Johnson and Burton agreed upon, it happened either during the previous consultation or through an exchange of signals from the dugout. It doesn't involve pulling Burton, which would be automatic if Darrell had to make a second visit to the mound, and there apparently isn't going to be an intentional pass. Johnson stands with one foot on the dugout steps, stone-faced as always, his arms resting on the railing, and does the only thing left for him to do after he's punched the decision clock. Like everyone else, he watches.

Burton comes to the stretch, sets, and throws. An outside fastball for ball one. Still uncertain whether they're trying to get him or working around him. The next pitch, though, tells the tale. It's a letter-high fast-ball. They want the out, here and now. Morgan fouls it off. Another fast-ball, another foul, this one down the left-field line. Now a slow curve that Morgan is out in front of and fouls off to the right. It's 1–2, and Burton wants him more than he's ever wanted anything. He snaps off a slider.

"It was the best slider I ever threw," he recalled to me. "A great pitch. I put everything I had into it. Everything. It was right at Morgan, and you can see him initially bailing out on it." You can. But it breaks at the last moment and Joe, being the extraordinary hitter that he was, somehow recovers. "Then, when he realized it was going to be over the plate, he just kind of threw his bat at it."

He does. It's pure reflex, an instinctive motion that's available only to the very finest athletes. Morgan's simply trying to foul the pitch off, give himself another swing at something better. But he's a strong guy, Joe. So when the tip end of the bat makes contact with the ball, and the bat breaks, he still has enough muscle to hit it somewhere. That somewhere is center field. It's a bloop to center with nothing on it. Nothing, that is, except just enough loft to get it over the infield. It falls beyond Burleson and Doyle, in front of Fred Lynn.

Does Lynn again hesitate for a fraction of a second before breaking in on the ball? Perhaps. But it is the toughest kind of fly to pick up, and Freddie's first subliminal thought is undoubtedly that the powerful Morgan will drive it deeper. Does it make any difference? No one I talked to thought so. Consensus was that the ball was going to drop no matter how quickly Lynn reacted. And yet . . . it's one final moment about which to ponder what mighta been.

Lynn comes up throwing, trying to get Griffey at home, but that's futile. All it does is allow the runners to advance. Cincinnati leads, 4–3.

Burton hasn't pitched horribly, and to Joe Morgan, pretty damn well. Yet now, as Johnson replaces him with Reggie Cleveland, he's on the hook to lose the game and the Series. There are still two runners in scoring position, but when Cleveland strands them by getting Perez on a fly to right, there's no sense of relief. Probably, there's not a Boston fan in all the world who believes the Sox can come back in the bottom of the ninth and take this one back.

With three left-handers—Miller, Doyle, and Yaz—due up, Anderson replaces Carroll with his left-handed ace, Will McEnaney. It's a smart move. He knows that Johnson has little in the way of right-handed punch on his bench. If Darrell wants to hit for any of these lefties, so be it. Sparky can live with the matchups.

"Now here's McEnaney," broadcaster Curt Gowdy announces. "He's part of the new style in baseball. Specialist relievers who are groomed for their job from the beginning." Yep.

Johnson does go to the bench, and for Miller he sends up the best hitter he has left, Juan Beniquez (who can also replace Miller in left if the Sox tie it up). McEnaney looks sharp. Beniquez flies to right. Two outs for the Series.

Now what? Will he bat for Denny Doyle, his most consistent hitter? For a guy who was near .300 on the season and has eight hits in the Series?

"No way," Doyle told me. He was a little ticked off about it, more than twenty-five years later. "I should have gone up there. I was swinging the bat good; I was the only player on either team to hit in every game, you can look it up." I did, and he was. "I could hit left-handers as well as righties."

He doesn't get a chance. In one of Johnson's most baffling moves, one that can be based only on the wildest kind of hunch, he sends up Bob Montgomery instead. Now, Monty is a nice guy. And he is not a terrible baseball player. And granted, these are Darrell's other options: Bob Heise, Tim Blackwell, Doug Griffin, or one of his pitchers. Griffin is the best hitter of the bunch, but he's been injured and isn't 100 percent, while Blackwell's sub-.200 batting average is barely topped by Heise's .214. (Perhaps even Rick Wise, he of the onetime two-homer game, crosses the manager's mind. And perhaps he's rejected because, in a Series like this one, he may yet be called upon to pitch.)

No, it's to be Montgomery for Doyle, Monty who has hit just .226 during the year, with minimal power (2 homers in 195 trips) and scanty run production (26 RBI). More important, Bob is slow afoot, very slow; if he hits the ball on the ground, the fielder could boot the ball and still throw him out. Plus, there's an awful lot of moss on his bat. He didn't play in the Oakland series and has yet to appear against Cincinnati. Now, two outs from extinction, it's a very peculiar choice, all the way round.

I groan. I don't believe Monty can do a thing with McEnaney, and I'm right. He swings at the first pitch and grounds out to short. Two down, one to go.

Now the whole thing rests on the shoulders of Carl Yastrzemski and, really, what could be more appropriate?

Of the technological revolutions of the past couple of decades, none has had such a profound effect on baseball, how it is played and how it is viewed, as the advent of the personal computer.

The game has always provided a repository of statistics. It has always had dedicated scribes who, with typewriter or simple pen, would be willing to transcribe the details of each and every game. We can look back for more than a century and evaluate any player's statistics, for a season, for a year, even game by game. We can, if we wish, place two players side by side and attempt to reckon their relative worth.

It used to be a lot of work. Now, it's nothing. As the power available on anyone's desktop has grown, so have vast databases containing stats on everything under the sun. Players, and managers, can know in an instant what a pitcher is likely to throw in a given situation or which batter has a better long-term record against that pitcher. How does someone do at night against left-handers in the late innings with two or more runners aboard? We can discover this.

Players will use this abundance of information to plan how to attack a pitcher, and vice versa. Managers will use it to plan game strategy and to assist in specific, unforeseen circumstances. Some, like Tony La Russa, have been highly successful doing more or less everything according to the stats. Others, like Jimy Williams, prefer to rely on their baseball instincts.

The computer age has also spawned a new class of fan, folks who have become collectively known as sabermetricians (after SABR, the Society for American Baseball Research), those who seemingly spend all their waking hours crunching numbers and telling us things about the players we never thought to ask. The most prominent of these, like Bill James, make a living at it.

James began by publishing a yearly *Baseball Abstract*, in which he tried to make the definitive analysis of the players' performances in the previous season. This eventually evolved into the *Historical Baseball Abstract*, a thick, hardback book that encompasses all of baseball history and is updated only now and then.

The latest edition was published in 2001. In it, James takes on one of the longest-running controversies in the game: Is there such a thing as a "clutch" player? That is, are there, among all these athletes of roughly comparable ability, some who have a nonphysical dimension—James calls it "character" [quote marks his]—that allows them to perform better in the most pressure-filled situations?

The average fan, I think, strongly believes that there are. James, however, is a statistician. His beliefs are driven almost entirely by logic. And because he has been totally unable to quantify "clutch ability" through statistics, he has concluded: "I do not believe that there is any such thing as an *ability* to perform in clutch situations. It's just a lot of poppycock." The good players, he maintains, perform predictably well across the board; the lesser ones, more poorly. Give a man a long enough career, and everything eventually evens out.

Having said this, however, he admits that there are, and always will be, intangibles to the game that aren't susceptible to mere number-crunching analysis. Life is just more complex than that. So he qualifies his judgment by saying, "the fact that 90% or 99% of what is said about clutch performers in sports is nonsense does not mean that there is nothing here." And he cites for examples Don Drysdale, who pitched consistently badly in the heat of pennant races, and Bob Gibson, who with equal consistency pitched extraordinarily well.

James doesn't attribute such things to an excess or defect in "character." They are merely things that "happened" to two highly talented players. Nonetheless, they did happen. And so, James concludes, "It's a dangerous area to get into. . . . But if a player really does come through in big games or fail in big games, I don't think we can afford to ignore that [in our evaluation of him]."

There are no imperatives. People are free to believe in their gut instinct, or in cold, inalterable numbers. Yet even those who favor the statistical view are going to be forced to admit that if a player's performance in clutch games exceeds that of his career by a statistically significant margin, then there may indeed be something to the notion. In this context, we cannot fail to consider Carl Yastrzemski.

Yaz was a great player, no doubt. Taking all of his defensive, offensive, and "clutch" abilities into account, a pretty decent case can be made that he was the greatest player the Red Sox ever had. It's that "clutch" part that's the sticking point.

For his part, Yaz doesn't think there's anything mysterious about it. "I wanted to be in a clutch situation," he told me, "a tight game. My mental concentration was better. It's in the blowouts that you get lazy. But when the game's on the line, you go to a different level. It was *easier* for me to play in those situations."

OK. But what about statistically? Did Yaz *really* perform far above his normally high level when he was in the pressure cooker? The *Boston Globe* decided to find out.

They checked the numbers for the twenty-two biggest games of Yaz's career, all of them games in which a pennant, LCS game, or World Series game was on the line: the last two regular-season games of 1967, both of which the Sox needed to win the pennant; the 1967 Series against the Cardinals; the last two games of '72, which decided that pennant; the 1975 playoffs and Series games; and the 1978 one-game playoff against the Yankees.

In those 22 games, here's how he did: he hit .417, with 6 home runs, 19 runs scored, 25 runs batted in, and a slugging percentage of .702.

Now zoom in on the 1967 pennant race. It was the closest ever, with four teams, separated by a game or three down the stretch, vying for a Series berth—and with no playoffs in that era, only one of those four was going to the postseason. That September, Yastrzemski was in what can only be described as "the Zone." He went on a tear that, given the circumstances, is probably unequaled in all of major league history.

The team played 27 games, with Yaz in all of them. He went to bat 96 times and collected 40 hits (a .417 average, exactly the same as in the aforementioned 22 pressure games), with 24 runs scored and 26 driven in. In the season's critical last two weeks, he went 23–44 (an average of .523!), with 5 homers and 16 RBI. And in the final two games, the ones that ultimately decided it all, he was 7 for 8! The Sox won 16 of those 27 games, and the pennant.

Is there such a thing as a clutch performer? Well, if so, then we are looking at him.

Thus, it seems fitting if not poetic that, with two out in the bottom of the ninth inning of the seventh game of a World Series whose outcome now hangs by the thread of a single run, the batter should be Carl Yastrzemski.

I met Yaz just before Christmas of 2001, near one of his homes (the other is in Florida) north of Boston, after months of trying to set up the interview. Yaz doesn't like to do them. He is now, as he was as a player, a very private person. But I persisted, mainly because his agent told me that once you do get him to sit down, he's apt to enjoy talking. Happily, that proved to be true.

We met in the windowless upstairs office of a grocery store where he's well known. He was right on time. Yaz looked every one of his sixty-two years. He'd gone thick around the middle, and his face had the leathery look of someone who spent much of his time outdoors, which was in fact the case.

"In the summer," he told me, "I fish six days a week and play golf on Sunday." He wasn't joking.

We sat down. Carl was wearing a turtleneck pullover with the Nike logo on the collar. He had a serious expression that rarely changed over the course of our time together; there were just a few small hints, when he was most at ease, of the fun-loving clubhouse prankster his teammates had described. First thing, he set a pack of filtered cigarettes on the desk between us. From then on, he chain-smoked.

For me, this was one of the highlights of my long journey, meeting the main man, and for once the subject corresponded pretty closely to my expectations. I thought of Yaz as a solid, workmanlike, go-about-your-business kind of guy, and that's whom I found. Yet at the same time, I wanted to explode one of the myths about him, that he had been a man of modest gifts, a simple potato farmer's son who achieved greatness through a single-mindedness of purpose, a dogged determination to succeed, and the application of a fearsome work ethic.

Yaz himself pushes this version of his story pretty hard. When he was inducted into the Hall of Fame, he said in his acceptance speech: "Why am I here in Cooperstown? I was never blessed with superb physical strength. I had to work twice as long and twice as hard as many of my peers. . . ." And: "The race doesn't always belong to the swift. It belongs rather to those who run the race, stay the course, and who fight the good fight."

To me, that seemed like nonsense. Not that he didn't have all of the aforementioned qualities. He did. Not that he's insincere. He's not. But I figured he must also have been born with a world of talent.

Watch him play left field. Sure, he *looks* clunky out there, but that's mostly illusion. He moves with economy and, yes, a kind of grace. He always does the right thing, and he does it very, very well. That's not just the result of a lot of practice. Or watch him hit. In his prime, he had a beautiful, fluid swing, an exceptional eye, outstanding hand/eye coordination, and the ability to extract every ounce of power from his body as it uncoiled. Most who try never reach that level, no matter how much time they put in.

I knew that he wasn't just a baseball player, either. Before he made the decision to concentrate on one sport, he was a quarterback in football and good enough at basketball to receive scholarship offers from Duke, Florida, and dozens of other schools. This guy was an *athlete*.

So that was the first thing I asked him, whether his innate athleticism hadn't been downplayed.

"Well," he said, "I wasn't a big guy, you know. Six foot, 185 pounds. Not one of the big guys. It took a lot of hard work."

But still . . . I poked at the question for a bit, trying to draw him out. He wouldn't be drawn. He talked a lot about how he "had to be perfect" to be a power hitter in a home park unfavorable to left-handers, and about adjustments he made to his swing during years when he was trying more to hit for average. He did everything but answer the question, conceding only a terse "Yeah" when I said that he'd been a great basketball player, too.

Finally, I concluded that he was either very modest or that he was incapable of thinking of himself in terms other than the ones he'd defined for himself for so many years. I changed the subject. What about the other popular belief about him, I asked, that he had no sense of humor?

He paused, as he did after almost every question. Sometimes the silence went on for quite a while. He was no Bill Lee, saying the first thing that came to mind. I wondered at first if this was because he wanted to give particularly thoughtful answers, but as the interview went on I decided that wasn't it. It was more, I came to believe, that he is very, very careful. He didn't provide me with depth of insight; he just avoided anything that might be misconstrued or considered controversial. It was, most likely, the instinctive reaction of a basically shy person who has been thrust into the public arena and been manhandled by the press for decades.

"Nah," he said. "That's because the fans only see you on the field, not in the clubhouse. I like to clown around as much as anyone, but during the game I'm very serious. Once I put on the uniform, I became a prick."

I laughed, and so did he. At himself, I thought. And perhaps also at those who think they know someone to whom they're connected primarily by newspaper and TV stories.

At the age of forty-four, after an extraordinary twenty-three seasons of putting on red stockings, Yaz took what in another profession would be called early retirement. Though he continues to tutor young hitters for a couple of weeks each spring training, and though he has a sometime job in public relations for the Sara Lee Corporation, he doesn't have to work, ever again. It's not a bad deal, and he knows it.

For two hours, we talked about his career, the character of the different teams he played on, his two World Series experiences, changes in the game since he broke in—of the latter, he listed as most important the lowering of the mound, the increase in glove size, pitch counts, and the advent of the five-man rotation.

But in the end it all came down to a consideration of a single at-bat. Game 7, bottom of the ninth, two down, a one-run deficit. Talk about the ultimate clutch.

I asked Carl with my finest mock-serious face on if he remembered that at-bat. He laughed. There are moments in life that you couldn't forget if you had access to a lake full of nepenthe. For Yaz, this was one of them.

For me, it all fuses together here. The game, as I watch it with Uncle Oscar in 1975. The game, as I reviewed it on tape a quarter-century later. And the game, as I recalled it with Carl Yastrzemski.

"He can do it," I say to Oscar. We've agreed—and who cares if McEnaney is left-handed—that there is no one we'd rather see up in this situation than Captain Carl.

They're not going to pitch around him, not with Fisk up next and Lynn to follow. McEnaney is going to go right at him, strength against strength. He delivers a fastball outside. Ball one.

Was he trying to hit one out? I asked him.

"I guess it was pride," Yaz told me. "Yeah, I was thinking *home run* all the way. No question. I wanted to tie that game. I really did."

McEnaney throws. Another fastball. This one catches the inside corner. Strike one.

"He was left-handed," Yaz said. "And a sidearm pitcher. With a good sinkerball. That's tough on a left-handed hitter, but I'd faced them before. I knew what to do. What you want is to wait until the last possible moment before swinging. If you don't do that, you're going to open up too soon, and you'll just pull it foul. So I waited on him. I waited pretty good."

Once again, McEnaney delivers, and it's yet another fastball. But this one is letter-high, right in Yastrzemski's wheelhouse.

"It was a mistake," Yaz said, "that pitch. He got it up, which is what a sinkerballer doesn't want to do. I had a good cut at it."

Yaz connects. It's a long fly to center field, deep.

"You have to time your swing just right," he said. "If you don't, you'll wind up hitting the sinker into the ground. I wanted to drive it, still thinking *home run*, but I dropped my hands a little too quickly. I got underneath it too much. Instead of driving it, I hit it too high into the air. Still, my first thought was that I'd done it. If it didn't make it out, I believed it was gonna be off the wall."

The ball is hit a long way, but it's a longer way to the bleacher seats. It's not a tough play for Geronimo. He goes back and, right at the warning track, hauls it in. Yaz has given it a terrific shot, and fallen a few crummy feet short.

The Red Sox, despite being given plenty of opportunities to score, have been shut out since the third inning. The game, and this most magnificent World Series that we wanted to go on and on, is over.

I groan. Probably I unfairly curse Yastrzemski's name; I don't remember.

"This is a very good team," Oscar says. "They'll be back in it next year. Our time will come."

And will come, and will come.

> *"Losing after great striving is the story of man, who was born to sorrow, whose sweetest songs tell of saddest thought, and who, if he is a hero, does nothing in life as becomingly as leaving it."*
> —ROGER KAHN, *THE BOYS OF SUMMER*

History, as they say, is written by the winners. True enough. How often, though, do we reserve a special place in our hearts for the other side? As Roger Kahn went on to say, about the perennially snakebitten Brooklyn Dodgers, "The team was awesomely good and yet defeated. Their skills lifted everyman's spirit and their defeat joined them with everyman's existence, a national team, with a country in thrall, irresistible and unable to beat the Yankees." He could just as easily have been writing about the Red Sox.

As I watched the final at-bat of the seventh game of the 1975 World Series on tape, in 2001, I knew that it wasn't over for me yet, and that it wouldn't be until I had met the last, and perhaps most important, of the boys on my list. Jim Burton, the loser of the ultimate game of the ultimate Series. How would he remember the experience now?

I discovered to my delight that he was alive and well, and that he lived with his wife and three daughters in Charlotte, North Carolina, only a few hours' drive from my own home. I got in my car and went to see him, and I wound up with an interview that, for its simple, disarming honesty, was all I could have hoped it would be.

Jim met me at his office. He has a small printing business, located in a nondescript one-story stone building on the outskirts of the city. He shares the building with a tenant who has vacated, so there was a "For Lease" sign out front. Inside, the space was pleasant and well lighted. It appeared efficiently organized. We used the conference room.

Burton was tall and rangy, still pretty youthful looking. His hair had receded, revealing his high forehead, but what was left was thick and brown. He was wearing what might be the same metal-rimmed spectacles that he wore twenty-five years ago. He was dressed very casually, in a green plaid shirt and jeans, and looked a lot like my neighbors back in the mountains of Virginia.

I found him to be a thoughtful, soft-spoken man who measured his words carefully. He was perhaps a little nervous about being interviewed—it surely happens infrequently now—and moved his hands a lot. After a while, he seemed to relax, if not actually to warm up to the process. He had a very agreeable presence, a solidity, and a little wry smile that women probably find way cute. I had an eerie déjà vu feeling, as if I'd met him before. Or perhaps he was just the way I had expected him to be.

He told me that he'd grown up in rural Michigan, a bit north of Detroit. His dad owned his own tool and die business, and the family was comfortable. It was a great childhood. There was baseball in the summer, ice hockey in the winter. Jim and his two brothers were into hunting and trapping, as well as team sports.

"All boys," he said. "That's what I was used to. My own kids are all girls, though, and it's been an adjustment. It's . . . different."

"Anyway, I was throwing something all the time back then," he recalled. "Which develops arm strength. Now kids don't do that as much. Their athleticism is greater than ours was, but the subtler things have been lost, I think."

Burton was drafted out of high school, but he didn't consider baseball as a vocation at that time. Instead, he went to the University of Michigan, from which he graduated. He had an excellent college career, and it was at Ann Arbor that he first began to believe that he might make it as a professional. The Red Sox were believers, too. They drafted him in the first round of the supplemental draft in '71 and sent him to Double-A Pawtucket. From there he moved up to Triple-A Louisville, Kentucky, and then, in the heat of the '75 pennant race, joined the parent club.

"I feel I had the skills to have a longer career than I did," he said. "If I hadn't been with a contender, I would have had some time to get my feet under me. But when the team is trying to get to the World Series, you don't have that opportunity. Each game is important."

Did the 1975 Red Sox feel like a special team to him?

"I don't know if there was a special feeling," he said. "I was a rookie; I had nothing to compare it to. I was just happy to be there. But it *was* a tremendously exciting group to be with. We kept surprising ourselves. And one thing I did find was that at that level you had to have total concentration, yet be relaxed at the same time, or you wouldn't do anything. It's hard."

It must also be hard sitting in the bullpen during a Series, I said, not knowing if and when you're going to get in.

"Sure," he said, "you have a lot of nervous excitement as a reliever, a lot of anticipation. During that seventh game, some of the guys out there, when they saw the coach in the dugout heading for the phone, they said, 'I hope that call's not for me.'"

What about him? How did he feel when he actually did get the call?

"I was surprised," he said. "I had pitched so little the last month of the season. You're not gonna be your sharpest when you have so few innings. So I never expected to be summoned in that situation."

"But there were left-handed batters coming up," I said, "and the other left-handers, Lee and Moret, had already pitched in the game. You were the last one left."

"Yeah, that was probably his thinking," he said. "But I tell you, I wasn't ready. I was nervous. I didn't want to go out there. Warming up, my whole body went numb. It was surreal, like an out-of-body experience. In those days, they sent a golf cart to bring you in, and when it came for me, I knew I couldn't ride in it. I had to trot in from the bullpen just to feel my feet on the ground. Otherwise I think I might have floated away."

Burton's shoulder was also sore, he told me. It had stiffened up in the cold.

"But once you're out there, the adrenaline takes over and you don't feel any pain. It didn't have anything to do with my walking Griffey. That was from nervousness, and lack of activity. After the walk, I was able to settle in and relax a little."

And he pitched pretty well. Geronimo was out sacrificing Griffey to second. Pinch hitter Driessen grounded out. One more batter to get and he'd be out of the inning. Did he think he was going to make it?

"I don't know. Probably not," he said disarmingly. "Joe Morgan was up. He's a great player, and they always seem to find a way to get it done."

He remembered the last pitch to Morgan, of course.

"Yeah. You know, over the years Morgan has always given me credit for making a good pitch in that situation." He chuckled. "Which doesn't change the outcome, unfortunately. But I threw that pitch because of the one before it, which was an inside fastball that he fouled off. I was surprised at how fast he came around on an inside pitch like that, and I decided I better not try it again. Fisk came out. We discussed it and decided on the slider.

"That's what it was. I wound up and threw it exactly where I wanted it, as hard as I could throw one. My slider wasn't a tight one; it was more like a 'slurve' that started in close to a left-hander and broke a lot, away from him. That's what that pitch did. It fooled Morgan, and you can see him start to bail out at first."

You can, but it's not by much. And his recovery is amazingly fast.

"Then he kind of threw the bat at the ball." Just trying to foul it off? "Maybe. But he got the end of the bat on it and blooped the fly to center. I turned, and the first thing I saw was Freddie Lynn going back a step or two. And I thought, 'Oh, no.' I knew Morgan hadn't hit it solidly. I could see that Freddie had no play."

And that was it. Jim Burton came out of the game after surrendering the Series' deciding run. He was sent down to Pawtucket after the season and didn't see any major league action in 1976. He began to feel it was in his best interest to leave the Red Sox. I asked him if he felt his World Series experience derailed his career.

He thought about it. "Probably. I didn't have a good year at Pawtucket after that. It hurt me mentally. And I became a negative focus for a lot of people after '75. I was the scapegoat. Darrell Johnson got a lot of flak for even putting me in." He shrugged. "But I'm not bitter about it now; I have no regrets," he said, and I believed him.

It took management another year to trade him. He went to the Mets' Triple-A team in Tidewater and then suffered a further demotion to the Single-A team in Lynchburg. He had elbow problems. By the end of 1977, he was out of organized baseball. Jim Burton had gone from playing for all the marbles to the final exit door about as fast as you can.

Yet he seemed at peace with what had happened to him and quite happy with his postbaseball existence.

"A lot of athletes struggle with reassimilating," he said. "And I did, too, in that my sense of identity and self-worth were tied up with athletic success. A lot of guys try to leverage who they were into something else, but that wasn't an option for me. Except with the stars, it doesn't help you for long in the business world. I also didn't play in an era when most players could exit the game wealthy. So I really needed something else to do. For me, transitioning out of thinking of myself as a professional ballplayer took four years, from '78 to '82. I moved back to Michigan, but I couldn't find anything there. It wasn't until I began running my own business that the separation became permanent. It's so time-consuming that it finally *forced* the transition."

He wound up in Charlotte, a city he'd never even visited, because a friend told him of an opportunity to open up a franchise printing business there. He checked it out, liked what he saw, and moved. He's now been at it for twenty years.

"I knew I wanted to own my own business," he said, "like my dad did. And when this came along I grabbed it, and I've succeeded at it. Not that I'm that great a businessman. I'm not. I don't have really good business instincts; I'm not a risk taker. I'll let someone else try out some new technology before I invest in it. I see myself more as a mule than a racehorse. But I have honesty and integrity, and I work hard. I persevere."

Not a bad prescription for success, I said.

To wind things up, I told Burton I'd read about some trips to Haiti he made. I asked if he wanted to talk about that.

"Sure," he said. "I have a strong faith, and part of that directs me into mission things. I heard through my church about some Haitians who wanted to start a print shop there. So we helped put one of them through an education in the business, here in Charlotte, then went down there to help them set up the shop. I've been there twice now. The shop is entrepreneurial, but it also works through the mission to help print educational materials for the schools. When you spend time in the third world, it gives you a more healthy perspective on your own life."

He thought for a moment, then went on. "Once I was riding with the local pastor down there through a slum area that was worse than anything I'd ever seen. I couldn't believe it. 'What makes these people even want to live?' I asked him. 'Suicide must be rampant.' The pastor shook his head. There's very little suicide in Haiti, he told me, much less than in the U.S." He paused. "I don't know. Here we have everything we could possibly want, and we're medicated to death. We can't cope with anything."

Did he think about baseball much anymore? I asked.

"No," he said. "Don't get me wrong, I love sports. I could probably become a sports junkie. But I have no time for athletics now. You look back and you realize that baseball is such a small part of your life, when you think about it. There's so much that's more important."

"One pitch, a fly to center, and it had stopped. Summer died in New England and like rain sliding off a roof, the crowd slipped out of Fenway, quickly, and with only a steady murmur of concern for the drive ahead remaining of the roar. Mutability had turned the seasons and translated hope to memory once again."

—A. BARTLETT GIAMATTI,
"THE GREEN FIELDS OF THE MIND"

Coda:
The Greatest Ever?

Was 1975 the greatest World Series ever played? Probably.

Yeah, sure, the complainer argues, *you say that, but you're a Red Sox fan. Of course it would be, to you* (perhaps forgetting that my team lost).

Some would no doubt opt for the 1960 edition, when the Pirates defeated the powerful Yankees on Bill Mazeroski's ninth-inning homer. Or 1971, with Roberto Clemente leading the Pirates past the heavily favored Orioles. Or even, and it pains me to say it, 1986: the Mets, behind by two runs and down to their last strike in the tenth inning of Game 6, miraculously pulling out a victory, then winning the seventh at Shea Stadium.

Well, perhaps.

Applying the highest superlative to one sporting event among many similar ones is always to some degree an exercise in futility. Individual preferences cover a broad range. The observer's degree of attention paid varies according to who's playing. And comparing different eras (modern vs. dead ball, all white vs. integrated, etc.) is difficult.

There's no doubt that my particular vision is colored by my loyalties. On the other hand, the matter is not entirely subjective. There are a few common yardsticks by which such things may be measured.

Take length. Surely to qualify as one of the finest, a Series should be a roller-coaster ride, featuring abrupt reversals of fortune. At a minimum, it must go the full number of games, so that either team may win it all on the final day. Or, to put it another way, the two contestants should be rel-atively equal.

So let's do some elimination.

The Series began in 1903. In that year, and 1919–21, it was played according to a best-of-nine format. Otherwise, it's been the more familiar best-of-seven. That's ninety-seven Classics, as of this writing (Fall 2001). There was no postseason in 1904 or '94.

Of them all, only a third—thirty-three—have gone the limit. We'll keep those and discard the rest.

Now, as to the games themselves. We can likely agree that maximum tension is generated (and enjoyment thus promoted) when a contest is decided by a single run. Let's then say that our seventh game must be a one-run victory for the winner. That pares the list down to only thirteen.

Keep in mind here that close games are actually quite the exception rather than the rule in baseball. In fact, counterintuitive though it may seem, there is a high probability that the winning team in any given game will score more runs in a single inning than the loser scores in nine. Over a reasonable sampling of games, it's statistically certain to be true more often than not. If you don't believe this, check the box scores on any day with a full schedule. Then, unless you're Pete Rose, find someone who's foolish enough to bet against it.

Comebacks and late-inning rallies that change the outcome are, of course, yet more scarce. (The team that scores first will win about 65 per-cent of the time.)

So we'll jettison those games in which the winning team took the lead and the loser came back but always fell short. Another five gone.

How about Series in which, though the final game was close, most or all of the others weren't? Like 1940, when Game 7 was the only one decided by one run. And 1960—exciting as its final game was, in the other six the Yankees outscored the Pirates by 46–17! And 1997? Only two close games. (Besides, the Series was won by the Florida Marlins, for God's sake. The Marlins. *Puhleeeze . . .*)

Now we're down to just five. They're all good ones.

1912—Smoky Joe Wood has a remarkable Series to lead the Red Sox past the Giants in eight games. (Game 2 in this prelights era ended in a tie called on account of darkness and was replayed in its entirety.) Wood wins Games 1 and 4 as a starter, gets routed in the first inning of Game 7 and takes the loss, then bounces back in Game 8 to pitch three innings of relief and get the victory over Christy Mathewson. New York gets a run to break a tie in the top of the tenth inning of the final game, but Boston comes back in the bottom half and takes advantage of a pair of errors to score two. Four one-run games and two come-from-behind victories.

1924—The Washington Senators rally from behind to win Game 7 in the twelfth inning. Walter Johnson, a two-time loser in the Series, gets the victory with four innings of shutout relief. There are three other one-run games.

1975.

1991—Jack Morris of Minnesota dominates the Atlanta Braves. He pitches 23 innings, gives up all of 3 runs, and caps his bravura performance with 10 innings of shutout ball in the 1–0 finale. That Series also featured three extra-inning contests but only one comeback victory.

Then there's 2001. It was pretty damn good, with Arizona beating the Yankees. It featured four one-run games, two of which went into extra innings. The winning team came from behind three times, all in the ninth inning—twice to tie, once to win. Both game-tying ninth-inning comebacks involved two-run homers with two outs. The seventh-game victory required that the Diamondbacks mount a final rally against the greatest closer in postseason history. And Randy Johnson was magnificent, picking up two wins as a starter and a third in relief on no rest.

Does it measure up? Well, I think you have to consider that the Series was won by the Arizona Diamondbacks. This is a team whose home field is called the Bob, a ballpark with a swimming pool beyond the center-field fence for "fans" whose attention is not sufficiently engaged by the game itself. It's a team that couldn't even sell out the first two Series games in its brief (four-year) history. It plays in a town whose leading newspaper, prior to Game 1, felt compelled to publish a detailed explanation of the rules of baseball (what's a hit? what's an out? etc.) for those "fans" unfamiliar with them.

Call me prejudiced, but at this point I can't stomach the notion that anything involving the Diamondbacks might be termed great. Still, had the 2001 Series been closer in other aspects, I might have been persuaded to abandon this stance. But it wasn't. Yes, the Yankees turned two seeming losses into improbable victories. Yet when they were beaten, they were trounced, once by 13 runs and once by 8. A third result was as much of a blowout as a 4–0 game can be, given the losers' utter bewilderment at the plate. In fact—the two great clutch homers aside—Yankee hitting was woeful throughout. In seven games, they managed a total of just 14 runs and 43 hits. The team batting average was .183, worst ever for a 7-game Series.

Now compare '75. In *six* of the games, the winning team came from behind, and in one, it came from behind twice. The winning margin was a single run *five times* out of seven. Two games went into extra innings; two more weren't settled until the ninth. Overall, Boston scored 30 runs on 60 hits, Cincinnati 29 runs on 59 hits. The Red Sox batted .251 as a team, the Reds .242. The Boston pitching staff's collective earned run average was 3.86; Cincinnati's was 3.88.

Talk about close. That's more than remarkable, it's unique.

The overall balance of the Series, that alone ranks it among the finest. But the foregoing are all statistical considerations. Baseball games are not only about numbers. The less tangible things also count.

For example, a sense of justice is achieved when the better team, having been pushed to its limits by a determined underdog, finds a way to win. The greatest teams always do. And, though others may beg to differ, I believe this is what happened in 1975.

In addition, the World Series should ideally showcase the premier talents of its day, and three of the final five did just that.

The 1912 Series spotlighted a sextet of giants: Tris Speaker, Harry Hooper, Honus Wagner, and Rube Marquard, along with Wood and Mathewson.

The 1924 Series had Hall of Famers Goose Goslin, Frankie Frisch, Sam Rice, Hack Wilson, and Freddie Lindstrom, as well as the Big Train, Walter Johnson. Not bad.

In contrast, Kirby Puckett is the sole '91 participant now in the Hall. Of the rest, Chuck Knoblauch, still active at this writing, has a chance of making it in. Jack Morris is close, though he's eligible and has had little support so far. And Tom Glavine, also active, is a real possibility.

The 2001 Series is too recent to call. Roger Clemens and Randy Johnson are Cooperstown locks. But the rest . . . only time will tell. Knoblauch, maybe. Mariano Rivera, yes if he plays long enough. Derek Jeter likewise. Curt Schilling, Mike Mussina, Bernie Williams? Unlikely. Perhaps some of the younger guys, like Luis Gonzalez and Alfonso Soriano, will make it. All in all, it could be a pretty big crop, or a party of two. We shall see.

But of '75 there is no doubt. It delivered, in spades. Johnny Bench, Joe Morgan, Tony Perez, Carlton Fisk, Carl Yastrzemski—all in Cooperstown;

Luis Tiant, who should be there; Pete Rose, who would be if he hadn't screwed up his personal life; and a number of other outstanding talents whose careers aren't far short of Hall of Fame caliber, like George Foster, Dwight Evans, Fred Lynn, and Ken Griffey Sr. Not to mention Jim Rice, unfortunately sidelined with the wrist injury, who has a fair chance of making it via the veterans' committee. And of course Sparky, enshrined as a manager.

Memorable plays are an important ingredient, too—ones so indelible that they can be referred to with initial caps (e.g., the Strikeout) and everyone will know what you're talking about—and once again '75 came through: the Perez home run on a Bill Lee eephus pitch, preceded by Rose's savage breakup of an inning-ending double play. Carbo's dramatic homer in Game 6, followed later by Fisk's. Evans's spectacular catch, pulling in a Joe Morgan line drive just before it left the ballpark. And of course the infamous blown calls that changed the complexion of Game 3: first, Ed Armbrister's interference with Fisk on an attempted bunt, then the putout of Geronimo at third that nobody saw because they were all watching the argument at home plate.

Then there's defense, so often overlooked. As Yaz told me, "Over the course of a season, defense is as important as good pitching. And the fans appreciate it when they get it." They got it here. Both of these teams had proved to be outstanding defensively during the regular season, and both played that way throughout the Series, turning in one fine effort after another. Yaz, Lynn, and Evans made spectacular outfield plays routine. Morgan and Concepcion showed why they were the premier middle-infield combination of the day. Bench continued to redefine the role of the catcher. Of the 59 total runs scored, 57 were earned.

Finally, there is the size of the audience to consider. It may be unfair to the old-timers, but we can't truly know how good the 1912 and '24 Series were, because only a relative handful of people saw the games. Millions watched in '75, and a complete visual record is available on videotape. We can savor the great moments, over and over if we want to.

Factor everything in and I think we have our answer to the initial question. Maybe not a definitive one—there are few such in baseball—but . . .

Was '75 the best?

Yeah, it was.

Epilogue:
Coulda Shoulda

The Red Sox have not won a World Series since 1918, after which they sold Babe Ruth to New York and thereby inadvertently laid the foundation for a winning Yankees tradition that has persisted for more than eighty years.

Those long decades of continual defeat have inevitably given rise to an ever-growing body of legend and lore, like barnacles encrusting a lone rock jutting from the shallows along the chilly New England shore. Of these, none has been more persistent than the story of the Man at the Bar. It's a tale that has been told and retold, so often that—though some may claim authorship and others swear on the Bible that it really did happen to a friend of a friend—I believe it can now be certified as an authentic urban myth. It also happens to nicely encapsulate, within the framework of 1975, something of the deep, unfathomable longing felt by Boston supporters when the lights of evening are extinguished and the rest of the city sleeps.

Though I've encountered any number of variations, the story goes more or less as follows.

It is a dark and stormy night, many long years after the 1975 Series. It's late fall, or early winter. Our reporter—who may or may not be an actual journalist but is unquestionably a devoted fan—is walking home, his collar turned up against the cold, his face wet from the nasty, drizzling rain. He passes the neighborhood tavern, glowing gold and friendly in the gloom, and is drawn to it. Anything to get out of the miserable Massachusetts weather for a few minutes. He goes inside.

The bartender may or may not be Irish. He probably should be, just as the setting wants to be South Boston. Our reporter seats himself. Other than the bored fellow serving drinks, there is only one other person in the place, the Man at the Bar, sitting several stools away. He stares morosely at his half-filled glass of beer and mutters occasional words under his breath that no one else can hear. Otherwise, there is only silence.

Our reporter knocks back his whiskey and, properly fortified for the remainder of his walk home, is preparing to leave. Just then, the Man at the Bar raises his glass to the light. He stares at its contents with moist eyes, as if somewhere in there lies the key to understanding his own bitter life's frustrations, his victories and defeats, the hard reality of aging itself. Once, this man too was a boy, and it was October, and his heart leaped as the pungent smoke from burning maple leaves lifted into a sky unbearably blue. He gazes for a long moment, holding our reporter spellbound. He sighs one great, terrible sigh. Then he shakes his head and, just before putting the glass to his lips, says:

"We never shoulda taken out Willoughby."

Postscript:
Requiescat in Pace

One of the things my Uncle Oscar loved most was *Dr. Pick*, a twenty-four-foot sailboat unaccountably named for a stuffed rabbit that was my brother's childhood companion, and was itself named after our first pediatrician. Oscar would sail that boat at every opportunity. He went for extended solo sails long after reaching an age where it seemed safe for him to do so. But no one tried to talk him out of it. He was a skilled sailor and way too Yankee stubborn to reason with. I often thought that he would one day go out on Nantucket Sound and fail to return, and that if it happened, it would be a fitting way for him to leave the world, doing something that brought him peace. After all, he had instructed us that he wished to be cremated and his ashes scattered at sea.

When *Dr. Pick* was destroyed in a hurricane in 1991, I wondered how long my uncle would outlive his boat. Not long, I suspected, and I was right. He passed away a few months later, in early 1992. In accordance with his wishes, we took his ashes down to the Sound one sunny but cold afternoon and gave them to the water. I didn't say anything about the Red Sox, but Uncle Oscar had died without having had the opportunity to see his beloved team win a World Series during his adult lifetime.

My dad, a few years Oscar's junior, is still waiting. Expectantly.

Resources

For my source material, I relied heavily on videotapes of the games, most of which I purchased on eBay. If it didn't exist, I don't know what I would have done. Sadly, there is nowhere one can go to purchase the complete tapes of this Series.

Two books were also by my side at all times: *The Baseball Encyclopedia*, 10th ed., by Jeanine Bucek et al. (New York: Macmillan, 1996); and *The World Series*, by Jordan Deutsch et al. (New York: Dial Press, 1976).

The wonderful Giamatti quotes are drawn from a compendium of his baseball writings: *A Great and Glorious Game*, by A. Bartlett Giamatti (Chapel Hill, N.C.: Algonquin, 1998).

And no real baseball fan should be without *The New Bill James Historical Abstract*, by Bill James (New York: Free Press, 2001).

Other books that proved useful to me were the following:

Robert Adair, *The Physics of Baseball* (New York: Harper Perennial, 1994).

Robert Benson, *The Game* (New York: Jeremy P. Tarcher/Putnam, 2001).

Larry Colton, *Goat Brothers* (New York: Doubleday, 1993).

David James Duncan, *The Brothers K* (New York: Bantam, 1996).

Peter Gammons, *Beyond the Sixth Game* (Boston: Houghton Mifflin, 1985).

Bill Lee and Dick Lally, *The Wrong Stuff* (New York: Viking, 1984).

Christopher Lehmann-Haupt, *Me and DiMaggio* (New York: Simon and Schuster, 1986).

Jim Prime and Bill Nowlin, *Tales from the Red Sox Dugout* (Champaign, Ill.: Sports Publishing, 2000).

Dan Riley, *Red Sox Reader* (Boston: Houghton Mifflin, 1991).

Dan Shaughnessy, *The Curse of the Bambino* (New York: Penguin, 1991).

Curt Smith, *Our House* (Chicago: Masters Press, 1999).

John Thorn, ed., *The Armchair Book of Baseball* (New York: Collier Books, 1985).

Luis Tiant and Joe Fitzgerald, *El Tiante* (New York: Doubleday, 1976).

Carl Yastrzemski and Gerald Eskenazi, *Yaz* (New York: Doubleday, 1990).

Don Zimmer and Bill Madden, *Zim* (New York: Total Sports Publishing, 2001).

Appendix

1975 World Series Team Rosters and Regular-Season Statistics

Boston Red Sox

Position Players	G	AB	H	BA	HR	RBI
C—Carlton Fisk	79	263	87	.331	10	52
1B—Cecil Cooper	106	305	95	.311	14	44
2B—Denny Doyle	97	325	97	.298	4	36
3B—Rico Petrocelli	115	402	96	.239	7	59
SS—Rick Burleson	158	580	146	.252	6	62
LF—Carl Yastrzemski	149	543	146	.269	14	60
CF—Fred Lynn	145	528	175	.331	21	105
RF—Dwight Evans	128	412	113	.274	13	56

Bench						
OF—Juan Beniquez	78	254	74	.291	2	17
C—Tim Blackwell	59	132	26	.197	0	6
OF—Bernie Carbo	107	319	82	.257	15	50
IF—Doug Griffin	100	287	69	.240	1	29
IF—Bob Heise	63	126	27	.214	0	21
OF—Rick Miller	77	108	21	.194	0	15
C—Bob Montgomery	62	195	44	.226	2	26

Injured—Did Not Play						
OF—Jim Rice	144	564	174	.309	22	102

Starting Pitchers	G	IP	W/L	ERA	Saves
Luis Tiant	35	260	18–14	4.02	0
Rick Wise	35	255	19–12	3.95	0
Bill Lee	41	260	17–9	3.95	0
Reggie Cleveland	31	171	13–9	4.43	0
Rogelio Moret	36	145	14–3	3.60	1

Bullpen					
Jim Burton	29	53	1–2	2.89	1
Dick Drago	40	73	2–2	3.84	15
Dick Pole	18	90	4–6	4.42	0
Diego Segui	33	71	2–5	4.82	6
Jim Willoughby	24	48	5–2	3.54	8

Cincinnati Reds

Position Players	G	AB	H	BA	HR	RBI
C—Johnny Bench	142	530	150	.283	28	110
1B—Tony Perez	137	511	144	.282	20	109
2B—Joe Morgan	146	498	163	.327	17	94
3B—Pete Rose	162	662	210	.317	7	74
SS—Dave Concepcion	140	507	139	.274	5	49
LF—George Foster	134	463	139	.300	23	78
CF—César Geronimo	148	501	129	.257	6	53
RF—Ken Griffey Sr.	132	463	141	.305	4	46

Bench						
OF—Ed Armbrister	59	65	12	.185	0	2
IF—Darrel Chaney	71	160	35	.219	2	26
OF—Terry Crowley	66	71	19	.268	1	11
IF—Dan Driessen	88	210	59	.281	7	38
IF—Doug Flynn	89	127	34	.268	1	20
C—Bill Plummer	65	159	29	.182	1	19
OF—Merv Rettenmund	93	188	45	.239	2	19

Starting Pitchers	G	IP	W/L	ERA	Saves
Don Gullett	22	160	15–4	2.42	0
Jack Billingham	33	208	15–10	4.11	0
Fred Norman	34	188	12–4	3.73	0
Gary Nolan	32	211	15–9	3.16	0

Bullpen

Pedro Borbon	67	125	9–5	2.95	5
Clay Carroll	56	96	7–5	2.63	7
Pat Darcy	27	131	11–5	3.57	1
Rawley Eastwick	58	90	5–3	2.60	22
Clay Kirby	26	111	10–6	4.70	0
Will McEnaney	70	91	5–2	2.47	15

Index